TEACHING POLITICALLY

Teaching Politically

GLOBAL PERSPECTIVES ON PEDAGOGY AND AUTONOMY

May Hawas
Bruce Robbins
EDITORS

FORDHAM UNIVERSITY PRESS   NEW YORK   2025

Copyright © 2025 Fordham University Press

All rights reserved. No part of this publication may be reproduced, stored in a retrieval system, or transmitted in any form or by any means—electronic, mechanical, photocopy, recording, or any other—except for brief quotations in printed reviews, without the prior permission of the publisher.

Fordham University Press has no responsibility for the persistence or accuracy of URLs for external or third-party Internet websites referred to in this publication and does not guarantee that any content on such websites is, or will remain, accurate or appropriate.

Fordham University Press also publishes its books in a variety of electronic formats. Some content that appears in print may not be available in electronic books.

Visit us online at www.fordhampress.com.

For EU safety / GPSR concerns: Mare Nostrum Group B.V., Mauritskade 21D, 1091 GC Amsterdam, The Netherlands, gpsr@mare-nostrum.co.uk

Library of Congress Cataloging-in-Publication Data available online at https://catalog.loc.gov.

Printed in the United States of America

27 26 25   5 4 3 2 1

First edition

Contents

Introduction
May Hawas and Bruce Robbins   1

Melville's Democratic Pedagogy: *Moby-Dick* Takes
On Hobbes's *Leviathan*
Bonnie Honig   20

Liberal Education and the Politics of Discussion
Benjamin Mangrum   37

Teaching While Arab
Mona Kareem   58

Whose Politics? Teaching Palestinian Literature
Nora E. H. Parr   72

"Don't Speak or Laugh! Greece Is in Danger!": Censoring Dissident
Discourse on So-Called National Issues in Greece
Dimitris Christopoulos and Dimitri Dimoulis   89

The Politics of Mentorship
May Hawas   106

Teaching Literature Politically: Some Examples
Bruce Robbins   125

Baking and Breaking Bread, or Daniel Defoe and the Catastrophic
Imagination
Rishi Goyal   140

Foundations for Nauru Prison Theory: Australian Border Violence, Art, and Knowledge Production
Elahe Zivardar and Omid Tofighian   151

Politics Was in the Very Air We Breathed
Conversations with Khaled Fahmy and Ahdaf Soueif   170

CONTRIBUTORS   191

INDEX   195

TEACHING POLITICALLY

Introduction

May Hawas and Bruce Robbins

An Arab can't imagine pedagogy not being political.

It sounds provocative. But in the Arab world, to say otherwise—that teachers at universities somehow exist outside the sphere of politics (however variously politics is understood), or, even more dangerously, that their job is to embody and promote detachment from politics while consecrating the value of reading books—sounds self-contradictory.

The platitude, of course, does exist. But parroting it almost always sounds like being a sellout. At best, bureauspeak. Making a serious claim to scholarly detachment in the specific context of teaching at the university level in the Middle East more often marks monumental self-deception or simply a denial of the pragmatic realities of life. The biggest universities in the Arab-speaking world are, as of this moment, largely free and public. Politics doesn't necessarily mean political action, but it means, at a minimum, acknowledging the inextricability of university education from the workings of the state. Even if the state itself were wholly stable, which as a political concept it never is, the terms of employment of a university academic are pretty much those of a civil servant. The language(s) that the university encourages; the curriculum allowed (or not); the microcosmic society represented on university campuses that are guarded (as in the case of Egypt, for instance, but in other countries as well) by security forces or the police; and even the student groups (when allowed to convene), which are miniature versions of the political parties functioning in the country, all make it impossible to *not* see the university as a microcosm of the workings of the state and its (empowered or embattled) body politic. Nor is it feasible to pretend that a pedagogical culture across the humanities that promotes a self-protective prefatory maxim of "stay away from religion, sex, or politics" is anything else except subservience to the (conservative) leanings of a state. To ignore the political vocation of teaching at universities in the Arabic-speaking world, then, is to actively dismiss or miscomprehend the historical movements of Arab academics and public university students that have sought to claim independence from state intervention.

Across the Middle East, long-standing movements for university independence and academic freedom—movements concerning what to teach and what to say, or how a country should or should not act—reflect the desire for autonomy, an autonomy that has been denied.[1] The aim of this autonomy is the freedom to *be* political. The university was never an enclave cordoned off from the public. Rather, the university is emblematic of publics that, over the course of their existence, have faced top-down interventionary measures to disempower them politically.

For students, this situation may have unexpected epistemological advantages. Strained resources and state authority on university campuses translate into the larger recognition by the university population that what students and faculty say or do is risky because it may enter the public sphere. But this also means that what they do, if given a chance, automatically bears political resonance. The campuses may differ, the contexts may differ, the countries across the Arabic-speaking world may differ: but the students' closeness to the political spirit remains comparable. The inextricability of the institutions from the state—deep or superficial—enables faculty and students to see that public issues such as poverty, economic instability, lack of employment, war, and geopolitics, whether within or outside the region in which they live, have immediate significance to their lives. Whether they believe they can meaningfully affect the societies in which they live, given the authoritarian contexts in which they live, is a different issue. Defending autonomy, in these contexts, almost always means defending the right to act, not the right to stay silent.

This is obviously not the way academics understand autonomy everywhere. Once we reach the Anglosphere, autonomy allows a loophole for lack of intervention. This time, the professionalization of pedagogy equates autonomy with individualism. To be autonomous doesn't mean having the right to be political, but the right to be *apolitical*. Being autonomous means staying away, and even making an injunction for others to stay away, from politics (petition-signing, boycotting, whatever), lest one compromise public support for one's core function. A core function that includes teaching as well as research. Clearly the measure of democracy is the degree to which choosing to act or not to act is treated as a protected political right. But when did the purpose of pedagogy turn into aporia?

One reason for the existence of this volume is the recognition that terms like autonomy and independence mean something very different in global contexts. All universities, it turns out, can be national allegories, not just those of the Third World. But what changes is the understanding of autonomy, and its complex intertwinement with professional responsibility, citizenship, and individual freedom.

In Europe and Latin America, for instance, where the majority of universities are public and higher education is either free or subsidized, the public resonance of the pedagogical process, or the reflective relation between the state and the university, is articulated in a way somewhat similar to that of the Middle East. While nations vary greatly in terms of discursive freedom and general resources available to students, there is an assumed, mutually reflective link between the university and the state, with students positioned to be citizens who are accessing public services. Campus dissent, understood broadly, is often contextualized as something more nationally oriented than an objection to university management. Think of how the crackdown on student protests for Palestine in German universities, for instance, was carried out not through a particular university administration, or political lobby, or political party, but through an application of the law of the state. People participating in such protests were seen to be contravening security laws, not campus laws. And the intellectual backlash to the German decision was concerned not with whether the ministry of interior affairs, for instance, should actually have the authority to intervene in principle, but rather with why Germany was taking this stance on Palestine. So the issue wasn't primarily the principle of state intervention (or which authorities, if any, can be allowed on campus), but the topic (the kind of activity being banned).

And if we are going to speak of politics and teaching, it would be impossible not to speak of Palestine. The global reactions toward the biggest current atrocity on the world's conscience bring to the fore precisely these differences about autonomy. We are faced here with a seeming conundrum: a lack of active protest in Arab countries, which refutes the supposed importance of politics to Arab university campuses, and the explosion of protest across Western campuses. If there is freedom to express your opinions, then, somewhat predictably, there will be more vocalization. The global diaspora of not just Arabs, but generally, migrants and the dispossessed, has had much less reservation about being vocal. The genocide in Gaza has of course been felt keenly among Arab populations—along with the accompanying shame, anger, and resentment about the inability to protest for fear of reprisal in authoritarian contexts where the prisons are already crowded and protest is forbidden. If the streets and squares in the Arab world remain quiet, grassroots actions that are not punished, such as arranging voluntary aid for Gaza or boycotting products with links to the IDF, have reached an all-time high.

Meanwhile, across Western campuses, there has been an explosion of protest in various forms, as student encampments, teacher walkouts, group resignations from learned societies, and the acceleration of the BDS movement mark the effort to stop the war on Gaza. As the outpouring of compassion and righteousness in marches and protests increased, so did the backlash from the ostensibly "apolitical" university administrations, which suddenly started to look very much like the lands of the un-free. If the political activity showed us the admirable bravery of autonomous agents to exercise their right for political self-determination, the crackdown on protest in the United States and other countries emphasized that, whether it is articulated or otherwise, universities are never nonpolitical entities.

So what does it take to forget or to remember Palestine? Individual autonomy, or lack thereof? If politics are inherent to education, and even if war does—and should—galvanize people into action, war shouldn't be the only reason for doing so. Empathy simply entails the recognition that violence is being perpetuated: whether by the power of veto or by the bombs. Recognizing atrocity shouldn't be the *first* trigger to empathy; it should be the last straw before the rage of disobedience. If we have freedom to act politically, autonomy cannot mean waiting for some "appropriate" time to exercise it. Instead, it means understanding that one is, whatever one's realistic capacity to act, inherently a political agent.

Above all, what does one actually do with the choice to *not* act? An apolitical premise in the form of autonomy makes the purpose and privilege of freedom of discussion questionable. It is popular to speak about queer theory and climate change theory, especially in abstruse language weighed down by aesthetics, and, perhaps more tangibly, it is political to write petitions and go on marches—the freedom is both admirable and real. But political expression remains a choice for those who are interested. If liberal democracy means teachers have a right to be political, then teachers should also have a right to be apolitical, and the subject matter remains unchanged in either case. As if to be political in the world of mass knowledge and mass violence today can be a choice. If it doesn't lead to a heightened political consciousness, that is, fostering empathy to students' surroundings and their role in the local or larger world, what is the point of teaching to begin with? What is the point, in other words, of freedom?

In an eloquent piece, Geoffrey Galt Harpham, who has done a great deal to historicize the American liberal tradition of pedagogy, and has done it well, somewhat resignedly addresses the reemergence of politics in literary studies:

Of course, literary scholars have the right to speak out and the right to free assembly; indeed, as articulate and presumably informed citizens, they have something like an obligation to enter the public realm wherever they might contribute. But this responsibility derives from citizenship, not from academic credentials. It does not derive at all from literary study itself. The relation between the immediacies of the political arena and works of art—which become regarded as art by virtue of their ability to detach themselves from their contexts and speak to people across boundaries of time, space, and culture—is never more than indirect, analogical, and, above all, variable from reader to reader, moment to moment, context to context. Literary study may be political in some larger or more general sense, but it has no necessary political directionality, and can easily accommodate positions on the left, right, and center of the political/cultural spectrum. To suggest otherwise, as many on both sides of the culture wars have done, is to attribute to literary study itself a kind of purposiveness and commitment that properly belongs to individuals in particular circumstances.[2]

For Harpham, the state—citizenship—lies outside the university itself, and if literature is seen to do anything, it is precisely to enforce the idea of nonaction in the shape of autonomy. Harpham is neither the first nor the last claimant for autonomy, whether of literature, criticism, pedagogy, or otherwise. Yet there is a contradiction in an education (rightly) claimed as American with its groundbreaking dedication to democratic discussion and emphasis on meritocracy on the one hand, and, on the other hand, the simultaneous dismissal of this education as civic. Harpham has every reason to be proud of what he calls the "American Revolution in Education," which supersedes others, including British and European pedagogies, in its foregrounding of originality and discussion. But why can't we call that pedagogical vision an inherently political one?

He asserts instead that only "individuals in particular circumstances" determinedly find or dismiss any "purposiveness and commitment" to (literary) pedagogy. It's not clear whom Harpham has in mind. Is it refugees, migrants, the poor? Perhaps Harpham is thinking of people like Mr. Ramirez, whom he presents in his compelling book *What Do You Think, Mr. Ramirez? The American Revolution in Education*. Mr. Ramirez, a professor of comparative literature who was once a "teenaged refugee from Cuba, washed up on a Florida shore," is described as being exemplary of the "tired, poor, wretched refuse" who benefit the most from American education.[3] Harpham insists that education allowed Mr. Ramirez to progress beyond his original washed-up state into a person who is invited to have an opinion. Yet the highest peak of autonomy is supposed to mean the right not to have an opinion at all. To be American, Mr. Ramirez needs to believe that he has the right to have an opinion, but to be a normative academic, Professor Ramirez needs to have the freedom of indifference. These are two different points of educational teleology.

Harpham is certainly on point in more than one sense. Accessing higher education *is* a civic process, but certain communities seem more ready than others to admit it. Those concerned with the fate of historically deprived communities are perhaps more ready than others to consider the potential significance of teaching for the community. One is reminded of bell hooks describing how her earliest teachers in segregated schools believed that "to educate black children rightly would require a political commitment."[4] Such groups are more ready, in other words, to consider purposiveness and commitment as part of the professional expertise of teachers, in spite or because of the discomfort that it entails; and they are thus perhaps more ready to accept that the teacher has a political vocation.

Of course, Mr. Ramirez was always autonomous: what he didn't have was support. If we think of political autonomy as the highest peak of freedom rather than a way of being that is articulated differently according to necessity (not choice), then we risk making autonomy (and therefore a- or de-politicization) a goal, the culmination of educational teleology, achieved at the end point of civilized humanhood, when people don't, so to speak, need to be "formed" any longer. The time for the American revolution in education has passed. These students now come to us as fully formed political adults—all we need to teach them is how to detach from their contexts across time and space, then to tell us why the literary text sounds compelling. Yet teaching is not a detached profession: it is holistically part of its contexts.

To say that teachers automatically have a political vocation is also to imply that the same cannot be said of all ways of making a living, however valuable and even indispensable they may be to the common life. Can teachers legitimately claim to have a vocation when not everyone does? If so, it's because in teaching, the stakes for the nation-state lie not merely in the fact that the work is done, but in *how* it is done. This is true to one degree or another for the teaching of any subject that deals with human and societal growth: from literature to sociology, and from medicine to economics. Teachers have a vocation because the result of the process of teaching is to produce new citizens.

For those who believe in democracy (not everyone does), what kind of citizens a democratic society should try to encourage is a crucial political question. For some decades the word citizenship has been out of fashion, but it serves as a useful reminder that stories of individual and familial formation like the ones we discuss in class have as their indispensable backdrop the existence of the nation-state—for the moment, the social unit in which questions of the common life are most open to shared decision-making. The issue is what kind of nation-state we want. Conflicts involving the university, from critical race theory to gender and sexuality, don't simply reflect the way groups and individuals see the institution, but help decide what kind of nation-state those groups and adults wish to inhabit.

We put a hesitant emphasis on "adult," which is more than a chronological marker. In the first paragraph of "What Is Enlightenment?" Kant defined enlightenment as emergence from self-imposed tutelage. Translations vary: some say "minority" or "nonage" rather than tutelage. The original German is *"Unmündigkeit,"* meaning literally minority, in the sense of childhood, or inability to speak for oneself. But for Kant, and for us, adulthood is certainly a goal. We do not assume that everyone of a certain age already possesses it. If teaching means enlightening, it is thus a paradoxical and politically questionable profession: speaking to others in order to help those others become capable of speaking for themselves, or tutoring others so as to help them become adults who no longer seek or need tutelage. In that sense, teaching adults does not assume that they already function as full political subjects. If these are the assumptions, then it's not hard to see why it is not just the project of enlightenment in general that would come under somewhat hostile political scrutiny, but teaching in particular. Naturally enough, the effects of that scrutiny include self-reflective questioning on the part of the teachers themselves.

One example of that scrutiny comes from Sonali Thakkar's *The Reeducation of Race: Jewishness and the Politics of Antiracism in Postcolonial Thought*. The antiracism that became international doctrine after World War II, Thakkar argues, answered the Nazi idea that race was biologically given by insisting that every identity was historically constructed, or plastic. What was constructed could be constructed differently. Everyone was "educable." The anthropologists who developed this doctrine, like Franz Boas and Claude Lévi-Strauss, were assimilated Jews, and they had every right, Thakkar says, to affirm their own plasticity or educability, if that's what they wanted. But as applied to other racialized groups, educability might not feel equally desirable. As applied to Blacks, for example, to be told you were educable might be understood as meaning that you should not affirm your Blackness as it is, or your desire to remain within that Blackness. Educability seemed to entail willingness to assimilate to the majority (white, Christian) culture. Thus the argument that racists should be educated out of their racism becomes an argument that everyone should be educated out of their racial identity. The labor of education, which assumes that people *need* to be educated, becomes an insult, even a vehicle of racism in its own right. But wait. The assumption here seems to be that in an ideal world, there would be nothing but autodidacts. In other words, the case against education in the former colonies easily becomes a case against education as such. By Thakkar's standards, any social collectivity would be justified in telling any would-be teacher, Who are you to think you have anything to teach us that we need to know? The argument would apply as well to class, or sexuality, or disability as to race. Those who have had a collective experience of discrimination and suffering have nothing to learn from anyone—or the only thing they have to learn is that on that particular subject the teachers in fact have nothing to teach that is worth learning.

Thakkar's book only *implies* this critique of the project of education. It does not make the argument explicitly. If it did, it would be courting paradox, calling into question its own effort to reeducate the educators. Yet the implication has to be called out and confronted, for even if it is buried out of sight, it underlies and informs a great deal of contemporary scholarship, and as such it undermines the confidence that teachers ought to feel in the political value of what they do. It might seem that the vocation of teaching shouldn't need defending from fellow teachers, but it does, and that defense involves taking a position on who is an educable subject. It requires that the category of the educable subject should include the victimized subject, just as it includes the victimizer; after all, it is the victims who are sometimes the more egregious victimizers, as the Israelis have shown again and again. It is also true that no one can teach well who does not also see themselves as an educable subject.[5] No one should feel politically demeaned by the assumption that everyone has a need for education, and (despite the word's politically perilous history) reeducation, even if the contents of that education are and must be open to continuing political debate.

This is true even as this education takes place, or perhaps especially because it takes place, in the university, the main venue of "credentialing" professions and the main platform for empowering individualist and competitive self-gain within them.[6] If teaching is inherently a practice of communal, political purpose, how do we square this idea of communal team spirit with the individualist need for advantage in a professional society? John Guillory has argued that when literary study was professionalized, literary criticism, ostensibly the basic method of engaging with society for literary study, was removed from the public sphere of journalism into the "autonomy" enshrined by the fact of professional work and professionalized university education. Not only are all scholarly professions distanced, according to Guillory, from being channeled into "agencies of government, or into the media public sphere," but the humanities are especially distant because of their relative marginalized importance in society and the "autonomy" of their scholars.⁷ "Autonomy" doesn't just mean, as it did for Harpham, the right or even the ideal to be apolitical, but it makes being apolitical a responsibility.

By removing the political capacity from critical method, and from literary study, political engagement by such "professionals" becomes something of a stigma. "For every Edward Said, Stanley Fish, David Bromwich, Michael Bérubé, Judith Butler, or Louis Menand," Guillory writes dismissively, "there are thousands of scholars who have little access to venues beyond their classrooms and specialized scholarly journals." It is the public intellectuals, apparently, who have been wrong all along. Guillory continues: "This same circumstance permits literary critics a great measure of intellectual autonomy, the obverse of their relative marginalization."⁸ Asking academics to wallow in narrowmindedness, isolation, and professional "marginalization" because it gives them freedom is like calling to maintain leper colonies for the sake of the residents' own independence.

Let's also set aside for a moment that the academic networks and organized societies of literary scholars referred to in *Professing Criticism* seem to be imagined as bookcases of textual commentary rather than intellectuals (that is, normal people engaged in some way with public work). Better to think that for every name Guillory mentions, there are also hundreds of unnamed others, affected by such scholars or otherwise, who live and work across the world, and who have drawn on critical methods to contribute to their students' professional growth and meet the needs of their local communities. What is needed here is a bigger scope of vision for the professional work that literary criticism does, and a wider perspective onto the world and the people who create it.

What is also needed is a more specific look at how criticism is intertwined within the academy with teaching. Critics haven't simply sold their political souls for the devil of professional credibility. The critics and scholars mentioned in Guillory's book—imagined so colorfully to be at war between discipline, scholarship, and criticism—were university teachers, and much of their theory came from classroom practice.⁹ Even if a journalistic public was supposedly lost to critics with the move to the university sphere, *teaching* sets up a context where professionals are required to face an audience of (would-be) citizens. The flimsy rationalization of professionalization doesn't do away with the need for politics: professionals don't stop being public citizens. The students are part of the public, and they are still an audience. The only requirement on the part of the teacher-critic is to accept the vocation. As academics, negating the political capacity of teaching literary study is an exercise in critical self-effacement and professional self-disparagement.

As the 1970s feminists have taught us, the personal is political, and politics is more than the sum of parties and movements and isms. Without taking a position on how far this expansion can go before losing its focus on the common good and the shared fate of the community, we have invited our contributors in this volume to think personally and freely: to think about who they are, as teachers, intellectuals, writers, cultural workers, and students, and of the meanings they want to bring to and take from the cultural discussion. From there, we ask about the political role that the profession plays in society, namely: What is our work supposed to do for the adults enrolled in our programs and the adults reached by our intellectual and activist work?

The collection encourages teachers to conceive of what they do as a vocation. This cannot be taken for granted. In defense of their claim to expertise, which is forever vulnerable to interference from representatives of the community, whether angry parents or angry governments, teachers have invested in the ideal of professional autonomy. The more invested they are in their autonomy, the more likely they are to resist a view of their profession as political, or as subject to judgment by the values of the community. The danger is of course a self-congratulatory complacency that is of little use to either profession or discipline. But the protection that autonomy promises is not an illusion. There is no easy resolution of this dilemma. As we note above, it's a source of discomfort. But there is much to learn from experiences of discomfort. It's for this reason that we have invited our contributors to add to their chapters elements of their own pedagogical experience, including its political challenges.

We had in mind educational manifestos of the likes of Paulo Freire's pedagogy of the oppressed, calls by Raymond Williams and Stuart Hall to include working-class voices in literary study, and bell hooks's rationale for teaching to subvert authority, but we were also mindful that teaching politically can mean different things. This volume brings together a number of academics, activists, public intellectuals, artists, journalists, and novelists. Naturally, for our contributors, teaching politically manifests differently: the effort to make up for the failures of the state; the criticism of a particular community in order to find an alternative; the reaction to an event of brutality; or even a personal journey toward becoming a politically invested teacher, someone a little more, or less, perhaps, than only autonomous.

We have asked our contributors what meaningful action they found themselves taking at critical junctures once they assumed, either willingly or unintentionally, a pedagogical role. We have asked them how their pedagogical consciousness changed in response to perceived crises, whether that has meant war, censorship, revolution, detainment, or historical changes in government. Predictably, this has made our contributors reflect on not just the nature of the crisis by which they came to understand their pedagogical-political positions, but also the specific connections between being a teacher (and therefore a leader with professional expertise), a citizen (and therefore a contributor to the community), and an intellectual (a voice for the sake of a community).

In asking our contributors what it means to teach politically, we did not feel we had to ask them to focus on the largest challenges, which are also the most familiar. The most obvious is the economic precarity of the teacher workforce, which has incited much advocacy and action on campuses. The corporatization of universities and the budget cuts to the humanities by states worldwide had already led, even before the devastations of the Covid-19 pandemic, to a depressed academic job market and dire economic precariousness for graduates. This precariousness entails erratic and unjust employment contracts and loose academic specializations as employees find themselves wearing several hats to retain the right to teach at all. Of course, we are all thinking of what the labor depression means to the profession. Economic precarity comes at a long-term professional cost. Scholars and intellectuals struggling with their own precarity inevitably find themselves questioning the values of their own field even as they address and try to inspire potential students and future graduates. To be, by job description, responsible for raising hopeful new generations while at the same time feeling caught in a job culture of hopelessness because of direct government dismissiveness of your occupation as a pedagogue is a dire state of affairs, objectively and subjectively.

"Politics is not education," David Bromwich declared in his denunciation of what he called "group thinking."[10] Group thinking is certainly not advocated here. But who says that politics *is* group thinking, which is to say not really thinking at all? Chanting slogans at a rally affords a sense of solidarity that is all too rare and has its value even if it is not strictly speaking educational. In any case, trying to foster individual political capacity, as in Kant's famous formulation, is a very different thing, though it doesn't contradict and can certainly foster the creation of meaningful solidarities. In this spirit, we did not ask our contributors to list examples of personal threat. It is not only in countries that are regularly described as undemocratic that the lack of academic freedom puts scholars at risk of bodily harm, legal persecution and imprisonment, and, at best, social and professional marginalization. In the Middle East, with which a number of our contributors are professionally concerned, the cultures of fear propagated by governments around education manifest themselves in persecution of faculty and students by the biased party politics of the administrative body of the university, in the spread of unofficial informers among colleagues, or in politically charged student groups working to enforce establishment orthodoxies and societal taboos. In the United States and Europe, which are supposedly among the most democratic states in the world, that is often the case for scholars who are critical of Israel. In Australia and Greece, both constitutional democracies, talking about issues of displacement and refuge in the countries' past or present stigmatizes speakers as threats to national security and the public peace.

Still, while we want to acknowledge that education faces different political situations in different countries and regions, we do not seek a mechanically achieved checklist for geographical distribution. What we do want to locate are crosspoints for comparison. Citizens of countries in the Arab world are not the first to complain about the demand by the global market that they represent the uniqueness of their country or culture rather than dilemmas and imaginations that their culture or country might share with others, but they are well placed to join the chorus. It might be strangely surprising how straightforwardly and, by now, even predictably, conflicts about the university—over method, content, freedom, outreach, impact, or even utility—repeat themselves worldwide. Strange, because, after all, universities emerged in very different historical contexts. Some were initially a place to gain some European veneer of etiquette. Others were primarily religious institutions. A few started as vocational places for apprenticeship or gateways into authority and the civil service in imperial contexts. Yet in looking today at the questions and conflicts raised about the role of teachers in university, despite historical and geographical circumstance, what stands out is a resounding sameness.

As such, we highlight here the significant sameness that educators have experienced as they traveled between countries and regions, taught in different institutions, and worked in systematic higher education and nonsystematic spaces for public knowledge. Questions repeat themselves about what to teach or how to teach it, who should teach and why, who gets to learn and why, how much or how little students need to know, and what preserves or goes against societal traditions and pedagogical values. If such discussions manifest differently in democratic and nondemocratic contexts, the core of the issue remains that the pedagogical problems faced by any kind of educational institution for adults in the world crystallize, and are potentially resolved, as part of the process of defining the nation-state. In their roles as mediators between state and individual, educators come second in importance only, perhaps, to the immediate heads of families. On a global level, educators broker the process of membership to the public. This is true whether the nation-state is democratic or dictatorial.

It is, of course, more likely that the nation-state is somewhere in between. For Dimitris Christopoulos and Dimitri Dimoulis it takes censorship and censure of academics to show the state's desire to cover historical atrocity. They remind us that silencing happens by defining topics that, though they can be discussed in public universities, are not "public" in a stronger sense. In Greece, a constitutional democracy by any measure, implicit and obvious censorship takes place, and its consequences bear heavily on both academics and media practitioners. Their essay takes as its starting point how words like "Bulgarian" or "Macedonia" turn overnight into hot-button issues to be pored over by court judges and members of parliament with the larger aim of eliminating the history of national atrocity. The threat of turning public discussions about history, the state, violence, or minorities into issues that ostensibly threaten public security, and therefore should *not* be talked about, contradicts the rationale for having a constitutional democracy in the first place. Thus, even within ostensibly democratic institutions, academics seek their own ways to speak out about taboos, to ensure that in the spirit of a public education, what concerns the public is actually discussed by the public.

"Public" is a hazy word. Is there a singular public, "the" public? Those who think so would probably be thinking of the mainstream media, and it would be the owners and controllers of those media that would get to decide on what public opinion is. Decades of attacks on the institutions of higher education from the journalists of the mainstream media make it clear that publics are in fact plural and often in conflict with each other, though the conflict may be aimed at determining what "the" public will feel. The enormous significance of today's social media, which has an entirely different set of gatekeepers, some political and some merely algorithmic, further complicates the definition of the term; the Israeli bombing of Gaza, ongoing as we write, seems for example to have permitted a great deal more criticism in this medium than in the older media. Even as a component of the hyphenated term "counter-public," the word "public" exerts a pressure toward consensus.

That is another sense in which teaching, as a public activity, is a political vocation. The potential to invite and reconcile divergent viewpoints is one of the profession's capabilities, though perhaps more often hypothetical than practical. Teaching in closed lecture halls and supervision rooms appears to be, or is even required to be by the contractual terms of employment, an activity bounded by the walls of campus and by the number of those who have paid to attend. That population is inevitably restricted. Helen Small has argued that higher education as a whole cannot plausibly claim to be necessary to the functioning of democracy, and the claim becomes more ridiculous when pressed by a single discipline or even the humanities as a whole.[11] Still, the population that has access to higher education has to count as a segment of the public, and a nonnegligible one. Globally, and with minor exceptions, the percentage of those with a tertiary education has followed a solid upward curve in the past forty years (with countries in North America having some of the highest percentages of BA degree holders).[12] There is democratic pressure to increase those percentages, but much of the insistence that higher education serves the few rather than the many comes on the contrary from university administrators seeking to cut pay and pensions, cancel tenure lines and whole disciplines, and increase workloads. Or it comes from local, state, and national governments seeking to dismantle programs and decrease public spending. It is hard to say how often the motive is ideological: a recognition that institutions of higher education tend to encourage thinking that is not just "critical" in an empty, sloganeering sense, but *politically* critical. What is sure is that the motive, both inside and outside the university, is often economic competitiveness for the institution, for the individual, for the nation: wins rather than losses. They are not concerned, as Coach Ted Lasso is, with kindness. Although the fact is that the university serves the public, it is not strange then that the point needs to be repeated, pursued into unfamiliar places and expanded upon.

We have focused in this book a great deal on literature. Postcolonial studies, the pioneering academic formation that took on the job of overcoming Eurocentrism, found an initial home for itself in the study of literature. That seemed at the time to make sense: literary studies specialized in the survival of endangered cultural particularity, and that was self-evidently the case for the cultures of Europe's colonies just as it was for Europe's own cultural past. Today the academic division of labor looks very different, and that is a sign of postcolonial studies' success; it has stimulated scholars in other disciplines to overcome its limits while preserving its primal impulse. If literary studies has retained a special place in the academy's efforts to achieve what Edward Said called worldliness, that place is reflected in the texts to which our contributors bring their attention. Our intention is certainly not to imply that teaching must always be the teaching of texts—though if our examples inspire others to follow the lead of our contributors, we would not be unhappy.

In the American liberal arts tradition, the teaching of literary texts has also been an exemplary model for democratic discussion. But how specifically do teachers contribute to or help form this liberal tradition? Is teaching directly an allegory of radical democracy where the authority of the teacher must be overthrown or renounced? Is it properly thought of as transgressive, as suggested in bell hooks's *Teaching to Transgress: Education as a Practice of Freedom*? Or is it better understood as a practice of freedom which, like other democratic practices, can never simply be antiauthoritarian since the goal is an alternative exercise of power, or authority, that is democratically shared?

For Bonnie Honig in this volume, pedagogy at its best is a form of democratic theater in which student mutinies are to be welcomed. In her reflections on teaching Melville's *Moby-Dick* as political theory set against a particular American landscape—surf and turf, as a colleague remarks—Honig makes use of allegory, faithful friend to many readers of politics, in order to show both Melville's attention in his famous whale story to Hobbes's Leviathan, another monster of the sea, and his insistence, against Hobbes, on the vulnerability of the absolutist tyrant to something like the power of the people. Thus it is *Moby-Dick*, and not Hobbes's *Leviathan*, that has become a democratic Bible, ritualistically read and reread—and thus it is that, for Honig, *Moby-Dick* deserves the honor and the authority, even if students in the classroom mutiny against it.

On the other hand, Benjamin Mangrum questions how far the politics of discussion at the American university really prepares citizens in American civic life, as is often assumed. Discussion creates a common, specifically public culture, but what if discussion becomes the be all and end all of the pedagogical encounter, and results in an uncurated multiplicity? How does a principle of "anything goes" really help to progress liberal democracy in times of crisis?

The principle of "anything goes" becomes further complicated when the teacher, as well as the text, embodies areas that have a history of being, at best, Othered, or at worst, enslaved or militarily attacked, by the same country. Mona Kareem narrates the experience of teaching Arabic literature as an Arab in the United States, not least while knowing that some of the students were army recruits. She describes the difficulty of being able to read Arabic literature simply as literature without having it turned into a moralistic lesson or anthropological archive. For Kareem even to have this discussion about her own teaching requires having to present it within a theoretical framework that is American enough (in this case, the topic of someone teaching "ethnic" subjects in an American classroom). Kareem's topics and curriculum would be unthinkable in certain Arab countries such as in the Gulf, or questionable on grounds of societal conservatism, for instance, in North Africa. Yet her syllabi, and her own performance in the US, offered as representative of the diversity of a liberal tradition, end up underlining the superficiality of a diversity that doesn't prioritize empathy.

Just as "diversity" can turn into an umbrella term, so can "sameness." In her essay, Nora Parr recounts the experience of teaching Palestinian literature in England. Provoked by the suggestion of teaching a given novel in the framework of disability studies, Parr steps back to reflect on the various frameworks by which Palestinian writing makes it into syllabi. They get the subject taught, which is good. (This cannot be taken for granted. Students are grateful for it.) But much is lost by virtue of these angles of vision, even those that would claim political solidarity with the ongoing plight of the Palestinian people. Not least, the Palestinian people themselves, who are more commonly taught than employed to teach, more often written about than invited to write.

Empathy also doesn't flower without some planting. How do you teach empathy without a body politic? Arab pedagogy has a history of treading a fine line between state-building and public mobilization. In the Arab case, unlike the Greek, persecution and harassment of intellectuals don't have to go via the courts at all. This has created parallel histories of mainland and diasporic Arab criticism. May Hawas argues that for the Arab pedagogue, the ultimate choice is between one vocation and the other: either a societally ingrained if high-risk form of professional-political mentorship that specifically targets a readily receptive body politic, or an exilic, more individually inclined criticism in a world utopia of migrants. While the two positions might overlap, the first emphasizes the role of teaching, the other, the role of criticism.

We have become used by now, despite detractors, to hearing that criticism starts the political conversation precisely by teaching how to distance oneself from the text, and from there, to question seemingly self-evident, specifically national truths. At the metropolitan heart of the Global North, in New York City, students are likely to be very aware of their relative privilege—perhaps even too much so. In the examples of political pedagogy recounted by Bruce Robbins, some of the resistances that need to be overcome include the hasty and uncritical acceptance of a writer's antitotalitarian sentiment (in the case of Milan Kundera) as an adequate politics, and an equally hasty and equally uncritical acceptance of a writer's detached view of race and racism in America, in the case of Chimamanda Ngozi Adichie's *Americanah*. Class is not definitive of politics, of course, but one task of would-be political teaching in the United States is getting students to remember that class is a factor at all, and for a writer whose prose and perspective are as attractive as Adichie's, that is a tall order, even within the genre of the upward mobility story. But the most surprising student resistance is perhaps the resistance to any form of national or civilizational self-flattery. Even on the subject of atrocity, it is difficult to get students to admit that anything like moral progress has ever occurred. Surely even in antiquity everyone had the same scruples against the massacre of noncombatants that we have now?

Perhaps it is not the goal of moral progress that brings people to collate, but the fear of isolation. During the Covid-19 pandemic, Rishi Goyal, professor of emergency medicine at the Columbia University Medical Center as well as Columbia's Institute for Comparative Literature and Society, found himself teaching in an emergency, but also about one. The panic that he was encountering, he writes, had something in common with that primal fear of other people that he, like Honig, associates with Thomas Hobbes. Like Robbins,

Goyal reiterates that exposing students to often discomforting knowledge about the nation-state, especially historical, ultimately encourages forging paths toward democracy.

If it takes commitment to expose students to discomforting knowledge, it takes a distinct kind of pedagogy to attempt to do it outside the university, in makeshift classrooms, digital platforms, and intellectual networks of those on the margins. This is especially true if the kind of primal fear mentioned by Goyal is not felt on the part of the mainstream, but by others facing the ongoing, everyday violence of governments. The university has become the chief nexus for modern professional and vocational formation, but education, in the broadest sense, does happen across the cultural ecosystem. This includes the kind of teaching that takes place at university, as well as the kind of edification accomplished in public writing, journalism, publishing, and translation.

Of course, such work proceeds in more nebulous and less predictable ways. Moving beyond and within the university ecosystem, cultural actors engage more directly in a merged form of activist pedagogy. Writing on Australia's system of border detention centers in the Pacific, writer and artist Elahe Zivardar and academic, translator, and activist Omid Tofighian call for the establishment of new forms of pedagogy that take into account the horrors of the contemporary incarceration system. Zivardar, who fled Iran to Indonesia and then to Australia, was detained on Nauru Island from 2013 to 2019. She was finally resettled in the US. Tofighian has collaborated with and helped make visible the creative work produced by such detainees. Many of them, like Zivardar, are former political writers and creatives who have fled oppressive conditions and have sought cultural expression to teach others about what they are going through. In their essay, Zivardar and Tofighian describe how their latest projects that aim to disseminate knowledge about the prison industrial complex create a theoretical discourse for imprisonment and borders, but also set up a cultural format with which to urge prisoners and publics to create new, more equal forms of knowledge and knowledge sharing. If this isn't the kind of public knowledge that is disseminated by systematic education, it is a reminder, as in all forms of marginalized production, that it can and should be. Pedagogy, in such ways, is inseparable from public outreach, knowledge production, and social movement building.

What blurs social movement building and teaching is the desire (the vocabulary is inevitably as clumsy as the desire itself is multiform and inchoate) for some sort of tangible social transformation. In a generous conversation between Egypt's two most prominent international intellectuals, Ahdaf Soueif and Khaled Fahmy discuss how political consciousness can be inadvertent, appearing when individuals find an urgent reason to want change. The heart of the pedagogical vocation—in their journalism, activism, creative writing, and scholarship—lies in relating one's relevance to the public good. Politics, as Soueif poignantly puts it, is in the air we breathe. Fahmy follows with a similarly arresting line, that the intellectual's role is not just to address the public, but also to listen, and through listening, to be part of the fabric of society.

So which is it? Are teachers supposed to listen or talk, read or speak, educate or be reeducated? Teaching politically might aim to achieve societal reform or build ethical citizenship, or it might respond to a moment of emergency or prolonged authoritarianism, or it might be grounded in literature as well as in any other discipline. But it is always oriented towards the public. We may disagree on what the public good is, or we might even disagree on how we should define a public while remaining committed to the world at large. But even if that self-questioning comes with the process of teaching politically, the biggest silencer of our own autonomy will always be our choice to stay silent.

Notes

1. For an overview of the kind of challenges faced by higher education and its inextricability from the state, the deep state, and the public, as well as the politicized responses toward various challenges, from independence movements to civil war, by faculty and students across the Arab world, see (on Syria) Oudai Tozan, "The Evolution of the Syrian Higher Education Sector 1918–2022: From a Tool of Independence to a Tool of War," *Globalisation, Societies and Education*, October 10, 2023, https://www.tandfonline.com/doi/full/10.1080/14767724.2023.2265854; and (on Iraq) Imad Harb, "Higher Education and the Future of Iraq," *Special Report* 195, United States Institute of Peace (January 2008), https://www.files.ethz.ch/isn/46082/sr195.pdf. On Egypt, for the 9 March movement, see Menna Omar, "University Independence in Egypt: The Struggle Continues," *Legal Agenda*, September 10, 2014, https://english.legal-agenda.com/university-independence-in-egypt-the-struggle-continues/; for the historical view, see Hilary Kalmbach, "Reform, Education, and Sociocultural Politics in Nineteenth-Century Egypt," in *Islamic Knowledge and the Making of Modern Egypt* (Cambridge: Cambridge University Press, 2020). For Lebanon, see Helen Murray's vividly comprehensive recent PhD thesis, "Universities, Conflict and the Public Sphere: Trajectories of the Public University in Lebanon" (University of Sussex, 2023), https://sussex.figshare.com/articles/thesis/Universities_conflict_and_the_public_sphere_trajectories_of_the_public_university_in_Lebanon/23483666; and for a historical overview of Lebanon's vital student movements (in specific relation to the 2020 protests), see Kareem Chehayeb and Tala Majzoub, "Lebanon's Student Movement: A New

Political Player?," *Arab Reform Initiative*, September 7, 2021, https://www.arab-reform.net/publication/lebanons-student-movement-a-new-political-player/.

2. Geoffrey Galt Harpham, "Politics, Professionalism and the Pleasure of Reading," *Daedalus* 134, no. 3 (Summer 2005): 68–75, 68. Also see Geoffrey Galt Harpham, *What Do You Think, Mr. Ramirez? The American Revolution in Education* (Chicago: University of Chicago Press, 2017).

3. Harpham, *What Do You Think*, 3.

4. bell hooks, *Teaching to Transgress: Education as the Practice of Freedom* (London: Routledge, 1994), 3. See also Jarvis R. Givens's historicization of Black education in his biography of Carter G. Woodson: *Fugitive Pedagogy: Carter G. Woodson and the Art of Black Teaching* (Cambridge, MA: Harvard University Press, 2021).

5. On the self-consciousness necessary to pedagogy, see for example Carol R. Rodgers, *The Art of Reflective Teaching: Practicing Presence* (New York: Teachers College Press, 2020).

6. John Guillory, *Professing Criticism: Essays on the Organization of Literary Study* (Chicago: University of Chicago Press, 2022).

7. Guillory, 58.

8. Guillory, 59–60.

9. For an exposition of lecture and teaching notes of the likes of I. A. Richards and T. S. Eliot, among others, see Rachel Sagner Buurma and Laura Heffernan, *The Teaching Archive: A New History for Literary Study* (Chicago: University of Chicago Press, 2021).

10. David Bromwich, *Politics by Other Means: Higher Education and Group Thinking* (New Haven, CT: Yale University Press, 1992), ix.

11. Helen Small, *The Value of the Humanities* (Oxford: Oxford University Press, 2014).

12. Organisation for Economic Co-operation and Development (OECD) Data, "Population with Tertiary Education," Adult education level (1981–2022), https://data.oecd.org/eduatt/population-with-tertiary-education.htm.

Melville's Democratic Pedagogy
Moby-Dick *Takes On Hobbes's* Leviathan

Bonnie Honig

> We get along with everyone, and it is well that we do, for at sea one either befriends one's companions or fights.
> —ALEXIS DE TOCQUEVILLE, WRITING TO HIS MOTHER, ON BOARD *LE HAVRE*, BOUND FOR NEW YORK, APRIL 26, 1831

> You see how well I mesh with the landscape.
> —TOCQUEVILLE, A FEW WEEKS LATER, WRITING TO HIS FATHER FROM A HILLTOP OUTSIDE NEW YORK CITY, NEAR SING SING

Teaching *Moby-Dick*

Teaching is like theater. Instructors issue invitations, and sometimes students respond. When it works, it can be magic, but there is no predicting exactly when or how it will happen. It may be that the room has good vibes, the scheduled meeting time works for everyone (so there is no rushing in late and hastening off early), or the topics and texts of the course are somehow timely. Sometimes the times, spaces, and texts of the course speak to the lives of those in the room or to the moment of the universe, even if in unintended ways, and the resonances surprise us all. I assume that when this happens in the theater, when the room and the news and the audience all meet, the actors leave the stage marveling at what has happened that night. So, too, I continue, almost ten years later, to marvel at my experience teaching *Moby-Dick*, at Brown, in the fall of 2014.[1]

I had taught the novel before, but it was different at Brown. It was partly that we were on the East Coast, not far from where whalers like those imagined by Herman Melville once sailed off and the lucky ones returned home. It was partly that I had just moved to Brown, so my course was added late to the roster of course offerings, which meant that it drew mostly transfer students who registered later than others. These were advanced undergraduates, so they knew well how to do the work but, since they were also new arrivals to Brown, they had the enthusiasm of first-year students. Also, these students did not all know each other already, so they were a bit of a motley crew, united only by their excitement about the proposed adventure of reading *Moby-Dick*.

The room was our ally. It was perched at the top of a tower with huge windows on two sides. One student compared it to the *Pequod*'s crow's nest, where Ishmael and other sailors served as lookouts. We saw no whales from our perch, but we could see all of Providence. That room assignment felt providential.

It felt providential as well to discover that the father of one of my students was then serving on a submarine. When the father heard about our class, he decided to read *Moby-Dick* along with his son. The son would bring their Skype conversations into the classroom. It was he who first pointed out how like the crow's nest our classroom was. He had a bird's-eye view every week, he said. By contrast, his father's perspective was submerged, more like that of the whale. Differences of perspective matter, we learned. So did differences of generation.

I recall opening my class that year saying: many people *say* they have read *Moby-Dick*, but after this semester, when *you* all say it, it will be true. We read the novel alongside Alexis de Tocqueville's *Democracy in America*, which appeared a few years before *Moby-Dick*. *Democracy in America* is another big book that people *say* they have read. Reading these two nineteenth-century texts together, I told the students, would allow us to approach them comparatively, the one theorizing American democracy on land, the other at sea. When I recently repeated this description of the course to my cinema studies colleague, Veronica Fitzpatrick, she said: "Surf and turf." And so it was.

Melville's *Moby-Dick* is a novel about irreconcilable conflicts and enthusiasms that drive some to their demise, taking others down with them. We experience with the characters the existential thrill of discovering who we are and what we stand for when, facing the implacable, we realize that either the whale will win or we will. If the whale is whiteness, then defeating it is a win for democracy. If the whale is nature, then learning that it cannot be defeated teaches a humility before larger forces that most humans have yet to learn. If the whale is a tyrant, or if Ahab is, then the story told is of the power of ordinary people to rise to great heights against domination. But great heights are also precarious; people who attain them may be frightened to find themselves up there.

Tocqueville and Melville looked at more or less the same thing but saw it very differently. Tocqueville was struck by the propulsive liveness of democratic life and by its propensity for social equality in America. He once saw a plumber and a gentleman tip their hats to each other on a street in New York and could not get over the radicality of it. He saw in America something like the egalitarian sociality that had struck him on board ship as he crossed the Atlantic. Melville saw the massive hierarchies that remained. It was only at sea (and not always there) that he could imagine a multiracial, multiethnic assemblage of people working together in common cause. He named the ship in *Moby-Dick* the *Pequod* for the Pequot tribe, nearly destroyed and scattered over two hundred years earlier by an epidemic and the Pequot War. The sea was not for Melville a mise-en-scène of American amnesia.

I have a habit of writing papers for my classes as I assign the students to do. That way, we are in it together, I tell them. In the end, for my paper that year, I decided to partner *Moby-Dick* with Hobbes's *Leviathan*, focused on how each offers up a pedagogy for their politics. Melville draws directly on Hobbes, quoting from *Leviathan*, the book that Hobbes named for a fantastical biblical monster of the sea. But it was Ahab that was Melville's most Hobbesian creation. Ahab, who sought to captain his ship with absolute authority, while the men on board found some small liberties and carved out larger ones, too. Not enough to save them, though. This was Melville's critique of Hobbes: Give a man absolute authority because you fear violent death? He will take you down, Melville made clear. Where Hobbes saw an absolutist sovereign whose stabilizing powers would check men's ambition, Melville saw how such a sovereign's enthusiasms would go unchecked.

Hobbes understood the importance of education to absolutism's reproduction, just as Melville understood the democratic need to counter national or official pedagogies with freeing forms of learning and imagination. Hobbes gave to the sovereign the power over language, but Melville gave to language such power that no one could ever be sovereign over it. Hence *Moby-Dick*'s pun-filled phantasmagoria of words, pointing dizzyingly and comically in several directions at once. In place of Hobbes's obedient *cives*, Melville conjures an unruly crew capable of navigating great storms *because* of their differences, and not in spite of them. Do they model a democratic sovereignty-to-come? Neither absolutist, nor doomed, but free, uncharted, and equal? All hands on deck, Melville all but says, as he invites us on board to find out.

Freedom in Context

As Melville wrote in the 1840s, American sovereignty was expanding and consolidating as the United States became for the first time a "continental nation." In 1848–49, Americans were aware of the upheavals and revolutions in France and Europe, and were concerned to avoid them in the US. In 1850, Clay's "compromise" let California join the Union as a free state and let New Mexico and Utah (newly taken in the Treaty of Guadalupe Hidalgo, which ended war with Mexico) declare themselves either free or slave states. Thus, the country "plugged the leaks" that threatened to "sink the ship of state."[2]

US sovereignty was also expanding demographically, through force and law. It moved over the moving bodies of its population, forcing some into motion, and others into confinement, through the forced resettlement of native people and through the Fugitive Slave Act (federal law of 1793, again in 1850), which was affirmed by Judge Lemuel Shaw, Melville's father-in-law, in a case decided in 1851. The act held that fugitive slaves claimed by "owners" must be returned, even in free states. No person of color could be safe from capture. This was true not just for fugitives; free people were kidnapped along the North/South borders, too, before the Civil War. These are some of America's own "disappeared." There have been many since, including children on the border with Mexico during the Trump years, taken from migrant parents and placed with far-away families. The US, which came into its own as a "continental nation" by criminalizing fugitivity, has continued on that path. Its fame as a nation of immigrants and a classless society in which all are free and anyone can make it if they just strive hard enough—that is just part of the story.

Hobbes's *Leviathan* is not now thought of as a great defender of liberty, but its defense of absolutism was on liberty's behalf. Leviathan was supposed to underwrite the *freedom* of its members. "By liberty is understood . . . the absence of external impediments," Hobbes said (chapter 14, *Leviathan*). In *Leviathan*, Hobbes argued, the authority of the sovereign monarch or Parliament was absolute, and its power vast, but the people could count on having freedom of movement. For Hobbes, control over the movement of our bodies is the definitive criterion of freedom for the sake of which we enter into a social contract in the first place. It is a fairly minimal requirement, a low bar, as many of Hobbes's critics have pointed out, to say that we are free insofar as no one physically impedes our movements.[3] And yet for many on US territory, now, as in the 1850s, that low bar is hard to clear. For many poor people, indigent people, or people of color, such impediment is a routine, sadly familiar, condition of life. In the US today, some are stopped, frisked, killed by police, while others routinely walk the streets or drive by unmolested. For Hobbes, this means—quite simply—that some are free and others are not. In some contexts, what looks like a low bar can be a radical claim and its minimalism can be clarifying. The word *arrest* means simply "stop." Freedom of unimpeded motion in the US of the 1850s would have been a radical idea for many denizens of the country, just as it is now.

Hobbes did not allow for contestations of sovereign violations of freedom. The sovereignty of Leviathan is absolute, not democratic. Sovereign commands cannot be questioned, sued, called to account, or put on trial, in Hobbes's view. That is because the sovereign is not a party to the Hobbesian social contract. Written during the English Civil War and in the wake of the 1649 trial and execution of England's King Charles I, *Leviathan* is Hobbes's effort to establish the conditions of civil stability. Among the many causes of instability charted by him are the seventeenth-century code of private vengeance, the ambition for glory, pride, and religious enthusiasm (what we call fundamentalism). Vengeance, glory, and enthusiasm are destabilizing passions that undo civil authority and lead to civil war.

Hobbes argued that civil peace can be had only if we build on a different passion: instead of vengeance, glory, and enthusiasm, which pit people against each other, politics can be founded on a passion that *unites* us: the fear of violent death. We all share that fear, or that is Hobbes's wager, anyway.[4] If the sovereign can incite that passion in us, or if Hobbes can incite it through his writing, then we will not do anything rash to unsteady the ship of state. Hence "leviathan," a terrifying sea creature whose awesome powers are frightening enough to keep us in line if we ever forget our oath, the social contract, which commits us to submitting without question to sovereign authority for the sake of civil peace. For Hobbes, that submission is worth it. The fear of violent death underwrites the many benefits of civil peace: the peace and predictability secured by the social contract enable knowledge, trade, commerce, scholarship, and science to flourish.

In sum, Hobbes is here juxtaposing two forms of life—the combative heroic form (motivated by vengeance, glory, pride, enthusiasm) versus the peace-seeking bourgeois (who fears violence and wants to be left to enjoy private pursuits like knowledge, trade, art, and science). This contrast is represented in Melville's *Moby-Dick* by two characters: Ahab, the glory-seeking ship's captain, whose quest for private vengeance puts everyone at risk; and Starbuck, his first mate, who just wants to make some money whale-hunting and go home. Notably, though, between these two characters, Melville imagines a host of others: a diverse and motley crew boards the *Pequod* precisely because they do not fear violent death more than anything else. They hunt whales, after all. This means they take their lives in their hands and they know it.

Indeed, the famous Ishmael at the center of the novel says quite clearly at the beginning that he would rather risk death than keep working his boring job on land. There is no more anti-Hobbesian sentiment than this. Ishmael joins up with Ahab because he longs for adventure. Game for the hunt, he and the crew get more than they bargained for. The captain lures them into a mad quest after a few weeks at sea, appealing passionately for their support in hunting down the white whale he has named Moby-Dick. When the crew swears an oath to join him, they enter unforgettably into an explicit social contract with their captain. ("Harpooners! Drink and swear, ye men that man the deathful whaleboat's bow—Death to Moby Dick!"). But Ahab does not join them. Like Hobbes's sovereign, Ahab is not a party to the contract.

Why Does Hobbes Animalize Sovereignty?

> Leviathan is the text. . . . Give me a condor's quill! Give me Vesuvius' crater for an inkstand! (Ishmael, chap. 104)

Hobbes's animalization of sovereignty supports his pedagogical purpose. Depicting the sovereign as a creature of the sea theologizes sovereignty (citing the biblical Book of Job, in which "leviathan" is a figure for God's omnipotent power), naturalizes sovereignty (by identifying sovereign violence with nature or the state of nature), and reunifies sovereignty (solving a problem known as that of the king's "two bodies" by adding a third). The first two depictions of sovereignty are well known to political theorists. But the last, which is opened up by reading Melville and Hobbes together, is not, and it is key to the work of *Moby-Dick* as *democratic* pedagogy.

In *The King's Two Bodies*, Ernst Kantorowicz traces the medieval history of how kings came to be seen as having *two* bodies (hint: it came over from Christianity): a material mortal body that is human; and the immortal body, or *corpus mysticum*, of the monarchy, a divine body. When the one, mortal body of the king dies, the other goes on, and this ensures royal succession without disincorporation (so the king can die without the kingdom dying). The king's two bodies are united in one man/figure, and the mystical or divine body of the king shores up the king's sovereignty (the Divine Right of Kings) and his good intent (so that he is assumed to rule for the public good and not for his private profit).

The doctrine of the "king's two bodies" was an early modern effort to make English sovereignty unassailable. Hobbes seems to enlist the doctrine for his own account of unified, absolute sovereignty when he calls Leviathan a "Mortal God," uniting humanity and divinity in a phrase. But, as Victoria Kahn points out in *The Future of Illusion*, the theory of "the king's two bodies" establishes a framework not just for unity but also for the very conflict that Hobbes sought to prevent. The "fiction of the oneness of the double body," Kahn says, eventually gave way.[5] Hobbes speaks of Leviathan as a "Mortal God," but "Godhead and manhood . . . [came to] stand in contrast to each other," as

Ernst Kantorowicz says in his reading of Richard II.[6] Once the two bodies of the king diverge, Kahn argues, they "morph into the distinction between person and office, which in turn played a crucial role in the dethroning of Charles I in 1649," the very event in response to which Hobbes wrote *Leviathan*.

Thus, Kahn goes on to say, "charisma is one effect of the king's two bodies" (it brings us the enchanted divine king), but "the other is *constitutionalism*" (which constrains the king).[7] The first effect, charisma, enchants and supports the office of kingship, but it also makes the supposedly stable office dependent upon the unstable vagaries of personal charm, which any particular ruler may have or lack. The second effect, constitutionalism, disenchants the office, making it more stable, and not dependent on the personal traits of the sovereign, and/but also rendering the king vulnerable to constitutional checks and even trial, which is to say, he is no longer absolute. The unity of sovereignty is now a duality and the unchecked sovereign is now checked, says Kahn.

Kahn assumes Hobbes is unaware of the problem, but he may actually be anticipating it when he gives the king a third, animal body.[8] Hobbes's sovereign does not have two bodies (à la Kantorowicz); he has three: mortal (human), immortal (divine), *and* animal (perishable).[9] As an *animal* in the state of nature, the sovereign is untouchable from inside the contract *even* if he betrays his office. The king's animal body represents a kind of immunized untouchability; the beast is beyond the law. Thus, Hobbes's animalization of sovereignty responds to the very problem Kahn identifies: the morphing of the two-body theory into a two-bodied standard by which to judge, try, and even kill a king. Hobbes's animalization of sovereignty heals sovereignty's split, and it also permits the ruler's predation.

But enter Melville. With this animalization, iconic, cultural, mythic, a door is opened. And Melville walks—or swims—right through it to put a thought in our minds. If the animal sovereign can be predator, might he not also be prey?

Moby-Dick: Melville's Response to Hobbes

Moby-Dick cites Hobbes's *Leviathan* more than once, in its opening pages quite directly—approaching what's been "said, thought, fancied and sung of Leviathan," from "a bird's eye view"[10]—and then more obliquely, throughout. Melville's novel is often read as a morality tale in which a mad leader, an absolute sovereign or captain possessed by hubris, is struck down, perhaps by the divinity he worships and disrespects. Ahab says repeatedly he wants to *know* God and wants an explanation for his suffering and that of all mankind. The whale on this reading is, as in the biblical Book of Job, a sign of God's great power to strike down an upstart.

But the text has a more democratic story to tell. The beastly sea creature of Hobbesian sovereignty does not just strike terror in the hearts of men or women. It turns out it is also vulnerable to democratic or popular overthrow and this not in spite of its beastliness but *because* of it. We can lose sight of this if we stay too focused on the captivating, mad Captain Ahab, and his doomed quest. But we must tarry with him, first. Ahab is bent on revenge against a whale he once hunted and who fought back. The whale bit off Ahab's leg and then got away free. Now Ahab has a prosthetic leg made of whalebone. That is his first vengeance, taking the bone from a whale, and it also suggests Ahab is, like Hobbes's sovereign, himself creaturely: with one leg made of whalebone, Ahab, too, has one foot, as it were, in the state of nature. Ahab has vowed to take his second vengeance, to hunt down and kill the whale that maimed him; he knows the whale's markings (it is notably a uniquely "white whale"), he has named the whale Moby-Dick (seeking like Adam to establish his mastery by naming, and miming Hobbes's own Nominalism, which insists that things are what their names indicate and are not to be understood by way of the essences attributed to them by the Schoolmen Hobbes mocks).

It will be weeks into the voyage before Ahab finally discloses to his crew the true purpose of the hunt—to find and kill Moby-Dick. At first, the men hesitate when confronted with their mysterious captain's strange plan. But he overcomes their misgivings with promises of money (a "gold ounce" coin, nailed to the mast as reward for sighting that whale) and the promise of glory. Ahab charismatically links the quest for Moby-Dick to an existential desire to see God and know the truths of the universe. The crew enters into his fantasy, sealing their consent with an oath and a shared drink from the same cup. This is Ahab's Hobbesian social contract: the men swear to join or serve him; he does not swear to join or serve them. Starbuck is the only holdout. He is the first mate and he thinks vengeance on a dumb animal is a bad idea. Starbuck would rather just hunt whales for money and go home when the job is done. He is the sort of man Hobbes would like to shape, a man of interests, not passions. Ahab lures him in, though. With threats and promises, Starbuck's submission is secured.

Also skeptical, and more charming, is Ishmael, who by turns is enthralled by Ahab and quite nervous about him. It is his line that opens the book—"Call me Ishmael"—one of the most famous lines in American literature. Ishmael is the narrator of the story and we see most of it through his eyes.

In the end (spoiler alert) the captain will go down and the ship with him as Moby-Dick once again has his way with Ahab. Since the whale is all-powerful, it is hard to see how *this* is a critique of *Leviathan*, rather than a novelistic *buttressing* of Hobbes's vision: after all, both sovereign figures in the novel, which is to say both Ahab and the whale, are terrifying, threatening, and violent. Both strike fear in the hearts of those around them, and both make the quiet life of knowledge, trade, art, and science look good. But there are other things going on as well in *Moby-Dick*.

A more subversive and democratic story emerges from the novel if we turn from Ahab to the men, especially to Ishmael, and from "the whale" of its subtitle (the invulnerable *Moby-Dick*) to whales, more generally, in their great power and vulnerability. Ishmael invites us to do this. He says he is drawn to the "great whale himself" (22)—this is why he joins up with the *Pequod*—but he says this long before he ever hears of Moby-Dick. So, the "great whale" to which Ishmael is drawn is not *that* great whale. It is *whales*. And this is one warrant for a reading of the novel in which the whale, Moby-Dick, is decentered and pluralized.[11]

Once we think of whales, we see how sovereignty's animalization, which was to secure sovereign absolutism, also renders sovereignty vulnerable to *democratic* powers. The men kill many whales during their time on the *Pequod*. And they overcome the panic induced by these creatures. In chapter 69, the funeral of a whale at sea is described as follows: "Thus, while in life the great whale's body may have been a real terror to his foes, in his death his ghost becomes a powerless panic to a world."[12]

Melville says in the next chapter, chapter 70, that "it should *not* have been omitted that previous to completely stripping the body of Leviathan, he was beheaded." Now, beheading is a term not normally used for hunting prey. It belongs to the lexicon of regicide. Charles I was beheaded; whales are killed or slaughtered. The choice of this word, beheaded, in the context of whaling is made even odder when we learn from Melville or Ishmael that with sperm whales there is in fact no distinction between head and body.[13] The head *is* the body. So it seems it is not actually possible to behead a whale.

How do we know this? By way of the story of Tashtego, a harpooner who falls into a whale's head when he is mining it for flesh, collecting whale spermaceti to be boiled for oil.[14] Tashtego is rescued, but Ishmael muses: "Had Tashtego perished in that head, it had been a very precious perishing; smothered in the very whitest and daintiest of fragrant spermaceti" (chap. 78).[15] Thus we find out that when we unpack the head of Leviathan it is not reason or will that we find, two kingly qualities, but sperm/flesh/blubber.[16] Leviathan is dethroned. It is all body, no head.

Or is it?

Later on, we are told not that the head is the body but that the whale has no body at all, that it is only head and tail.[17] The politics of whale head and body are worked out further in chapter 105, "Heads or Tails," which implies a wager but offers still more. Melville notes the legal requirement in England that anyone who captures a whale off the coast must give the head to the king and the tail to the queen. This, Melville notes wryly, is "a division which, in the whale, is much like halving an apple; there is no intermediate remainder." If the tail goes to the queen and the head to the king, then the one who caught the whale is left with precisely nothing. Melville asks why: Why should the queen and king between them get the whole of the whale that some ordinary fellow has caught? Why? On what authority? What grounds? "On what principle [is] the Sovereign . . . originally invested with that right?" he asks (chap. 105).

The answer, Melville says, comes from Edmund Plowdon [*sic*: Plowden], who happens to be (though Melville does not mention this) the sixteenth-century English jurist and member of the English court who formulated (along with Anthony Browne) the theory of the king's two bodies. It is Plowden, says Melville, who says that "the whale so caught belongs to the King and Queen, 'because of its superior excellence.'" That right can be delegated to any duke by the Crown. Indeed, Kantorowicz traces all of this back to debates in the 1560s over the status of the duchy and notes that in Plowden, the right to the whale is delegated to the duchy. But in Melville's chapter 105, the right belongs to the king. Plowden also says the queen needs the whalebone for her corsets, Melville says, mocking him: the bone needed for corsets is not actually in the tail but rather in the head. Why then would the Queen need the tail? Perhaps because she is a mermaid? Melville jokes.

The citation of Plowden signals that Melville is targeting the king's two bodies theory of sovereignty. If so, then Melville also has in mind the animal supplement by way of which Hobbes hoped to hold together the king's other two bodies and sovereignty's absolutism. Recall that Hobbes adds animality to sovereignty to cover over the failure of the king's two bodies theory, to counter the constitutional check that emerges out of it with the unchecked bestial, to resecure sovereignty with a third mask. But Ahab wants a reason for his suffering, and demands to see behind the mask. Melville admits the demand for justification can produce its own suffering (Ahab's own suffering illustrates the point). But Melville also seems to suggest that such demands may be their own redemption. He tilts the scales in the latter direction when he cites Plowden, only to then mock him. Plowden's way of carving up the world, allotting the deserved head or tail to the deserving king or queen, leaves nothing for the rest of us, Melville says. He asks Plowden: Is that what is on offer? The nothing of a whale-body? And the theory of the king's two bodies?

And then, at the same time, Melville says to Hobbes: And you? You are offering Leviathan? Well, that can cut many ways. Indeed, another scene in *Moby-*

Dick suggests a sustained engagement with Hobbes's *Leviathan*, both with its arguments and with its affective universe. The whales are not only hunted by the men, they are also processed on the ship. When the whale flesh is boiled for oil, aboard ship, the men sit around fleshpots and with their hands they squeeze the melted spermaceti, in order to liquefy globules of fat that resist the heat. This is wearing work, but Ishmael experiences it as a kind of joyous and loving social contract, very different from the fear-induced one imagined by Hobbes in *Leviathan* and from that exacted by Ahab from the crew. Squeezing the sperm oil with his crewmates, Ishmael gets high on its perfume ("I snuffed up that uncontaminated aroma," chap. 94). He notes with pleasure that sometimes he squeezes another man's hand in the fleshpot, mistaking it for a globule, and this gives rise in him to "an abounding, affectionate, friendly, loving feeling" (601). The joy is so powerful that he forgets "all about our horrible oath," by which he means the ship's Hobbesian contract to hunt down Moby-Dick under Ahab's absolute authority. Another collectivity has taken its place and another affect: love, not fear; brotherhood, not vengeance.

Forgetting the social contract? Confronting a leviathan that lacks a body (no people)? Melville here infiltrates the affect of *Leviathan* and retunes it. Normally trained to think of the sovereign as a head that rules over the body of the people that it incorporates (into a body), we see something rather different is going on with the whale whose head *is* its body. Could this be a *democratic* whale?

A democratic whale requires a democratic pedagogy and, once again, Ishmael shows the way. He makes the whale's anatomy his subject and says it is known best not by scientists who study it or even by ship surgeons who witness it, but by ordinary whale hunters who engage with it. Against Linnaeus, he invokes "Simeon Macey and Charley Coffin, of Nantucket, both messmates of mine in a certain voyage" (chap. 32) and, later, "practical cetology," which Ishmael himself practices when he peruses two whale heads hanging off the sides of the Pequod, one a right whale and the other a sperm whale. "Here, now, are two great whales, laying their heads together; let us join them, and lay together our own" (chap. 74). Two bodies! Lay them together, and join our own? It seems this is all that is left of Plowden's doctrine of the king's two bodies.

Ishmael studies his subjects like a practical cetologist. He walks across the deck from one side to the other. Recall how, for Hobbes, unimpeded freedom of movement is the definition of freedom ("By liberty is understood . . . the absence of external impediments," chap. 14, *Leviathan*). Freedom of movement is freedom, but here it is also knowledge. Crossing the deck, back and forth, to compare the two whales, Ishmael has an insight into their vulnerability. It turns out that that same "Mortal God" that Hobbes says is all-seeing is actually less than omnipotent. Indeed, the "puzzling question . . . concerning this visual matter as touching the Leviathan" (298), Ishmael says, is that the whale's two eyes sit at such a distance from each other (where human ears are located) that it is not possible for the whale to see what is straight ahead of him nor directly behind (chap. 74).[18] This is why ordinary whaling men in small boats can surround a sperm whale and force it into a "helpless perplexity of volition" (chap. 74). A "helpless perplexity of volition" is a significant phrase since, in chapter 6 of *Leviathan*, Hobbes establishes willing, or volition, as the last appetite in deliberation (a point since abandoned by deliberative democratic theory).[19] If, in Melville, the regal beast of sovereignty is easily paralyzed into volitional helplessness by a few whaling men working together, then the Hobbesian spell of absolute sovereignty, which is built on will not reason, is surely broken.[20]

In sum, Melville took seriously Hobbes's animalization of sovereignty in order to undo its symbolic powers.[21] Rather than reject Leviathan as others did (Harrington, Hobbes's contemporary, mockingly called it a "spit frog"), Melville shows that, fearsome as it is, Leviathan is nonetheless also vulnerable, especially if people band together against it. Leviathan can be hunted down, skinned, melted; it happens all the time. Casting such ordinary whalers as "knights and squires," Melville does not harken back to the glory days of aristocrats and nobles: he appropriates "glory" for democratic striving. He rejects the Hobbesian determination to cast glory aside, preferring to ennoble democratic purpose. Melville democratizes glory.

But a democratized glory requires people willing to step up, to assume its mantle or respond to its call. For that, Melville turns to parable, and he will end by addressing us directly.

He starts with the legal distinction between loose fish and fast fish, noting how hard it is to pin down. Loose fish are free; fast fish are caught by a line or a hook. But in real life, things get ambiguous. For example, a whale caught by one ship may get away with harpoons still in him. Is he fast or loose? Or he may be released because, although caught fast, he is still fighting and his movements threaten the ship that has caught him; so the crew cuts him loose. Then another ship may kill that wounded weakened whale and take it for themselves. The first ship will protest: our harpoons show we got him first! The others will say: yes, but we got him last. "Thus," says Melville, "the most vexatious and violent disputes would often arise between the fishermen, were there not some written or unwritten, universal, undisputed law applicable to all cases." (chap. 89, p. 571). What is that law? "American fishermen have been their own legislators and lawyers in this matter" and they live by two laws, which "found the fundamentals of all jurisprudence:" "Fast fish belong to the party fast to it. Loose fish are fair game to anyone" (chap. 89, p. 571).

But what if a fish is both fast and loose, swimming free, yet stuck with harpoons? Melville continues: "Alive or dead a fish is technically fast, when it is connected with an occupied ship or boat by *any medium controllable by the occupant or occupants—a mast, an oar, a nine-inch cable, a telegraph wire, or a strand of cobweb, it is all the same.*" The cobweb gives the game away. Melville is having a joke. But at whose expense? It turns out the question is not simply that of rightful property, it is empire. "What was America in 1492 but a Loose-Fish, in which Columbus struck the Spanish standard by way of waifing it for his royal master and mistress? . . . What will Mexico be to the United States? All Loose Fish," which is to say, free for the taking. And "What are the Rights of Man and the Liberties of the World but Loose-Fish? What all men's minds and opinions but Loose-Fish? What is the principle of religious belief in them but a Loose-Fish? What to the ostentatious smuggling verbalists are the thoughts of thinkers but Loose-Fish? What is the great globe itself but a Loose-Fish? And what are you, reader, but a Loose-Fish and a Fast-Fish, too?" Addressing us directly, that last line leaps off the page.[22] Wait, what *am* I? A loose fish? Or a fast fish, (too)?

Conclusion: University Teaching

I've proposed that we read Melville's *Moby-Dick* as a kind of how-to book that invites us to unfasten the fastenings of a still-Hobbesian sovereignty so that we might experience the freedom that is motion and become loose fish. Or looser fish, like Ishmael.

Melville hopes to loosen our fastenings by telling a story about a fast-fish come loose. Ishmael was bound fast to his work on land but he left it, unfastening himself to go on an exciting sea adventure. But—and here is the risk of that move—once on board, the now-loose Ishmael trades in the conventional social contract for one more awful: the Hobbesian oath to Ahab. Joining with the crew, Ishmael is under the total control of Ahab, and Ahab is insane. It turns out that this escapist adventure may make Ishmael more fast than loose after all. Loose fish need defending; they are easily entrapped into new oaths, new immobilities.

And so Melville also seeks to loosen our fastenings with his writing, which is shot through with precisely the kinds of neologism and wordplay that Hobbes said the sovereign of Leviathan must prevent. We know from Hobbes that it is up to the sovereign to control language and its meaning. Hobbes's sovereign holds the power of definition. Otherwise, he would be unable to control or prevent disputes, since so many of them are about language, and he could not enforce contracts, his primary responsibility, which require agreement on terms. Some people call this Hobbes's Humpty-Dumpty-ism because of this exchange in *Alice in Wonderland* that captures the Hobbesian mindset: "When *I* use a word," Humpty-Dumpty said, in rather a scornful tone, "it means just what I choose it to mean—neither more nor less." "The question is," said Alice, "whether you *can* make words mean so many different things." "The question is," said Humpty-Dumpty, "which is to be master—that's all" (*Alice in Wonderland*).

Hobbes wanted to write a book that could build a more uniform and stable polity out of unruly, riven people. He toyed with the idea of requiring its assignment at universities so as to keep in people's minds, current and present, the dangers of abandoning the social contract. Melville's heteroglossia aims to undo such an effort in almost every way, indulging in wordplay, cheekiness, irony, and more. One irony, since, is that there are now yearly readings of *Moby-Dick*, conducted communally over several days and nights, but there are none of Hobbes's *Leviathan*. In other words, only one of the two has become the Bible that the other aspired to be.

The further irony, of course, is that the world we live in, with cameras and digital surveillance everywhere, is one in which some of us are not free to move (ID's requested, hoodies suspected, public BarBQ'ing questioned), and those who think they are free of impediments are digitally trackable. It turns out the sovereign doesn't need the power of definition. The verbalists can be left to their wordplay as long as the sovereign and his partners control the algorithms and surveillance cameras. It is as if the whale's head has been redesigned: with its two eyes now coordinated and focused, ordinary people are no longer able to force a sovereign into a "helpless perplexity of volition" (chap. 74).

Those who mock, disclose, train, question, and thwart on behalf of specifically and radically democratic knowledge, practice, and pedagogy are Melville's worthy heirs. The university classroom is, at its best, one of their sites; not the scene of Leviathanic induction into static hierarchy but a space of play, (de)authorized learning, and even host to the occasional mutiny. When I taught *Moby-Dick* in 2014 at Brown, I made a few of the chapters optional, hoping better to secure the students' capacity and willingness to keep up. I will never forget how one day, as we all took our places at the table, one student protested loudly: "How could you leave out the chapter on the Town Ho? It is the best one in the book!" Others chimed in: "It has everything: a story within a story of a whale hunt, a mutiny, and an authority figure too stuck on his own power." I had not seen it coming. Today, state governors may police curricula and local school boards may ban books but, as long as *Moby-Dick* is read aloud, the mutinous spirit of democracy will not be quieted or quelled.

Notes

1. This article began as a Presidential Lecture, given at Brown University, in October 2017. Thanks to Brown President Chris Paxson for the invitation and to the Brown and Providence communities for their questions that day.

2. Michael Paul Rogin, citing Senator Henry Clay's words, in *Subversive Genealogy: The Politics and Art of Herman Melville* (Berkeley: University of California Press, 1985), 107.

3. This is what Hillel Steiner takes from Hobbes in *An Essay on Rights* (Oxford: Wiley-Blackwell, 1994).

4. See William Connolly's reading of Hobbes for the claim that fear of violent death is not natural or common but rather instilled in us by Hobbes's dramatic account of the state of nature as one to be avoided at all costs. William E. Connolly, *Political Theory and Modernity* (Oxford: Blackwell, 1988), chap. 2.

5. Victoria Kahn, *The Future of Illusion: Political Theology and Early Modern Texts* (Chicago: University of Chicago Press, 2014), 63.

6. Ernst H. Kantorowicz, *The King's Two Bodies: A Study in Mediaeval Political Theology*, with a new preface by William Chester Jordan (Princeton, NJ: Princeton University Press, 1997 [1957]), 31; quoted in Kahn, 63.

7. Kahn, *Future of Illusion*, 58.

8. Does Hobbes turn to animality to avoid what Kantorowicz calls a "curious change in Richard's attitude," in act 2, scene 3, as kingship seems to "disintegrate" into nothing? Kantorowicz describes this change as "a metamorphosis from 'Realism to Nominalism'" (in Kahn, 63). That metamorphosis may go further still. Benjamin will call it creaturely (as Kahn also points out, and as Diego Rossello has documented in "Hobbes and the Wolf-Man: Melancholy and Animality in Modern Sovereignty," *New Literary History* 43, no. 2 [Spring 2012]: 255–79), finding in Hamlet "the creaturely exposure of the person." Might Hobbes be said to have anticipated that, and perhaps sought to forestall it with his creature of sovereignty and his turn to nominalism?

9. Notably, these map onto Hannah Arendt's distinctions among three domains of human experience in *The Human Condition* (Chicago: University of Chicago Press, 2018): animal/perishable in Labor, mortal in Work, and immortal in Action.

10. Herman Melville, *Moby-Dick*, ed. Hershel Parker and Harrison Hayford, Second Norton Critical Edition (New York: W. W. Norton, 2002), 8n1.

11. But the focus remains on the whales, and not on all the animalities depicted in the novel, because we are concerned with the one animal that emblematizes sovereignty: Leviathan. It should be noted that Leviathan is a sea creature of some sort, not necessarily a whale, but Melville was making the connection, so I follow his lead. I should also note that Ilana Pardes (*Melville's Bibles* [Berkeley: University of California Press, 2008]), in her reading of the novel, points out there are many Jobs in *Moby-Dick*, and not just one, and so, I would say, why not also many whales, and not just one?

12. "A powerless panic" is quite the oxymoron. Panic, we know from Hobbes, is named for Pan, the satyr, part human, part animal, whose random screams would cause those who heard them to feel great fear but with no known cause. Hobbes says, "this passion happens to none but in a throng, or multitude of people" (*Leviathan*, 6.18). The throng that fears without direct cause worries Hobbes because panic is destabilizing. But the throng that fears is also a key element of Hobbes's project. *Leviathan* seeks to stimulate fear, so that we don't have to experience it directly for ourselves. We can just follow the fear purveyed by Hobbes, who is here in the role of Pan.

13. It may well be Hobbes who is mocked (along with so many others) when Melville has Ishmael say that the Greenland whale, until now taken by scientists as exemplary of whales, "is an usurper upon the throne of the seas . . . the Greenland whale is [now] deposed,—the great sperm whale now reigneth!" (chap. 32). Elsewhere Melville is more direct: he cites the opening lines of Hobbes's *Leviathan* in the opening pages of *Moby-Dick*. And there is a clear allusion to Hobbes in chapter 87, "The Grand Armada," when a herd of whales seen from afar is described as "sometimes embracing so great a multitude, that it would almost seem *as if numerous nations of them had sworn solemn league and covenant for mutual assistance and protection*" (chap. 87; emphasis added). Hobbes liked to say that his mother was frightened into birthing him prematurely, when she panicked at news that the Spanish Armada had sailed, so that "fear and I were born twins together." See also Joseph Adamson, *Melville, Shame, and the Evil Eye: A Psychoanalytic Reading* (New York: State University of New York Press, 1997).

14. Ishmael has elsewhere said that every time people light a lamp with whale oil they should not waste a drop because chances are some sailor has died for that oil. Whale oil is the pre–fossil oil of America's then new industrializing economy in the nineteenth century.

15. Ishmael's musing continues: "coffined, hearsed, and tombed in the secret inner chamber and sanctum sanctorum of the whale" (chap. 78).

16. The head is not immediately accessible to just anyone, no more than is "Plato's honey head" to which Melville immediately analogizes it (chap. 78). But which sort of head is *this*, this pun for two different male body parts? On this point, see George Shulman, whose essay "Chasing the Whale: *Moby-Dick* as Political Theory" in *A Political Companion to Herman Melville*, ed. Jason Frank (Lexington: University Press of Kentucky, 2014) tracks the figure and the work of "Leviathan" through Job, Hobbes, and Schmitt.

17. This brings us from Hobbes's Leviathan as a giant head of a peopled body (as in the frontispiece) to something like *The People's Monarch*, a contemporary image of Queen Elizabeth II, at Gatwick Airport in the UK, with the queen's face made up of snapshots of her subjects: all head no body.

18. "He can never see an object which is exactly ahead, no more than he can one exactly astern." It is as if for a human our ears were our eyes and we could see only from the side, even if "your bitterest foe were walking straight towards you, with

dagger uplifted in broad day" (chap. 74), as might happen in Hobbes's state of nature.

19. "In deliberation, the last appetite, or aversion, immediately adhering to the action, or to the omission thereof, is that we call the will; the act, not the faculty, of willing. And beasts that have deliberation, must necessarily also have will. The definition of the will, given commonly by the Schools, that it is a rational appetite, is not good. For if it were, then could there be no voluntary act against reason. For a voluntary act is that which proceedeth from the will, and no other. But if instead of a rational appetite, we shall say an appetite resulting from a precedent deliberation, then" willing "is the last appetite in deliberating." Hobbes, *Leviathan*, book 1, chap. 6.

20. Significantly, the idea that the whale is vulnerable to action in concert by ordinary men might have suggested to Ishmael that so, too, was Ahab, whom Leon Harold Craig takes to represent Hobbes's sovereign. It may be his awareness of this sovereign vulnerability that causes Ishmael to wonder at his own submission to Ahab's mission. Writing from a perspective different from mine, Leon Harold Craig documents many of the apparent allusions to Hobbes's *Leviathan* in Melville's great novel: "Suffice it to say, there is no shortage of features woven into *Moby-Dick* that are suggestive of Hobbes's *Leviathan*" (*The Platonian* Leviathan [Toronto: University of Toronto Press, 2010], 21). On Hobbes and Melville, see especially "A Melvillian Coda: *Moby-Dick* as Fourfold Allegory," 499–524.

21. Here the material whale, known so well by the practical cetologist, subverts the symbol or fetish of the theologized whale. See Ludwig Wittgenstein, *Philosophical Investigations*, on the distinction between the machine as symbol and the machine as it actually works. James Martel says that we can read the whale as a messianic figure in Benjamin's sense, disrupting the fetishes we project onto it. Martel's own work on fetish and Benjaminian messianism is very useful here; see James R. Martel, *Textual Conspiracies: Walter Benjamin, Idolatry, and Political Theory* (Ann Arbor: University of Michigan Press, 2011). I should add that this idea of literalizing or materializing the symbol or the fetish (e.g., the flesh) in order to work our way out from under it may well be taken to guide my reply to Eric L. Santner in *The Weight of All Flesh: On the Subject-Matter of Political Economy* (Oxford: Oxford University Press, 2016).

22. Indeed, in his book *Prophecies of Leviathan: Reading Past Melville* (New York: Fordham University Press, 2010), Peter Szendy points out that the French translator of *Moby-Dick* left that line out. For him, I guess, it literally leapt off the page.

Liberal Education and the Politics of Discussion

Benjamin Mangrum

In Mary McCarthy's novel *The Groves of Academe* (1952), a group of faculty at fictional Jocelyn College have convened to discuss their administration's decision not to renew the contract of a professor named Henry Mulcahy. The third-person narrator explains how each faculty member "felt called upon to stipulate, like a lawyer, his own degree of interest in the case, and to distinguish his own area of human solidarity from that of his neighbor, carefully set up boundaries and limits, eminent domain."[1] The reasons for supporting Mulcahy range from an appreciation for his teaching and writing to the desire to have a theist in the English Department. Some faculty are obliged by a sense of loyalty to support Mulcahy, but many others don't have strong personal feelings for their colleague. Instead, the novel depicts a larger imperative at work in the desire of each "to stipulate, like a lawyer, his own degree of interest in the case." No one *calls upon* the faculty to discuss Mulcahy's dismissal; they "felt called upon" by some unnamed compulsion. It's as though the law and order of academe stirs within each academic, demanding that matters of substance be considered through the practice of discussion.

McCarthy treats the silent rules and internalized norms at play in academic life with a deep-seated irony. For example, the participants are described as "neighbors," but their communal effort leads to a process of individuation, each participant identifying some private domain of a generalized feeling ("his own area of human solidarity"). The general becomes parceled out into the "boundaries and limits" of individual feelings. The discussion doesn't enable the participants to understand one another; it's a technique for separating the self from others. *I believe this, but she holds to that.* Indeed, in an inversion of the governmental right to "eminent domain," the participants expropriate a matter of public interest for private ends. The compulsion to deliberate within an academic community leads to the disarticulation of that community. In McCarthy's depiction, the politics of discussion is a politics of the ego.

I take McCarthy's skepticism as a starting point for considering how the politics of discussion fits within the history and institutional forms of a liberal education. The first section traces the changing rationale behind a liberal education. The second examines how the idea of small discussion-based classes entered higher education in the US. Together, these two sections demonstrate that the politics of discussion is rooted in the postwar politics of a liberal education. The third section extends the insights of the first two by considering how discussion-based practices inherit the norms of this complicated genealogy. I'll consider the extent to which discussion prescribes a common liberal culture—or at least a "common method" for liberal democracy.

Liberal Education and a Common Culture

McCarthy's novel is a useful starting point for understanding the politics of discussion because of two developments contemporaneous with its publication. The first and most immediate context for the novel was the Second Red Scare—a period of institutionalized anxiety about leftist politics in Hollywood, higher education, and US government agencies. The novel alludes to this context when one professor hastily refers to "Senator McCarthy, the Hiss trial, the crisis of liberalism in American universities" (93). Yet McCarthy's novel depicts this panic about communism as a smokescreen for private intrigue. A federal agent visited Jocelyn College a week before the president notified Mulcahy that his contract would not be renewed. Mulcahy uses this coincidence to argue that his past affiliation with the Communist Party led the college president to fire him. The federal agent had not questioned the president about Mulcahy's politics, but concern about the *appearance* of political pressure allows Mulcahy to coerce the president to renew his contract. The "crisis of liberalism" takes a backseat to the schemes and idiosyncratic delusions of the professorate.

If the institutional crisis of postwar liberalism surfaces in *The Groves of Academe* only to be casually dismissed, a different kind of crisis within liberalism nonetheless remains one of the novel's central preoccupations. This second crisis centers on what a liberal education can offer a politically polarized and socially heterogeneous public. These debates began much earlier but changed in important ways after the Second World War. A substantial body of scholarship has examined the history of these changes in the philosophy of liberal education. Discussion-based pedagogy reacted against certain elements of this evolving philosophy, but I'll later argue that contemporaneous discussion practices have not escaped the political problems that this pedagogy often purports to address.

Earlier conceptions of a liberal education aimed broadly to shape "Christian character" by inculcating generalized virtues or habits of thought.[2] In the classic conception of a liberal education, Christianity "provided the 'essential condition' for all knowledge and culture."[3] For example, John Henry Newman's *The Idea of a University Defined and Illustrated* (1858) offers one of the earliest and most influential theories. An English churchman and theologian, Newman views "liberal knowledge, or a gentleman's knowledge" as the "scope of a University."[4] He developed this theory in opposition to the idea of professional specialization that was gaining currency in Anglophone academic institutions. Industrialization and an increasingly professionalized society made demands upon education that Newman felt would be deleterious to "culture" and "character." Matthew Arnold would offer a secular version of this argument a decade later. According to Arnold, education in "culture" leads to the production of a certain kind of self, which "turn[s] a stream of fresh and free thought upon our stock notions and habits, which we now follow staunchly but mechanically, vainly imagining that there is a virtue in following them staunchly which makes up for the mischief of following them mechanically."[5] While there are major differences in these conceptions of education, both Newman and Arnold hoped that knowledge or culture would liberate the mind and guide the social life of the educated.[6]

The professionalization of research methods, a changing student body, and a link made in the popular press between education and middle-class commercial aspirations challenged this older conception of a liberal education.[7] The result was that, by the 1940s, most colleges and universities expressed ideals about a liberal education through a narrow set of requirements—namely, through decisions about the general education curriculum. Yet these attempts to achieve a liberal education through "general" or "universal" curricula were driven by a political impulse: college presidents and educators argued that the establishment of general education requirements would inculcate a common culture. Perhaps the most influential example was the report produced by a committee of Harvard faculty called *General Education in a Free Society* (1945). The report, often referred to as the Redbook, acknowledged the importance of specialized research but also argued that a general education would create a "binding experience" for high school and university students.[8] It envisions "education in a common heritage and toward a common citizenship."[9] The president of Harvard University, James Bryant Conant, presented a closely related rationale for liberal education in his book *Education in a Divided World*

(1948): "A set of common beliefs is essential for the health and vigor of a free society," Conant argues, "and it is through education that these beliefs are developed in the young and carried forward later in life."[10] In this view, common curricular requirements bind the self to "free society."

This need for a common culture derived in large part from midcentury political conditions. Worries about global communism led Conant to describe "the system of universal education as an instrument of national policy."[11] Conant believed that a general education could reinforce the culture of liberal democracy domestically, thus holding at bay the spread of communism globally. This notion illustrates how Cold War anxieties animated the reformulation of nineteenth-century ideas about "a gentleman's knowledge" toward liberal programs for a general education. Gerald Graff describes Conant's theory of general education as a "nationalistic conception of cultural unity" developed in opposition to the notion of "class struggle."[12] Whereas class consciousness divides, a general education unifies. This midcentury view held that an education in liberal culture would offer national unity against an external threat. In other words, the common values disseminated by postwar general education programs often dressed up American liberalism in the regalia of universalism.

The midcentury writer and critic Lionel Trilling offered a less nationalistic version of this support for liberal education. Trilling taught Columbia University's Colloquium on Important Books—an honors course that would later be the model for the humanities requirements in the university's general education program.[13] Trilling had been a student at Columbia and enrolled in the first version of the Colloquium. Drawing on this experience as both student and professor, he notes, "The American system, conceiving of literature as a necessary element, but only an element, in a general university education, supposes that enough has been done if the sensibility of the undergraduate has been engaged, although of course a great deal more than this is often accomplished."[14] Trilling's description includes more than a hint of irony, but he nonetheless concurs with the notion of requiring literary study in a general education curriculum because such a requirement makes good on what he calls a "moral impulse," that is, an attempt to "produce the judgment of 'what is really good and really evil in human life.'"[15] He believes that humanistic requirements in a "general university education" have a norming effect upon the "manner and style" of the student.[16] They do not disseminate "doctrine" or "systems, ethics, and creeds." Instead, educators increase "enlightenment and sensibility" both in "the private life and in the social life."[17] This education in sensibility creates more than "mere practical arrangements"; it fosters a particular "style of life."[18] Higher education is therefore in the business of shaping selves and fostering a wider liberal culture, an argument that revises but nonetheless has recognizable consistencies with Newman's argument about "liberal knowledge."[19]

A closely related cultural project informed the core curriculum at the University of Chicago. In the middle of the twentieth century, Chicago's core was considered "the most thoroughgoing experiment in general education of any college in the United States."[20] Prior to the adoption of the core curriculum, the undergraduate curriculum was entirely elective. The curricular requirements that replaced this lax system would expand substantially: from 1943 to 1953, the BA degree consisted almost entirely of general education courses. Anne H. Stevens explains that this curricular design collapsed under the weight of several problems:

> After completing the Chicago degree, students found they had to do additional coursework to be accepted into graduate programs anywhere but Chicago. The lack of personal choice in the program, its reputed rigor, and the length of time needed to prepare adequately for the exams, sometimes five or six years, kept undergraduate enrollments low.[21]

This form of general education was abandoned at Chicago in 1953, and the university returned to a two-year sequence of general education courses followed by two years of specialization.[22] While vocationalism, undergraduate enrollment, and preparation for graduate study exerted pressure on the midcentury shape of the Chicago curriculum, the liberalizing and generalizing rationales have persisted in the institution's culture. They were even invoked during debates over proposed changes to undergraduate course requirements in 1999, such that one protester reportedly yelled out, "Long live Hutchins!" (a reference to the president who established the university's core curriculum).[23]

McCarthy's *The Groves of Academe* ironizes these midcentury ideals about a liberal education. We see this irony in the novel's epigraph: *Atque inter silvas academi quaerere verum* ("And seek for truth in the groves of academe"). This epigraph, taken from one of Horace's epistles, invokes the pastoral (*silvas*), suggesting a kind of innocent, pure, and natural association between academe and truth. Yet in the first pages of the opening chapter, Henry Mulcahy fabricates a terminal illness for his wife, exaggerates his past relationship to the Communist Party, invents an unwritten commitment by the Jocelyn president to hire him permanently, and manipulates one of his students by relaying a distorted account of being "fired from Jocelyn" (19). If truth is to be found in academe, McCarthy's novel offers no reliable guides for this sylvan pursuit.

McCarthy's best-selling novel is a skeptical variation on an important midcentury development: the explicit connection between political deliberation and the ideals associated with liberal education. The less skeptical varieties of this connection held that liberal education was the answer to social and political ills. As Sam Reese explains, this midcentury view drew especially on two "liberal" tenets: "On the one hand, art and literature could be powerful tools in bettering the individual and helping them develop into a more sophisticated entity; on the other, intellectuals in the UK and the United States argued that art should be leveraged to engender a greater level of freedom for society as a whole."[24] In short, education sophisticates the self and betters society. I'll argue in the next section that challenges to this midcentury view gave rise to the theory and practice of discussion-based pedagogies.

A Genealogy of Discussion

Most justifications for discussion-based pedagogy are continuous with the midcentury argument that education inculcates liberal identity and a free society. For instance, Stephen D. Brookfield and Stephen Preskill's widely cited handbook *Discussion as a Way of Teaching* describes discussion as fostering "engaged pluralism," a term they adopt from the educator Richard Bernstein. This theory holds that pluralism may be fostered in the classroom because discussion can diffuse power: if a discussion is designed properly, it allows the participants to stand on more equal footing, thus mitigating inequalities produced by authority and social position.[25] Discussion activities "seek out multiplicity."[26] Whereas a lecture disseminates specialized knowledge, educational theorists argue that discussion multiplies the sites of authority that produce knowledge. Indeed, they argue that discussions do not require the exhibition of expertise in the subject matter, only in the method of facilitation—a dynamic that ostensibly allows for greater equality in classroom spaces.[27] This theorization suggests that discussion-based pedagogy amounts to preparation for—and perhaps even an instantiation of—civic life in a liberal democracy. When faculty use discussion, they not only "teach democratically," as Brookfield and Preskill put it, but they teach the procedures and ethos of democracy itself.[28]

Conant, Trilling, and others thought of an updated liberal education as the dissemination of a common culture, but Brookfield and Preskill's view illustrates how recent educational trends shift the terms of a "binding experience" away from the *curricular content* of a general education and toward the *curricular methods* of academic life. This shift in the mandate of a liberal education has developed slowly in the US since the Second World War, but this adjusted mandate still regularly draws on the postwar association between education and liberal democracy. The student's intellectual formation within classroom discussion takes its rationale from liberal democratic norms regarding civic society. As the subtitle of Brookfield and Preskill's handbook puts it, discussion-based pedagogies are "tools and techniques for democratic classrooms." This view illustrates an important but relatively recent rationale for the *forms* of a liberal education.

I'm not rejecting this rationale, but I am scrutinizing its genealogy and the kind of politics it has generated. Later in this chapter, I'll argue that the theory and practices of discussion depend upon a formalist conception of politics, which has failed to resolve the problems of selection and compulsion that harried earlier forms of liberal education. To better understand these problems and how discussion-based pedagogy inherits them, we need to investigate how the ideals of a liberal education came to be associated with discussion—an association that I trace in this section.

The fact that the term "discussion" names a mundane activity can create some confusion about its genealogy. The term seems so natural and innocent that it escapes notice. It has become an idea that, to borrow from Ludwig Wittgenstein, "is like a pair of glasses on our nose through which we see whatever we look at. It never occurs to us to take them off."[29] The ordinariness of discussion obscures its historical novelty as a pedagogical form. If we were to take the glasses off, if only momentarily, we would see the historical contingencies that have transformed this mundane activity into an apparatus for academic discourse.[30]

Another source of confusion is that "discussion" names dozens of loosely related pedagogical techniques across academic disciplines. For example, some instructors in the humanities and social sciences create discussion through a method called the "fishbowl," in which a subset of students in a larger class evaluate a focused passage from an assigned reading while the remaining students sit in a circle around the group and listen to their deliberations. The students observing the discussion do not participate in it, although they may refer to their peers' comments at a later moment in the class meeting. In contrast to this method, many law schools practice a very different kind of discussion during large lectures, using the term as a label for the "call out" method in which the lecturer identifies individual students and asks them to explain points of case law. Both techniques invoke Socratic dialogue as antecedents, although it's not clear that the institutional and professional settings of either clearly derive from the public function of philosophy in fifth-century Athens.[31] In any case, as Derek Bok explains, there is a relatively long history of modern research institutions conjuring the ghost of Socrates.[32]

Despite this wide variation in practice and its purported antecedents in the classical era, discussion-based pedagogies primarily developed in the US during the second half of the twentieth century. One of the primary sources for the legitimation of discussion was a growing body of educational research on active learning. This formalization of discussion has its roots in the educational philosophy of John Dewey and other pragmatists, but the scholarship on active learning first developed in the 1960s and then rose precipitously after 1980.[33] Research from this period found that few students had significant prior experience with discussions in an educational setting.[34] And when teachers were trained to incorporate discussion into their classrooms, researchers found that those instructors regularly posed questions only to answer them on behalf of their students. Discussion felt new and hard to implement.[35]

By the early 1990s, federally funded research on higher education urged college and university faculty to shift away from "traditional lecture methods, in which professors talk and students listen."[36] Some courses in the humanities and social sciences had already shifted to discussion-based formats—a shift I'll return to below—but this reorientation was somewhat slower to occur in other disciplines. For instance, educational theories on active learning influenced the design of some STEM classrooms in the late 1990s and 2000s. This shift in the design of classrooms allowed physics instructors to eliminate or at least reduce their reliance on lectures, focusing instead on *"tangibles* (hands-on activities) and *ponderables* (key questions on common misconceptions)."[37]

While discussion appears to enter STEM fields around the turn of the twenty-first century, it is more difficult to trace the history of these techniques with certainty in the humanities and social sciences because of the paucity of archival and firsthand sources on the classroom experience. In *The Teaching Archive*, for instance, Rachel Sagner Buurma and Laura Heffernan note how rare it is to find archives of teaching materials "organized and preserved by their creator with an eye to their future survival and potential use by others."[38] This paucity of firsthand classroom sources makes it difficult to determine the extent to which formalized discussion activities entered the pedagogical repertoire of the modern university. Still, if we take educational research as a proxy for the history of discussion-based pedagogical techniques, this research suggests that the techniques became somewhat common in certain subjects in the United States during the 1960s, growing in prevalence over the next forty years.

Using educational research as a proxy for the prevalence of discussion techniques in the classroom runs parallel with an adjacent development: the history of discussion-based course formats. In the United States, the oldest form of teaching at the college level was not the lecture (as is often assumed) but the recitation. "Although lecturing was not unknown," Lawrence Veysey explains, "the basic method of teaching in nearly every classroom in 1865 was the 'recitation.' The recitation was not a discussion group in the twentieth-century sense; it was utterly alien to the spirit of Socratic byplay. Rather it was an oral quiz, nearly an hour in length, held five times per week throughout the academic year."[39] Yet this method of teaching shifted in the late nineteenth century, with the lecture hall, the laboratory, and the seminar representing the three "basic types of instruction [that] came into prominence in the new American university."[40] The uniting feature of these three types of instruction was their emphasis on research. The antebellum university was a space for piety and elite enculturation, while the "new American university" came increasingly to center on the production of specialized knowledge.

The seminar, not the recitation, first introduced the seeds of discussion into American higher education, although this format was nonetheless oriented around expertise in a way that is at odds with present-day discussion-based courses. The seminar was first practiced at the University of Berlin in the 1830s and appeared in the US during the 1880s.[41] As Julie A. Reuben demonstrates, the seminar developed in American higher education as a counterpart to the laboratory. Educational reformers felt that professors in the social sciences ought to "teach the process of intellectual discovery by guiding students through a research project in small seminar classes."[42] In effect, professors would model research methods in the seminar, often inviting students to participate in their critical inquiry. The seminar thus foregrounded the professor's expertise and emphasized professionalized research. It centered practical methods in a way that is adjacent to, but still different from, the discussion-based courses that would become a common offering in US universities later in the twentieth century. The spirit of the seminar, we might say, was not an egalitarian or democratic space for the exchange of ideas.

It was only after the Second World War, but especially in the mid-1960s, that discussion-based courses became common in the academic humanities. Columbia University called for small discussion-based courses in its General Honors curriculum during the 1930s. However, as Graff explains, it was not until the 1940s that these changes were implemented:

> For one thing, the small discussion classes called for by the General Honors model were expensive, especially when, as at Columbia, they were "team-taught" by two instructors. Large-scale implementation would require a level of economic expansion well beyond the universities of the twenties and thirties. For another, the opposition of research scholars, who suspected discussion courses of dilettantism and who

saw general education programs as impediments to teaching their specialties, was able to keep such experiments marginal until after World War II.[43]

The discussion-based class posed a threat to faculty who felt that the university ought to be oriented around research. This insertion of discussion into the classroom was "political" at least in the sense that it challenged established perceptions of academic power, however modest those challenges may have been in reality. Within this vein of midcentury skepticism about the idea of discussion, faculty felt that it devalued expertise and might also require pedagogical changes that would undermine the ability of faculty to sustain the kind of specialized research that was often tested out in seminars and lecture halls. In its historical development, then, the politics of discussion-based classes centered on debates about both the nature of the university and the pedagogical role of the faculty's authority.

There is a notable exception within the genealogy of discussion-based courses: the revision to the curriculum at St. John's College in Annapolis, Maryland, during the late 1930s. St. John's was nearly bankrupt after the Great Depression, and the college adopted curricular changes first proposed (but never fully implemented) at the University of Chicago. The college instituted what Anne Stevens calls the "purest institutional embodiment of [the] ideal of general education."[44] Undergraduates studied exclusively within a four-year general education program, which consisted of discussion-based courses on "one hundred great books, . . . supplemented with lectures, laboratory experiments, and language tutorials."[45] St. John's is an exception in the genealogy of discussion-based courses, because it did not encounter resistance from research-focused faculty. It eliminated specialization at the undergraduate level, and it did so by relying almost exclusively on discussion-based courses—a curricular design that no other American institution of higher education had implemented at the time.

While few institutions would follow the St. John's model, discussion-based courses would become a staple in higher education later in the twentieth century. There were many reasons for this development, but perhaps the most important was a challenge to the research model of education that lay behind seminars, laboratories, and lectures. Louis Menand explains that the research model of the university, while supposedly focused on "disinterested" scholarship, had led many social-scientific and humanistic fields to aid the highly interested US State Department and other government agencies from the 1940s through the 1960s. This model of "disinterested" scholarship fell under scrutiny during the Vietnam War, as students, staff, and faculty questioned how knowledge production supported state-sponsored violence. This scrutiny in turn led to the revival of John Dewey's model of teaching as a collaborative process.[46] Collaboration would better approximate equality, this school of thought maintained, because more dialectical avenues for the evaluation and production of knowledge might bring to light authoritarian uses of that knowledge.

Dewey's writings on education, while not centrally concerned with discussion-based courses, nonetheless illustrate why the institutional turn toward these courses coincided with the scrutiny of "disinterested" scholarship. As we saw above, the notion of "liberal knowledge" transformed at midcentury into an emphasis on the dissemination of a "common culture," yet two political problems harried this transition—namely, the politics of selection and compulsion. Dewey touched on the first of these when he responded to the generalists' attempts to reorganize the curriculum at Chicago.[47] The vision of a so-called Great Conversation facilitated through common cultural texts was, as James Sloan Allen puts it, predicated on "the coherence of Western culture."[48] This coherence was produced through a hierarchy of knowledge: *these* texts and subjects are exemplary of a shared culture, while *those* aren't. Such a hierarchy illustrates that the design of a general education curriculum is a statement of values, implicitly asserting what counts as common culture and the body of knowledge that an educational institution deems requisite for participation in contemporary society. Yet Dewey noted that the university's attempts to institute this "hierarchy of learning" had "conveniently ignored . . . who is to determine the definite truths that constitute the hierarchy."[49] As subsequent debates about the literary canon would clarify, the very notion of a common culture or Great Books tradition hides the politics of selection. It takes "common knowledge" and "liberal culture" as self-evident baskets of content, when in fact both are constructions that cannot be separated from the historical contingencies produced by racial, gendered, and national politics.

The increasing importance of discussion-based courses and pedagogies has often presented a solution to the politics of selection in general education programs. Pedagogical theorists note how the top-down model of lectures and canonical lists of Great Books are instantiations of rigid power hierarchies, and they argue that discussion decenters faculty expertise while inviting students to think independently about course subject matter. For example, in *Teaching to Transgress* (1994), bell hooks defines discussion as both "action" and "subversive practice," particularly when it is a "collective struggle to discuss issues of gender and blackness without censorship."[50] According to hooks, discussion-based pedagogies make space for those experiences, identities, and issues that traditional pedagogies have suppressed.

There is a definite through-line between Dewey and hooks: both view education as a form of action. For hooks, critical discussion-based pedagogy not only prepares learners for civic action but also revises established hierarchies within educational institutions. Critical discussion "eliminates the possibility that [instructors] can function as all-knowing, silent interrogators."[51] Conservative academics, according to hooks, worry that critical discussions "will dismantle the bourgeois idea of a 'professor' and that, as a consequence, the sense of our significance and our role as teachers in the classroom would need to be fundamentally changed."[52] Dewey similarly argues that democracy depends upon "the breaking down of those barriers of class, race, and national territory which kept men from perceiving the full import of their activity."[53] He argues that the industrialization of society requires that educational institutions deliberately sustain "the liberation of a greater diversity of personal capacities which characterize democracy."[54] In effect, both hooks and Dewey maintain that passive forms of education work against the democratic aims of a liberal education.

The politics of selection in philosophies of general education have long been vulnerable to the criticisms levied against them by thinkers like Dewey and hooks. So far, we've seen that the knowledge that counts as "general" became suspect for both political and philosophical reasons. Yet hooks extends the hierarchy-of-knowledge problem beyond curricular requirements. She argues that addressing the political problems besetting American education requires not only a change in the *content* of the curriculum; it also requires a change in *pedagogy*. hooks maintains that critically informed and thoughtfully designed discussions can be "an interrogation of the biases conventional canons (if not all canons) establish."[55] According to this view, the design of the in-class experience, much like the design of a reading list, either challenges or reinforces social hierarchies.

So, the hierarchy-of-knowledge problem not only led to a change in the books, ideas, and disciplines taught in colleges and universities; it also provoked substantive changes in the methods of instruction. Such changes are, as hooks argues, essential for "creating a democratic liberal arts learning experience."[56] hooks's transformative pedagogy illustrates a subtle but crucial development in the idea of a liberal education. Dewey's older identification of the politics of selection asks questions about curricular content and institutional authority: Which texts and disciplines count as "general" knowledge? Whose understanding of "culture" receives institutional legitimacy? What powers within the institution will determine the structure of knowledge? hooks's advocacy extends these questions into new domains, calling attention to how the politics of selection is also a politics of the forms of pedagogy. She notes, for example, that professors "may attempt to deconstruct traditional biases while sharing that information through body posture, tone, word choice, and so on that perpetuate those very hierarchies and biases they are critiquing."[57] From this perspective, the methods of instruction matter as much as curricular content to the transformative power of a liberal education. Indeed, the body of the professor has become part of the curriculum. The forms and performativity of pedagogy are now essential components in this emerging conception of a liberal education.

So far, I have argued that midcentury conceptions of a liberal education retained a classic emphasis on changing selves, but the generalists of the 1940s and 1950s added to this rationale by insisting that higher education offers a binding experience and disseminates a common culture.[58] Later in the twentieth century, the legitimation crisis of higher education began to shift the pedagogical work of subject-formation away from prescriptive requirements about disciplines, courses, and texts, placing increasing emphasis on modes of instruction. The result is that the rationale for a liberal education has often come to be based less on the content of the curriculum than on the *methods of inquiry and discursive exchange* that students learn through the curriculum.

The Politics of Discussion

Discussion has become a central technique in a new philosophy of liberal education. This philosophy no longer takes its rationale from Important Books but from Important Methods. The postwar development of this view challenged faculty perceptions of research and authority, but it has also offered a way for disciplines to address the politics of selection. For example, professors can use discussion-based pedagogies to "teach the conflicts" surrounding disciplinary knowledge.[59] Or, discussion signifies a political disavowal of the professor's authority in what Henry A. Giroux describes as the "unarguably normative" arrangement of higher education.[60] For Giroux, a critical pedagogy "*produce[s]* rather than merely *transmit[s]* knowledge within the asymmetrical relations of power that structure teacher-student relationships." The forms of classroom instruction require attention because "what we teach and how we do it are deeply implicated not only in producing various forms of domination but also in constructing active practices of resistance and struggle."[61] Such accounts present critical, egalitarian discussions as an end run around the normativity of canon formation and the hierarchies of knowledge created by the disciplinary order of higher education.

I argued in the previous section that the development of discussion-based pedagogies is a proxy for the wider shift in American philosophies of liberal education: the pedagogical method has become the message. Or at least it has become a major element of that message. Yet the intellectual and political appeal of discussion can often lead to an under-theorized understanding of its politics. Discussion isn't a panacea to the politics of selection or the professor-centered classroom. Discussion-based pedagogies *transmit* knowledge, too, even if that knowledge is rooted in the tacit norms and procedures that structure the classroom experience.

Let's consider how compulsion subtly and silently operates in the uses of classroom discussion. At the most basic level, instructors lace discussion with compulsion by associating students' in-class contributions with a participation grade. Arranging classrooms in a circle or eagerly searching students' faces for reactions to a question or idea likewise becomes a *transmission* of knowledge. Such practices transfer norms once hidden in the seemingly self-evident value of Great Books into the forms of classroom space and discursive procedures. The effect of these pedagogical choices is to prescribe behavior. Literature reviews and exams also prescribe behavior, of course, but we don't tend to justify those assignments by invoking democracy or the cultivation of civic virtues like empathy and dialogue. The trouble comes, I think, when we too readily and uncritically confer upon discussion the mantle of democracy. Given the brief history of discussion-based courses and pedagogies, it's not even clear to me that these are preferable *forms* for a liberal education.

But what is clear to me is that discussion techniques have assumed the aura of a fetish, untouchable despite our constant touching and attempts at gratification. It's also clear to me that students perceive discussion-based teaching techniques as prescriptive and coercive at least as often as they enjoy their freedom and openness. For instance, in a study of the "culture of problems" in education, one student reported objections to being forced to analyze literary texts: "I have talked to some students that I know feel this way. They dislike the thought of being forced to pick apart why things went a certain way. One, they don't see the point, two, they sometimes have no clue what's going on, and three, they could care less why it happened."[62] The student explicitly associates the instructor's requests to analyze the literary readings as an act of compulsion—that is, they are "forced to pick apart" the assigned reading during class. From this perspective, the students don't "get to" participate in a democratic classroom; they feel compelled to perform before a monarchy that thinks of itself as benevolent.

The shadow of compulsion that falls over pedagogies of discussion has precedents in the liberal tradition. These precedents exemplify how liberalism has at times been in tension with democracy. John McGowan notes, for instance, that the history of compulsory education historically arose out of liberal elites who feared the *demos*. For intellectuals like John Stuart Mill and Matthew Arnold, the masses were ignorant and governed by "weak-willed susceptibility to outside influences." Compulsory education became a way to make the masses "ready" for democracy.[63] This indecorous history calls attention to a hazard in liberal philosophies that associate education with democratic participation. Might there be a similar class anxiety underlying our pedagogies of discussion?

We may see vestiges of this class structure when we assert that discussion activities prepare students for civil dialogue, public engagement, or responsible citizenship. If we wear our skeptic's hat and interrogate these assertions, we might ask what they imply about the masses who don't take our classes. Are we suggesting that those who lack a university education also lack a common culture? They've missed a binding experience, we seem to suggest, and as such our pedagogical values cleave "us" and "them." When democracy goes awry, it's easy to blame the undereducated, and the democratic virtues we associate with discussion-based pedagogy are then put to the service of class antagonisms.

Yet the student's response cited above calls attention to another level of compulsion that surrounds our practices of discussion. The survey response also invites us to consider how academic situations lead students to internalize instructional procedures and norms. We see this in the second kind of discussion that surfaces in the student's response—that is, how she "talked to some students that I know." It's tempting to see this as a rhetorical device that allows the student to displace her feelings onto her peers. However, the other interviews in the study bear out her impressions, and more important, her metacognition about the in-class experience illustrates how she has absorbed the picking-apart of a literary text and now deploys the same strategy when talking about academic discourse. The student presents three reasons why the in-class discussions are objectionable, expressing them sequentially and coherently. It's almost as if the student "sees through" the instructor's invitation to talk about the literary work, finding demands and stipulations beneath its surface. The student reads for depth, applies a hermeneutic of suspicion to the classroom-as-text. She then argues by invoking a deliberative process as the basis for her perspective. The *forms* of objecting to compulsory discussion nonetheless follow the *norms* of academic speech-acts.

This extracurricular discussion of classroom procedures illustrates a dynamic at play in a classic debate between C. J. B. Macmillan and James Garrison.[64] Drawing on Wittgenstein's philosophy, Macmillan argues that the enabling social conditions of modern education necessarily lead to the indoctrination of students, even though such an outcome is opposed to the goals of educational institutions. Here is the basic paradox as Macmillan sees it:

> In a modern democratic society, the desired goal of education is that each student develop a set of beliefs that are rationally grounded and open to change when challenged by better-grounded beliefs. In order to develop such students, however, it would seem that they must acquire a belief in rational methods of knowing which must lie beyond challenge, i.e., held in a manner inconsistent with its own content. Thus students must be indoctrinated in order not to be indoctrinated: a pedagogical dilemma or paradox.[65]

The desire for a "democratic society" requires that certain "methods of knowing . . . lie beyond challenge." But this is itself a kind of indoctrination, according to Macmillan, because it asks students to accept unconditionally a *method* as though it were axiomatic.

Garrison responds to Macmillan by saying that education should "inoculate" students to "indoctrination" by introducing doubt.[66] For Garrison, the problem of indoctrination centers on the dissemination of a single "world-picture."[67] By introducing students to multiple world-pictures, teachers circumvent the problem of indoctrination by showing the contingencies of values associated with any particular world-picture. If we were to agree with Garrison, we might say that discussion circumvents the problem of indoctrination, showing students how to understand different perspectives and scrutinize the received norms and inherited positions they bring to the classroom. Discussion inoculates but doesn't indoctrinate.

Yet it seems to me that Garrison's response misses the first-order problems posed by the politics of our pedagogical choices. The student who felt "forced to pick apart" a literary text but then employs a similar method in her criticisms is introducing doubt into the value of discussions in a liberal arts classroom. Yet I wouldn't say that she has been inoculated from indoctrination. Her response instead inhabits "the discourse of [her] readers," as David Bartholomae puts it. She's writing not for herself but for the professors interviewing her about her classroom experience with other professors. This kind of response invokes what Bartholomae describes as "a context beyond the reader that is not the world but a way of thinking about the world, a way of talking that determines the use of examples, the possible conclusions, the acceptable commonplaces, and the key words of an essay."[68] She draws on institutionally sanctioned discursive methods to criticize the discursive routines of her educational institution.

The emphasis on method in late-twentieth- and twenty-first-century liberal education produces this kind of discourse within students. Like its predecessors in the nineteenth and early twentieth centuries, the liberal discourse about discussion is wrapped up in a way of thinking about the world. It's worth taking the glasses off our nose and thinking about the limitations of this world-picture. Does requiring students to talk through their readings, experiences, and reasons imply that the "point" is the discussion? Have the forms of our pedagogy become ends in themselves? Is "the exchange of ideas" a compelling enough rationale for students who now have a multitude of digital platforms that readily facilitate discussions not curated by a professor? Does the pedagogy of discussion generate a liberal culture that sacralizes the multiplicity of discourse?

It is tempting to argue that we should address these questions about politics and pedagogy by discussing them with students. Graff, for instance, maintains that having students discuss matters of pedagogy and disciplinary knowledge ought to be the default response to the intellectual and political difficulties created by our disciplines. Graff has in mind the many academic methods that appear "odd" to students, such as the assumption that something "deeper" lies behind a writer's words: "I believe the best way of dealing with these apparent oddities is not to avoid them, but to build classroom discussions and writing assignments around the questions they pose and to let students debate these questions."[69] This is a recognizably liberal response to tensions generated by the liberal tradition. More speech is the solution to the politics of speech. Or, in the classroom, more discussion is the solution to the politics of discussion.

This solution can lead into frustratingly circular reasoning. If the links between democracy and discussion-based pedagogy are historically recent, should we use that pedagogical method to scrutinize its norms and assumptions? My worry is that an automatic association between democratic politics and pedagogical discussion can invite a hollow formalism within academic institutions. For instance, the claim that "student participation" is the guiding impulse behind discussion activities elevates the *method* of contributing discourse above the political effects and enabling conditions of the institutions in which the discourse occurs.[70] The commitment to student participation as an intrinsic good implies, *Stick with the form and a healthy democracy will follow*. It's an ahistorical sentiment, one that assumes there will be institutions to support discursive exchange. But what if the institutions undermine themselves? What if the commitment to open discussion delays action on existential crises or structural forms of injustice? The liberal proliferation of competing ideas and narratives can, of course, be useful in misinformation campaigns, and an uncritical commitment to discussion can license institutional feet-dragging.

I'm not suggesting that we abandon associations between discussion-based pedagogy and democratic values. However, I am suggesting that pedagogies which invoke only *forms* and *methods* as solutions to liberal paradoxes produce a contradictory and potentially self-defeating kind of politics. These ways of thinking about discussion lead us into conceptions of "human solidarity" produced by "carefully set[ting] up boundaries and limits," as McCarthy puts it (91). The political failure would be for discussion to lead only to individuation and detachment. If formal discussion has become part of the new Important Methods disseminated by liberal education, then the common solidarity we gain through such a method may become little more than a design of the self.

Notes

1. Mary McCarthy, *The Groves of Academe* (New York: Harcourt, Brace, 1952), 91. Hereafter cited parenthetically.

2. Julie A. Reuben, *The Making of the Modern University: Intellectual Transformation and the Marginalization of Morality* (Chicago: University of Chicago Press, 1996), 4–5.

3. Reuben, 83.

4. John Henry Newman, *The Idea of a University Defined and Illustrated: In Nine Discourses Delivered to the Catholics of Dublin* (Project Gutenberg, 2008), 111.

5. Matthew Arnold, preface to *Culture and Anarchy: An Essay in Political and Social Criticism* (Cambridge: Cambridge University Press, 1993), 190.

6. For more on "culture" and the shaping of selves, see Laurence R. Veysey, *The Emergence of the American University* (Chicago: University of Chicago Press, 1965), 197–203.

7. Anne H. Stevens, "The Philosophy of General Education and Its Contradictions: The Influence of Hutchins," *JGE: The Journal of General Education* 50, no.3 (2001): 184. On media portrayals of education and commercial aspirations, see Daniel A. Clark, *Creating the College Man: American Mass Magazines and Middle-Class Manhood, 1890–1915* (Madison: University of Wisconsin Press, 2010), 52–55.

8. *General Education in a Free Society: Report of the Harvard Committee* (Cambridge, MA: Harvard University Press, 1945), 102.

9. *General Education in a Free Society*, 5.

10. James Bryant Conant, *Education in a Divided World: The Function of Public Schools in Our Unique Society* (Westport, CT: Greenwood, [1948] 1969), 108.

11. Quoted in Gerald Graff, *Professing Literature: An Institutional History* (Chicago: University of Chicago Press, 1987), 167.

12. Graff, *Professing Literature*, 167. See also Stevens, "Philosophy of General Education," 184.

13. Louis Menand, *The Marketplace of Ideas* (New York: Norton, 2010), 36.

14. Lionel Trilling, *Beyond Culture: Essays on Literature and Learning* (New York: Viking, 1965), 217–18.

15. Trilling, 219.

16. Trilling, 222.

17. Trilling, 210.

18. Trilling, 223.

19. For more on the persistence of "shaping selves" in secular theories of education, see John McGowan, *Democracy's Children: Intellectuals and the Rise of Cultural Politics* (Ithaca, NY: Cornell University Press, 2002), 70–73.

20. Daniel Bell, *The Reforming of General Education: The Columbia College Experience in Its National Setting* (New York: Columbia University Press, 1966), 26.

21. Stevens, "Philosophy of General Education," 170.

22. This more modest form of a general education curriculum underwent complex revisions in subsequent decades. See Stevens, "Philosophy of General Education," 170–71.

23. Stevens, "Philosophy of General Education," 165.

24. Sam Reese, "Renaissance Women: Brigid Brophy, Mary McCarthy, and the Public Intellectual," *Contemporary Women's Writing* 12, no. 2 (2018): 212.

25. Stephen Brookfield, "Uncovering and Challenging White Supremacy," in *Educating for Critical Consciousness*, ed. George Yancy (New York: Routledge, 2019), 17. This diffusion of power is a design feature of certain kinds of American liberalism—consider, for instance, the Federalist Papers. Remarking on this federalist tradition within liberalism, John McGowan says that diffusion-by-design "accords with a fundamental liberal belief that proliferating sites of power is an excellent safeguard against tyranny." John McGowan, *American Liberalism: An Interpretation for Our Time* (Chapel Hill: University of North Carolina Press, 2007), 158.

26. Stephen D. Brookfield and Stephen Preskill, *Discussion as a Way of Teaching: Tools and Techniques for Democratic Classrooms*, 2nd ed. (New York: John Wiley, 2012), 18.

27. Brookfield and Preskill, *Discussion as a Way of Teaching*, 197. Graff illustrates this perspective by drawing on his experience: "I remember the relief I experienced as a beginning assistant professor [in the mid-1960s] when I realized that by concentrating on the text itself I could get a good discussion going about almost any literary work without having to know anything about its author, its circumstances of composition, or the history of its reception." Graff, *Professing Literature*, 178.

28. Brookfield and Preskill, *Discussion as a Way of Teaching*, 19.

29. Ludwig Wittgenstein, *Philosophical Investigations*, trans. G. E. M. Anscombe, P. M. S. Hacker, and Joachim Schulte, 4th ed. (Malden, MA: Wiley-Blackwell, 2009), 50.

30. By "apparatus," I mean a discursive formation "that at a given historical moment has as its major function the response to an urgency." Giorgio Agamben, *What Is an Apparatus and Other Essays*, trans. David Kishik and Stefan Pedatella (Stanford, CA: Stanford University Press, 2009), 2. I'll argue in the final section that there were two political "urgencies" that justified discussion-based pedagogies: the legitimation crisis of the concept of research specialization and the politics of selection. However, I should be clear that there have always been other rationales, including a body of research suggesting that certain discussion activities increase retention and improve quantitative outcomes like test scores. See, for example, Louis Deslauriers et al., "Measuring Actual Learning versus Feeling of Learning in Response to Being Actively Engaged in the Classroom," *PNAS* 116, no. 39 (September 2019): 19251–57.

31. For still another example of the conflation of discussion with Socratic dialogue, see Erick Wilberding, *Teach Like Socrates: Guiding Socratic Dialogues and Discussions in the Classroom* (London: Routledge, 2021).

32. Derek Bok, *Higher Learning* (Cambridge, MA: Harvard University Press, 1986), 86–90.

33. See pronouncements about the death of the lecture in F. S. Keller, "Goodbye, Teacher . . . ," *Journal of Applied Behavior Analysis* 1 (Spring 1968): 79–89.

34. Donald A. Bligh, ed., *Teach Thinking by Discussion* (Surrey, Great Britain: Society for Research into Higher Education and NFER-Nelson, 1986), 18–19.

35. Richard G. Tiberius, *Small Group Teaching: A Trouble-Shooting Guide* (Toronto: Ontario Institute for Studies in Education, 1990), 99.

36. Charles C. Bonwell and James A. Eison, *Active Learning: Creating Excitement in the Classroom*, ASHE-ERIC Higher Education Report No. 1 (Washington, DC: George Washington University, School of Education and Human Development, 1991), 5.

37. Paul Baepler et al., *A Guide to Teaching in the Active Learning Classroom: History, Research, and Practice* (New York: Stylus, 2016), 12.

38. Rachel Sagner Buurma and Laura Heffernan, *The Teaching Archive: A New History for Literary Study* (Chicago: University of Chicago Press, 2021), 45.

39. Veysey, *Emergence of the American University*, 37.

40. Veysey, 153.

41. Veysey, 153–54.

42. Reuben, *Making of the Modern University*, 66.

43. Graff, *Professing Literature*, 135.

44. Stevens, "Philosophy of General Education," 172.

45. Stevens, 172.

46. Menand, *Marketplace of Ideas*, 80. For an example of this revival, see Bonwell and Eison, *Active Learning*, 1.

47. For example, see John Dewey, *Democracy and Education* (New York: Free Press, 1916 [1944]), 109–10.

48. James Sloan Allen, *The Romance of Commerce and Culture: Capitalism, Modernism, and the Chicago-Aspen Crusade for Reform* (Chicago: University of Chicago Press, 1983), 108.

49. Quoted in Graff, *Professing Literature*, 165–66.

50. bell hooks, *Teaching to Transgress* (New York: Routledge, 1994), 67.

51. hooks, 21.

52. hooks, 140.

53. Dewey, *Democracy and Education*, 87.

54. Dewey, 87.

55. hooks, *Teaching to Transgress*, 39.

56. hooks, 38.

57. hooks, 141.

58. One might object that philosophies of education have always centered on self and society. But, as Dewey notes, both ideas "are quite meaningless taken at large, or apart from their context" (Dewey, *Democracy and Education*, 96).

59. Gerald Graff, *Beyond the Culture Wars: How Teaching the Conflicts Can Revitalize American Education* (New York: Norton, 1992). See Bill Readings's critique of this argument in *The University in Ruins* (Cambridge, MA: Harvard University Press, 1999), 112–14.

60. Henry A. Giroux, "Liberal Arts Education and the Struggle for Public Life: Dreaming about Democracy," *South Atlantic Quarterly* 89, no. 1 (1990): 114.

61. Giroux, 123.

62. Gerald Graff, "The Problem Problem and Other Oddities of Academic Discourse," *Arts and Humanities in Higher Education* 1, no. 1 (2002): 31.

63. McGowan, *Democracy's Children*, 122.

64. See C. J. B. Macmillan, "*On Certainty* and Indoctrination," *Synthese* 56, no. 3 (1983): 363–72; James E. Garrison, "The Paradox of Indoctrination: A Solution," *Synthese* 68, no. 2 (1986): 261–73.

65. Macmillan, "*On Certainty* and Indoctrination," 370.

66. Garrison, "Paradox of Indoctrination," 268.

67. Garrison, 268.

68. David Bartholomae, "Inventing the University," *Journal of Basic Writing* 5, no. 1 (1986): 8.

69. Graff, "Problem Problem," 41.

70. See, for example, George Brown and Madeleine Atkins, *Effective Teaching in Higher Education* (London: Methuen, 1988), 59.

Teaching While Arab
Mona Kareem

> We will remain powerless collaborators, in repressive tolerance if, in higher education in the humanities, we do not rethink our agency.
> —GAYATRI SPIVAK, "TEACHING FOR THE TIMES"

1

I have been teaching in the American classroom since my first year in graduate school, also my first year in the United States—talk about cheap labor. I mostly taught Arabic literature in translation, but sometimes I had to take on teaching Arabic language courses, to first- or second-generation immigrants, seated next to soldiers, future diplomats, and counterterrorism experts. I was part of the military industrial complex for a few semesters. I tried washing away my sin by teaching Arabic at community centers, or in the living rooms of Arab American families in Queens and South Brooklyn. Other times, I had to pick up English composition courses. During my first year as a graduate student, my professors—older, tenured, and white—did not bother to explain what a lesson plan is. "Teach world literature," they said, and at that point, the world was still Arabic to me.

I figured it would be safe, even ideal, to begin with our Nobel laureate, Naguib Mahfouz. Choose a novel that marks events familiar to an American reader (think World War I), a novel that explores issues, issues that can generate discussions, discussions that are conversations. Little did I know that generating discussion is the one hideous part of the American classroom experience. I assigned *Midaq Alley*, thinking it would be a safe choice, a reasonable one, with appealing characters, and a narrative arc for which the Americans yearn.

The book begins from the alley itself, the outer space, described shop by shop; each shop holds a character, each character is a door to a story, to a world. The narrator moves slowly through the landscape, as if taking the reader on a tour, which ends with the apartment building where the people of the alley reside when not performing labor. The reader may feel claustrophobic, overwhelmed, a feeling a first-time tourist in Cairo may recognize. It is that specific alley of which the novel is made, with its shops lined up in an order that brings them to interact throughout the day: it plays a role in the development of the narrative—how it moves, expands, retreats, and even escapes, and who emerges or withdraws throughout this motion.

When asked whether the alley represents Egypt, an allegory, Mahfouz replied that he did not intend it to be so, it did not occur to him; he then added, "but sure, why not." Decades after his statement, there I was, in an American classroom in a postindustrial town in upstate New York, 5 feet tall and 126 pounds small, a 24-year-old Arab woman with an accent, and I too was being made into an allegory. I stood excited to "generate a discussion" about Mahfouz's characters, how distinct and vivid they are, their love stories, and the usual family dramas that make them the protagonists of their own lives. There was also the typography of their speech, sometimes overlapping with the narrator's voice, yet rendered seamless in Davies's translation (2011).

I first read *Midaq Alley* many years ago. I remember laughing at many points, especially at the conversations between the men at Kirsha's café. But by many readers, or even those of us who watched the 1963 film adaptation starring Shadia or the 1995 adaptation starring Salma Hayek, *Midaq Alley* is best remembered for its young protagonist Hamida, a beautiful woman who dreams of leaving the alley and exploring the world. The novel situates her between the women of the alley, whose labor is confined to the domestic sphere, and her middle-class friends who are beginning to join the workforce. Hamida is also at the center of attention—she is the love object of Abbas, the young barber, as well as of Salim Alwan, the old businessman. We follow this love drama for a while, before Hamida decides to choose her world adventure over the two men. She leaves the alley, with a decision to cut any ties to the past, to never look back.

Hamida has done the impossible. For a novel published in 1943, a woman's escape or departure was a powerful feminist sentiment. In that decade, women's liberation was a major debate in Cairo's elite circles, and an important issue for liberal nationalists like Mahfouz. What is especially crucial about Hamida is the fact that she represents one of the earliest working-class feminist characters to appear in the modern Arabic novel. Yet Hamida was not the only young character hoping to leave the alley; others wanted out, such as Hussein. He too wished to enter the new metropolitan life, to pursue his aspirations for upward mobility, and to gain whatever liberties it might bring.

I was especially fascinated with Hamida's entry into the bourgeois world, which at the time was entirely colonial. The scenes in which Hamida begins to practice her sexuality, to give away her innocence, to attempt, for the first time, to own her body, to make it no longer a property of her mother, or of society at large. It is that feeling of excitement and fear, of danger and adventure, of sin and intention. I identified with Hamida, I saw myself in parts of her story, I related to her reclaiming of the body. I also recognized the alienation she felt in those moments, how freedom is an illusion: we first conceive it as a pure ecstatic abstract, yet it is never familiar, and more important, it is conditioned by social relations and settings. Hamida's freedom could not simply evade patriarchy, because patriarchy is everywhere. In the alley it is erected upon gender, and upon race with the British soldiers, or upon class in the bourgeois metropolis.

In the classroom, my American students had a very different impression of Hamida. It was a diverse class, mostly from New York City or Long Island, including students who were White, Black, and Jewish, in addition to one Egyptian student. They described Hamida as selfish, for having left her mother and Abbas. They had more compassion for Abbas than for her. They did not understand why his love was not enough for her: Why leave the alley for good, why not be in the middle of two worlds? Her escape and class-transgression, unheard-of for women of her generation whether in Egypt or the United States, was not seen as heroic, admirable, or even understandable. Although I was teaching at a moment when feminism had become a mainstream cultural phenomenon, Hamida was not once described as feminist by my students. Her entry into the bourgeois world was disturbing to them. They came just short of calling her a whore. Although Hamida's story indeed turns tragic, the novel explores the struggle itself, the process of breaking free, what freedom we come upon, and how class and gender interrupt such travel. The novel was not necessarily making an example of the runaway woman, yet this is how my students perceived it. Dare I say, this is how each Arabic novel I taught was perceived, or rather judged—on a moralistic basis, as a lesson to be learned.

From classroom to classroom, semester to semester, the American student's gaze became evident to me. I began to realize the similarities between Hamida and me, what my body looks like in a historically liminal space (brown, 120). Each teaching day, I felt interrogated. I once described it in a poem "as if going to a visa interview" at the US embassy. American students do not direct their questions to the writer, to the text; they direct them to me, the Arab, representative of four hundred million humans. They are not interested in the story, in where the character may go or end up, their aspirations, heartbreaks, or failures. They are not even interested in the political context, or the witty and cinematic style of Mahfouz, in this example. They pause at any point and pose an incongruous question like "But is this allowed in Arab culture?" I realized that, by default, the American student arrives with whatever stereotypical understanding they have of "Arab culture," which then results in a trial of the characters, and therefore of a culture. In one scene, and with a tone of surprise, I was asked, "Are men and women allowed to sit together?"

Gradually, the embassy interrogation began to make of me the angry Arab I was assumed to be. When that question was raised, "Do women and men sit together?," I found myself exploding. I answered in a high-pitched voice, "Stop scrutinizing every simple ordinary thing in the story." I then found myself using the pronoun "we" as in "we Arabs," that *we* are just like everyone else, *we* do ordinary things, *we* sit together at home, and *we* do have a drink! They succeeded, at that moment, in displacing me away from the text. That moment marked a shift in the way I interact with Arabic literature. I was suddenly no longer an insider, fascinated with the story, the stylistics, less concerned with themes and history. I slowly began to look at Arabic literature with the American gaze, first censoring and filtering, to include texts that may manage their moralistic policing, to trick or outsmart their gaze.

Being an Arab woman in the American classroom is complicated by both race and gender. I also describe it as giving testimony in court. My students were always interested in seeing how my personal experience intersects with that of the novel. I tried to draw their attention to how, when sexism appears in the Arabic text, they locate it as a problem of tradition and culture, while in the American context, it is simply sexism. The women nodded slowly, the men rolled their eyes. "Professor, is this true, is this how it is?" is a question I've grown used to. The late Magda al-Nowaihi described it as the "mimetic model of simple reflection" whereby, even when the teacher attempts to recenter students' attention on the aesthetic and how it helps create comparisons between human experiences, "they are still desperate, at the end of the day, to make the jump from knowing this Arab text, to knowing 'the Arab'" (27).

2

In the months I spent reading up on the politics of teaching, I encountered two relevant takes: that of postcolonial theory and the other of Arabic literature scholars. In *The World, the Text, and the Critic*, Edward Said contests Western humanities for traditionally isolating the text from its world by fixating on the aesthetic: "My position is that texts are worldly" (4). In the work of

Gayatri Spivak, who has written extensively about her experience in Western higher education as well as in the literacy classrooms she started in West Bengal, we see her too critiquing how the humanities train students to be preoccupied with aesthetics in the abstract. In *An Aesthetic Education in the Era of Globalization*, Spivak uses the description "not stylistically competitive" when critically discussing what texts appeal to scholars of postcolonial studies, as opposed to their favorite "sexy postmodern texts" (147). Spivak proposes a radical reconceptualization of ethical responsibility to reclaim the aesthetic: "By aesthetic education, I mean training the imagination for epistemological performance" (197). She frames the imagination as the connection between the aesthetic and the ethical.

This tradition of the humanities that major theorists like Said and Spivak attempt to critique and reimagine is far from the reality of Arabic humanities in the American classroom. The practice of close reading, which Bruce Robbins discusses in "Discipline and Farce," as reading a text with "nothing about who they were or when or why the texts had been written," is rather a dream for scholars teaching Arabic literature in the American classroom. In two edited volumes, published in 2017 and 2018, both focused on Arabic literature and pedagogy, scholars teaching in the United States come to agreement that they struggle to bring the attention of students to the aesthetic values and practices of Arabic literature (al-Musawi; Hartman). Their contributions, in these volumes, are spent discussing strategies and tactics that may trap the American student into appreciating the craft of Arabic authors. This is not to suggest that students are more concerned with the "worldly" in these texts; on the contrary, they are interested in neither. Most of the essays included in the two volumes, as well as in other sources I located online, were written by white scholars, many of whom have "good politics," specifically signaled by their stance on Palestine. Some propose new readings of problematic texts such as Hanan al-Shaykh's *Zahra*, some explain how the American classroom is a micro-representation of the US empire, others engage with critiques of area studies in US academia. Although these writings understand the inescapable political nature of teaching Arabic or its literatures to Americans, they can't help but conclude their essays by offering pedagogical solutions.

In "Untranslatability, Discomfort, and Ideology: Should We Teach Arabic Literature?" Stephen Sheehi proposes that we who teach Arabic literature "should locate the ideological and historical positions of a text's trajectory into the class and be prepared not to alleviate the discomfort of our students" (58). By "discomfort," Sheehi refers to the class-based and imperialist ideologies (liberal or conservative) with which American students arrive in the Arabic classroom. "Ideological" also means racist, although Sheehi does not use the word, perhaps because "imperialist" and "class-based" already indicate racist. However, I find it important to highlight this, because "racist" is a more familiar, recognizable, and shared diagnosis of how American students interact with world literature, as well as with American literature by writers of historically marginalized groups.

Sheehi makes a brilliant effort framing his take on the American classroom experience, with a focus on imperialism and the neoliberalization of education in the United States. Nevertheless, the professor and his students appear innocent in his essay, sitting together against a background of a vicious empire, whose presence he highlights throughout the piece. Sheehi sketches quick comparisons between a number of modern and contemporary Arabic novels through his students' impressions. He sees Mahfouz's work as rooted in "petit bourgeois sensibilities," which somehow does not appeal to his students, as opposed to the "cosmopolitan urbanities" found in Alaa al-Aswany's *Yacoubian Building* (57). For his students, Mahfouz's characters and stories are "dull," "flat," and of "familiar archetypes," as if it is Mahfouz's fault that his work is not intriguing to American students (57). Sheehi precedes his sketches with a section on Arab armed struggle, in which he discusses teaching Leila Khaled's autobiography, without much context on what locates her text as an example of Arabic literature.

In *Approaches to Teaching the Works of Naguib Mahfouz*, published six years before Sheehi's essay, Waïl S. Hassan refutes such reductionist readings of Mahfouz's work. Having taught courses devoted to the works of Mahfouz, Hassan reminds us that a "radical reconceptualization" is inherent whenever we read a text outside of its literary domain, and within so-called world literature. This type of reading, no matter how global we would like it to be, "remains tied to the particular location of its production, and therefore expresses a particular ideological worldview" (27). Building on Gaber Asfour's framing of Mahfouz's range of work as a "a museum . . . or a laboratory," Hassan argues for the laboratory nature of the novels, because "a laboratory contains tools, instruments, and specimens, each the product of a particular process . . . [and] a laboratory expands the field of time into the future and toward the discovery of new relations and configurations" (37).

For Hassan, as for Edward Said, who sees in Mahfouz's work a history of the novel form, the content of Mahfouz's work cannot be divorced from its context. Hassan reminds us that Mahfouz blends and adapts elements from Western and Arabic literary traditions that correspond with "his creative needs at every stage of the country's history." In this sense, the trajectory of Mahfouz's aesthetic transformation "multiplies interpretive possibilities" of the texts, instead of limiting them (39).

Sheehi's diagnosis of why his students "do not warm" to the work of Mahfouz is more a critique of the writer's realist phase than of his class politics (56). While referring to the critiques of al-Alim and Anis, Sheehi overlooks Mahfouz's treatment of social mobility and its intersections with colonialism, gender, and sexuality, especially in his realist novels. Sheehi also overlooks how Mahfouz's focus on the middle class documented and treated the emergence and transformation of this social class in postcolonial Egypt. His pre-Nasseri works are occupied with a conflict between two disparate classes (the colonial and the colonized) who hardly cross paths, unless the colonized commits a spatial transgression, meaning aspiring to social mobility. Giving the example of *Miramar*, Sheehi states that his students see the treatments of class and gender in Mahfouz's work as "one-dimensional," with a peasant-woman character like Zahra seeming "flat and robbed of agency" (57). On the contrary, my students condemned the working-class Cairene Hamida for having too much agency.

Mahfouz's humanist approach is too easily painted as that of a reactionary liberal intellectual class, and not as a literary realist device. This is not to argue that aesthetics and politics are separable, but to make the following reminders: that Mahfouz's aesthetics made attempts and continued to transform; that class relations are at the center of his work, even if painted through his petit-bourgeois gaze; that in the American classroom, the limitations in Mahfouz's works are amplified and grounded, rather than problematized toward a reading of his novels that evokes joy and learning, as well as conflict and critique—a reading that does not alleviate discomfort. For Sheehi, the question of teaching Arabic literature in the United States is an entirely ideological question, without an acknowledgment of how these very texts, given the power relations he outlines, turn from confrontation in the original context to collaboration, or "from oppositional to complicitous. No longer shocking their readers out of their apathy and prejudices, they simply confirm what we always knew about these people" (al-Nowaihi, 26). Rather than build on discomfort, Sheehi proposes we "break our class solidarity and alliances with middle-class writers in order to recognize the class and political components that drive culture production" (58). But to address the ideological question, or class alliances within culture production, would require us to read Mahfouz intertextually with his contemporaries; to revisit their debates and approaches to colonialism, class, race, gender, and sexuality; and to reflect on their understandings and aspirations for the text and its world.

Sheehi's experience with Mahfouz brings me back to an essay by the novelist Gina Apostol in which she analyzes Western expectations of the Third World writer: "What is it about the writer in the First World that wants the Third World writer to be nakedly political, a blunt instrument bludgeoning his world's ills?" Through Apostol's take on Borges and the First World critic, I begin to see Sheehi's call "to break alliances with middle-class writers" as a sentiment only vocalized against the Third World writer. Apostol counters this Western attitude by centering the perspective of the colonized who sees Borges to be political, offering "a template to think about politics," or "tools and specimens," as Hassan finds in Mahfouz's work. Both Hassan and Apostol recognize a realm of possibilities in the aesthetics and works of their two Third World writers. Borges, Apostol writes, "provokes us to imagine what 'identity' and 'nation,' the 'other' and the 'self' are, with cunning, humor, and incalculable, astonishing vision and precision."

3

When I returned to my readings with a sole focus on Arab scholars working in the United States, I found no mention of what it is like to be an Arab in this violent setting, for your livelihood to be dependent on teaching your people's language or literatures in a colonial context, or how we even derive value and fulfillment from doing such work.

When revisiting her experience of teaching Tayeb Salih's *Season of Migration to the North*, Rula Jurdi Abisaab writes that she wanted to provide an approach to the region's history that is different from what is being offered in history courses and textbooks; to give students "an intimate experience of the creative labor . . . that would take them to uncomfortable and ambiguous spaces" (133). Abisaab soon encountered the challenge of having her students treat a novel as only a novel, not "as a guide to understanding encounters or clashes between East and West." Similarly, Tarek El-Ariss explains how teachers within Middle East studies had to adapt and adjust their curriculum and approaches after 9/11. The event, he writes, "forced scholars to rethink curricula and devise new ways to engage this unique event." El-Ariss declares that his aim is to ground the study of Arabic literature in the humanities through a comparative lens of genres and traditions, and to lead courses that are "constantly negotiating the relation between aesthetics and politics yet always grounded in humanizing the other through engagements with his/her imagination" (131).

In both examples, the Arab scholars are aware not only of how the American student reads Arabic literature but also of how that student reads the Arab themself. Abisaab is an anthropologist who uses literature in the study of history; she finds in literature a generative and critical interpretation or writing of history. El-Ariss is a scholar of Arab/ic literatures and cultures who has witnessed the transformation of the Arab's image in the American classroom since the so-called war on terrorism. Both scholars, however, do not grant themselves the permission to reflect on what it is like to be an Arab teaching Arabic literature in the American classroom within the political contexts they outline. They are not alone in performing this self-removal, in presuming that this omission equates to being scientific and objective—an omission best marked by the absence of the authorial "I" in scholarly writings.

The Arab in the American classroom is disembodied, textually and physically, so that even when revisiting our experiences with a theoretical lens, we assume ourselves to be neutral, to be the better and wiser siblings; or perhaps we unconsciously turn our policed hypervisibility in the classroom into an invisibility in our reflections. If the immigrant Black woman professor is forced into the role of "the help" or "the mammy," then the Arab in the American classroom is assumed to play the interpreter whose loyalty lies with their contractor (Alleyne).

I was not surprised when my research around the politics of teaching, specifically on the disembodiment of the native teacher, led me to writings by Black educators on this subject. In each article of *Teaching While Black* (2022), Black educators have an understanding that their subjectivity is central to the classroom and learning experience. They also arrive to the classroom with a political commitment they wish to translate in their daily jobs. Although the journey is hectic, the goal is not blurry. What do we want from the American classroom, as Arabs? Do we want to politicize our students? Do we want them to appreciate our literatures? Do we want to foster a curiosity in them, for world literature at large? And to what purpose? Or to borrow from Louise Wakerakats:se Herne, a Mohawk Bear Clan Mother of the Mohawk Nation: "What do you stand for? Who are your people? What do you bring? What do you leave behind? What is your dream?" (Rosario, 201).

What I learned from the essays of Black scholars is that "as a woman, as a woman of color, and as a woman of color who chooses to be in academia as an educator, a huge part of my labor in the classroom is to (re)construct and maintain my personhood so that I can encourage, support, and be of service to my students as we do the work of deconstructing the structures that would deny us all our full humanity" (Alleyne, 176). The Black or Arab educator cannot escape being the native informant in the classroom; their personhood cannot possibly be made neutral or "professional."

To build on Alleyne's historical figure of "the help," Black educators are aware that they are "expected to solve the problems they present in their work" (Derricote, 141). On the contrary, Arab educators in their reflections, although burdened with this role, are not aware of the impossible and unrealistic responsibility they take upon themselves. Relentlessly, we chase pedagogical solutions and offer new readings. We have yet to learn to sit in discomfort with our students, to offer incomplete answers, to not feel responsible for the texts, to both uphold and deface these texts if necessary, without letting a given reading be representative of an entire literary domain, but rather of the ideological and stylistic differences and battles that make up the body of Arabic literature. To let Arabic literature be disembodied and reincarnated, as we ourselves are disembodied and reincarnated, classroom to classroom.

4

By the time I received my PhD, I managed to create a good recipe for my future American patients. This recipe is intertextual, nonlinear, unchronological, comparative, multilingual, transnational, internationalist, utilizing translation as a contact zone, analytical in discussion, yet creative in writing.

I began to construct my model for teaching Arabic literature to both inform and learn from my scholarship. As a scholar of literatures and cultures of the Arab Gulf, it took me years to realize how absurd it is to limit the study of literatures in the Gulf to Arabic writings, when the majority of the region's peoples are not even Arabic speakers. I was made aware of this when encountering Amitav Ghosh's "Petrofiction: The Novel and the Oil Encounter," which is a review essay of the two translated volumes of Abdelrahman Munif's *Cities of Salt* (1989, 1991). Ghosh praises Munif's work for tackling a muted encounter, that is, of oil extraction as a form of colonization. Ghosh then extends a critique not only to Munif's writing but to "writing as we know it" for not adjusting to the new reality of a geography like the Gulf, where people, especially working-class people, have no common languages or cultures that may aid in their struggle to seize the means of production, or the production of history, as well as the production of literature (11).

In light of this critique, my work as scholar and teacher began to center around a new constructed module based on geography. I now teach writings from the Gulf by writers who work in Arabic, English, or Malayalam. I use translation as a transit zone, exemplary of the Tower of Babel that is the Gulf region. In my course "The New Arab Gulf: Migrants, Weirdos, and Rebels," the American student is merely a spectator at a distance, only gestured toward as a colonizer, mocked, or flirted with in texts. The Global South is at the center, and on its northern side, the American realizes that, all along, they're merely a corner! That world is unattainable to them, and as such, it cannot be summoned to court, or scheduled for a visa interview.

To outsmart the enemy, to maneuver his gaze, I decided to follow each assigned text with another that somehow counters it, or weaves into it as a different yet simultaneous thread. For example, after teaching *Cities of Salt*, where the natives of Arabia are antagonized and deprived of their land, as well as of the right to battle their colonizers, I follow with Sonallah Ibrahim's *Warda* (2000), where people of the peninsula do fight and resist, but are nevertheless defeated by the British and their oil sheikhs. This practice of intertextuality not only expands our experience of history but also showcases the laboratory nature of modern Arabic fiction, and how Arabic literature plays a major role in writing the people's narrative against official histories.

I find the work of Sonallah to be unique in its effect on students; although they are often appalled by his communist politics, they nevertheless respond to his work, because it touches their own experiences of living under capitalism (in the example of *The Committee*), and because of its transnational landscape. Sonallah composes a unique journalistic aesthetic that allows him to embed a counter-history, necessarily a radical history, to treat theoretical questions as open wounds, whether in *That Smell*, *Warda*, or *Beirut, Beirut* (1966; 2000; 1988). Hosam Aboul-Ela describes Sonallah's work as "nonfiction fiction." From Sonallah, I learned to seek anticapitalist fiction, such as the work of Albert Cossery, a francophone Egyptian surrealist whose short novels are attractive and amusing to my students for their mixture of absurdist plots, historical contexts, extreme emotions, and his subversive anticapitalist call to withdraw from society, from production, and by extension, from art and culture, as well as from politics. Cossery's fiction is different from the militant or committed novels of Sonallah, yet his anarchist, anticapitalist, and nonconformist critiques shock my students out of their American individualist ideals.

I also began to question the traditional approach in English and comparative literature, or writing and composition courses, of limiting writing assignments to critical or research papers. I shifted my mentality and reminded myself that I am first a writer, before I became a scholar, and how my courses can be unique when approached through the lens of the creative writer. I realized that expecting criticism from American students implicitly means granting them too much power, since criticism assumes one to possess expertise over the text, or to be on even ground with the text. This is not to argue against critical writing; on the contrary, my aim is to complement analytical writings, practiced within the humanities at large, by approaching creative assignments as also a form of critical thinking.

In fall 2019, I taught a course titled "Readings in Contemporary Arabic Literature" that consisted entirely of short-form writings and creative writing assignments. Students wrote flash fiction, short stories, poems, film reviews, and autobiographical essays. In that course, my students were not allowed the chance to create full impressions or partake in the "mimetic model of simple reflection"; they were forced to sit with excerpts and passages and to engage

Arabic literature only through its presence on the page (al-Nowaihi, 27). They were challenged to imitate the assigned texts, and to make something out of their imitations, to explore and experiment in dialogue with Arabic literature. I learned from that course to tap into the creative and experimental, the imagination as Spivak had proposed, to activate a set of cognitive skills in the Arabic literature classroom, and to challenge linearity in every sense. Moving forward, I only assigned excerpts of novels, to avoid allowing the voyeuristic reader to feel too comfortable.

Poet Hilary Plum, who is not an Arabic speaker or scholar, reflects on her experience of teaching literature in translation in the creative writing classroom. Her reflections were refreshing to read and came in conversation with my experiment to bring the workshop setting into the Arabic literature classroom. Plum finds teaching literature in translation in a writing workshop "natural" because the workshop model "emphasizes creativity as dialogic and dialogue as a creative practice." Teaching in translation, Plum explains, also challenges ideals of authorship, turns them from the individual to the collective. Moreover, teaching translation as creative writing naturally recenters the aesthetic "on the level of word, phrase, syntax, diction, metaphor, image, and so on." Thus, teaching Arabic literature in relation to creative writing liberates it from its violent place within area studies and critical languages departments (Plum).

Plum describes her students as "hungry to read." She is aware of the classroom power relations, how teaching literature in translation "asks readers to bear witness to our own positions. Here's a text that is addressing us; it both was and wasn't written for us." She provides an example of how, when once she intended to teach a story by Hassan Blasim, the course organizers were more bothered by a passing mention of oral sex, and less so by the grotesque context of the Iraq-Iran war. Unlike the Arabic scholars I read, Plum does not feel responsible, eager, or pressured to offer context or answers. She wants her students to become "skilled at reading"; she aspires to teach "reading," not in its form of expertise and critique—what I would like to call "authoritative reading"—but on an equal footing, out of curiosity and joy. In this sense, a big part of teaching literature in translation, especially Arabic literature in my case, requires a constant micromanagement of power in the acts of reading, writing, and discussion. It requires rejecting the paternal discourse of responsibility and care, and replacing it with a transnational, multilingual, and nondisciplinary model of experiencing literature only in fragments, in airwaves, or perhaps as bottled messages lost across the ocean.

Works Cited

Abisaab, Rula Jurdi. "Arabic Poetics through a Canonical Translation: Teaching Tayeb Salih's *Season of Migration to the North*." In *Teaching Modern Arabic Literature in Translation*, edited by Michelle Hartman, 132–47. New York: Modern Language Association of America, 2018.

Aboul-Ela, Hosam. "Nonfiction in the Novels of Sonallah Ibrahim: The Horizons of Translation." Center for the Study of the Middle East, Indiana University, Bloomington, March 31, 2022.

Alleyne, Lauren K. "You Is Kind, You Is Smart, You Is Important: The Black Female Professor as 'the Help.'" In *Teaching Black: The Craft of Teaching on Black Life and Literature*, edited by Ana-Maurine Lara and drea brown, 172–77. Pittsburgh: University of Pittsburgh Press, 2021.

al-Musawi, Muhsin J., ed. *Arabic Literature for the Classroom: Teaching Methods, Theories, Themes and Texts*. London: Routledge, 2017.

al-Nowaihi, Magda M. "For a 'Foreign' Audience: The Challenges of Teaching Arabic Literature in the American Academy." *Middle East Studies Association Bulletin* 35, no. 1 (2001): 24–27.

Apostol, Gina. "Borges, Politics, and the Postcolonial." *Los Angeles Review of Books*, August 18, 2013. https://lareviewofbooks.org/article/borges-politics-and-the-postcolonial.

brown, drea. "A Question of Victory: Teaching Claudia Rankine's *Citizen: An American Lyric*." In *Teaching Black: The Craft of Teaching on Black Life and Literature*, edited by Ana-Maurine Lara and drea brown, 117–24. Pittsburgh: University of Pittsburgh Press, 2021.

Derricote, Toi. "Baring/Bearing Anger: Race in the Creative Writing Classroom." In *Teaching Black: The Craft of Teaching on Black Life and Literature*, edited by Ana-Maurine Lara and drea brown, 139–43. Pittsburgh: University of Pittsburgh Press, 2021.

El-Ariss, Tarek. "Teaching Humor in Arabic Literature and Film." In *Arabic Literature for the Classroom: Teaching Methods, Theories, Themes and Texts*, edited by Muhsin J. al-Musawi, 130–44. London: Routledge, 2017.

Ghosh, Amitav. "Petrofiction: The Novel and the Oil Encounter." *New Republic*, March 2, 1992, 11.

Hartman, Michelle, ed. *Teaching Modern Arabic Literature in Translation*. New York: Modern Language Association of America, 2018.

Hassan, Waïl S. "Teaching a Seminar or Mahfouz." In *Approaches to Teaching the Works of Naguib Mahfouz*, edited by Waïl S. Hassan and Susan Muaddi Darraj, 25–40. New York: Modern Language Association of America, 2012.

Hassan, Waïl S., and Susan Muaddi Darraj. Introduction to part 2, in *Approaches to Teaching the Works of Naguib Mahfouz*, edited by Waïl S. Hassan and Susan Muaddi Darraj, 13–22. New York: Modern Language Association of America, 2012.

Mahfouz, Naguib. *Midaq Alley*. Translated by Humphrey Davies. Cairo: American University in Cairo Press, 2011.

Plum, Hilary. "Teaching with Arabic Literature in Translation: The Creative Writing Workshop." Interview by M. Lynx Qualey. *ArabLit*, January 22, 2018. https://arablit.org/2018/01/22/teaching-with-arabic-literature-in-translation-the-creative-writing-workshop.

Robbins, Bruce. "Discipline and Parse: The Politics of Close Reading." *Los Angeles Review of Books*, May 14, 2017. https://lareviewofbooks.org/article/discipline-and-parse-the-politics-of-close-reading.

Rosario, Nelly. "Th/Inking in Black: Notes on Teaching Creative Writing." In *Teaching Black: The Craft of Teaching on Black Life and Literature*, edited by Ana-Maurine Lara and drea brown, 201–14. Pittsburgh: University of Pittsburgh Press, 2021.

Said, Edward W. *The World, the Text, and the Critic*. Cambridge, MA: Harvard University Press, 1983.

Sheehi, Stephen. "Untranslatability, Discomfort, and Ideology: Should We Teach Arabic Literature?" In *Teaching Modern Arabic Literature in Translation*, edited by Michelle Hartman, 41–61. New York: Modern Language Association of America, 2018.

Spivak, Gayatri Chakravorty. *An Aesthetic Education in the Era of Globalization*. Cambridge, MA: Harvard University Press, 2012.

———. "Teaching for the Times." *Journal of the Midwest Modern Language Association* 25, no. 1 (1992): 3–22.

Whose Politics? Teaching Palestinian Literature

Nora E. H. Parr

A colleague was putting together a disability studies reading list for a new class. With core texts in place, they sought fictional representation of disability from the non-Western world and wondered if I could recommend something from Palestine. There was one text, they said, that had an autistic narrator—at least according to the blurb on the back—and asked if this was a good candidate for the syllabus. An autistic narrator was news to me, but sure enough, J. M. Coetzee's blurb on the back cover of Adania Shibli's *Minor Detail* (2015; trans. 2020) diagnosed the novel's Palestinian narrator as "high on the autism scale."[1] The work's author, whom I happened to be in touch with at the time, wasn't so keen on the reading, but of course it's hard to turn down a blurb from such a well-known figure. The cause of the author's disquiet, as indeed other readers have since remarked, was that in diagnosing the narrator, Coetzee pathologized the protagonist's response to a military occupation. In labeling the character with a disability, as the novel's author put it, the burden of smooth social interaction became the single responsibility of a character—and not, say, the grave inequalities that condition some of the character's interactions, through which Coetzee proffers his diagnosis.

Coetzee was not wrong about the ontology—many of the interactions between the protagonist and her interlocuters are painfully awkward, but this is not the character blocking or missing social cues. The character is, rather, painfully aware of the social and political context she is operating within. The difference in interpretation is reading this awkwardness in its political context. The nameless character—living in the West Bank—had used the identity card of a colleague (who lived in Occupied East Jerusalem) to access areas (in the south of Israel) that the Israeli military deemed off-limits for Palestinians. The character thus interacts with Israeli characters on her journey knowing that at any point they might identify her as an "infiltrator." She is walking on eggshells worried about being caught. She has, after all, set off in search of the details of a murder of a Bedouin woman in 1949 that had been referenced in the newspaper. She sought more details of a story that had been buried along with the Palestinian past in Israeli archives. Her awkwardness—stuttering, mumbling, shyness—speaks to fear, not to her cognitive function—even if she is on the spectrum.

Minor Detail was not, I advised my friend, a good candidate for her disability studies reading list. The interaction left me upset; I felt the book had been badly treated by the blurb. But teaching, I later reflected, gives us the chance to do something different, something better. So, I corrected myself to my colleague: the book was not suited for a disability studies seminar *unless* they wanted to offer something a little different—a lesson in mediated reading and the problem of approaches. For the sake of this chapter, I will call this approach "teaching politically." In a nutshell, I mean this as teaching a text at the same time as teaching about the frameworks that are being imposed and limiting its interpretation.

That the interpretation of texts is influenced and limited by the politics they circulate within is not, of course, news. We've all read Edward Said's "Permission to Narrate" and *Orientalism*,[2] after all. In contemporary teaching on Palestine, and on Palestinian literature, however, there remain (and are some new) rather pernicious limitations that I want to address. These limits restrict the kinds of texts we teach, the stories we give our students privileged access to, and thus the parameters of Palestine that we explore. And it often begins with a simple course title (a subgenre that we know holds much information about disciplinary structure, and the things that count as "knowledge").

First, then, a brief assessment of where and how Palestinian texts are taught; for what purposes, for what aim? This assessment uses the Open Syllabus database of more than 7 million aggregated reading lists, in addition to 32 syllabi sourced from online course listings, and 13 syllabi from my own friends and colleagues. Analysis of this pool reveals three "types" of courses in which Palestinian literature is taught. These can be summarized as "conflict courses," "survey courses," and "themed courses." Each course type tends (quite reliably) to ask Palestinian fiction to perform a certain function, and therefore imposes a very specific set of limitations on the possible interpretations of the work. Whether we expect to "learn about the conflict" through fiction, to "understand Palestine" through literature, to "learn to empathize with the other" via a novel, or to explore a theme—from disability to human rights, postcolonialism to trauma—the questions it is possible to ask begin with the way the work is presented,[3] and tend not to respond to the universes within which the works are created. This is not necessarily a bad thing, and indeed the tension between what classrooms ask of novels and what authors use them to express can be pedagogically harnessed. It just requires time and attention spent understanding the frames of mediation and making space to ensure the texts are allowed to challenge/speak to these frames.

In the three sections that follow I read work by authors that (1) never appears on university reading lists (Ahlam Bsharat, b. 1975, Tamun, West Bank); (2) is grossly overrepresented (Ghassan Kanafani, b. 1936, Accre; d. 1972, Beirut); then (3) the experimental case of what reading Adania Shibli (b. 1974, Shibli, Israel) on a disability studies course could mean. Each reading challenges the knowledge arcs presented by the three course types (the conflict, the survey, and the special topic). Read alongside each other, the works show that, when it comes to teaching Palestinian literature, the question of "teaching politically" is best approached at a remove. Not a removal of politics, but a stepping back and asking: Whose politics are shaping our approaches to texts, to text selections, to the structure of syllabi? What is conditioning the reading and reception of Palestinian literary texts in today's classroom?

The "Conflict"—Limitations of Sovereignty and Binaries

This first section looks at courses on "the conflict," which is perhaps the most ubiquitous type of course in which a student encounters Palestinian literature. The section begins with a brief overview of the way knowledge tends to be framed in these classrooms—expectations of what "a conflict" *is* and how one goes about understanding one. Next, a reading of Ahlam Bsharat's novel *Trees for the Absentees* (2013) shows how this way of structuring knowledge seems to exclude the sort of reflections and thinking represented in *Trees*. The "knowledge arc" (or the way information is structured) of "conflict courses" is the same across syllabi in English, comparative literature, history, religion, and political science departments (as represented in the sample examined here). Whether a course is "The History of the Arab/Israeli Conflict," "Palestine in Context," "Israel/Palestine through Fiction," or even "Palestinian Literature," the tendency—even my own—is to sketch out "the conflict" within a linear sense of its history, then find texts that fit into this narrative. What most of these syllabi share is a definition of "conflict" that follows a particularly Euro-American understanding of what is at stake. In each of the syllabi I have taught (someone on leave, a course given over to a grad student), sourced online, or been sent by colleagues, "the conflict" is understood as one thing: a dispute over the sovereign control of a defined territory. A few courses began with larger questions like "What is 'the conflict'?" that start unpacking assumptions about the core issues of "conflict" for those living it, but then proceed structurally along the same lines as other syllabi, following a predictable pattern of analysis that jumps from one war/battle to another (i.e., 1948, Refugees, 1967, 1973, 1982, etc.). In reading *Trees*, I want to illuminate what following this trajectory and approach misses, and how reading Bsharat's work might lend a "conflict course" the tools to redefine the very terms within which "conflict," and even "Palestine," are defined.

The narrative arc of a "conflict course" is most obvious when classes are structured into a "two sides" binary that looks alternatively at Israeli and Palestinian material but is present as an underlying assumption in all examples. One classic structure is a class that begins with a week on Zionism—the Jewish nationalist movement that began in Europe and sought a sovereign homeland for a Jewish people. The next week sets out a parallel track and discusses Palestinian nationalism. This typically includes materials written by late Ottoman or British Mandate–era Palestinian political figures—sometimes in their diversity showing the Pan-Arab, Ottomanist, Greater-Syrian-ist, or Palestinian aims of political organizing. Whether or not forms of political independence other than the nation-state are discussed in this overview of Palestinian nationalism, students are left with the idea that these other ideals fell away for a focus on the nation-state, and that at some point Palestinian and Jewish nationalisms became parallel projects. This is, certainly, a comfortable and understandable framework for students in most Anglo-European classrooms. The ramifications are huge. This "in search of a nation state" framework drives the rest of the course content, so that readings follow key moments in the gain or loss of land but leave out the story of alternative ideas of political sovereignty, or indeed freedom and justice.

Courses styled around the "conflict" search for texts that explain key moments in a history of Palestine and Israel understood as a dispute over land ownership. In one course, for example, weeks 4 and 5 look at, respectively, Atzmaut (Israeli Independence Day) and the Nakba (the displacement of Palestinians from their homes and villages). This again posits land, and sovereign control of it, as the core of the issue, where Israel won the land, and Palestine lost it (one party has control, the other does not). Many Palestinians, however, understand Nakba as an ongoing process,[4] and see the "catastrophe" (the direct translation of "nakba") as the result of a settler colonial system. It is not the inverse or parallel of Atzmaut. Even more important in Palestinian writing than the loss of access to land is the consequence of the Nakba, and the sociocultural significance of generations of displacement and disenfranchisement.

When comparing Nakba to Israel's marking of its independence, the story is limited as one of historic loss, and not one that loudly reverberates across time. The meaning of loss and how it informs fiction does not become the center of focus. Instead, courses continue on to other key moments in land control, moving from the occupation of the West Bank in 1967 (a turning point in Arab-world discourse, which is rarely mentioned; the moment is marked only as "defeat"), past the peace talks of the 1990s, and the Intifadas ("rising up" in which Palestinians organized to demand self-representation and later in protest against failed peace talks), and finish with a week on "where things are now." According to the arc of "the conflict" narrative, things now are "stuck." There are no peace talks, no one knows if a one- or two-state solution is the answer, and no political leader has emerged to find a way out. A look at Bsharat's novel shows the damage done by the end point of this narrative arc of conflict, and how very much it leaves out that is central to Palestine, Palestinians, and their experiences over the past several generations.

In *Trees for the Absentees* Ahlam Bsharat does not write about any "moment" or event that is marked in the narrative of the "conflict" outlined above. Yet her work, like that of so many other unread Palestinian authors, deftly represents the fabric of life created by the Nakba and all that followed. It depicts Palestinian life in the West Bank under occupation, and the shape of the impact of decades of repressive policies on the lives of young adults. The novella is set between a village and its neighboring West Bank city of Nablus. It represents the *longue durée* of disenfranchisement through: the character of the protagonist's grandmother, a ghost from the Ottoman era, and the ancient architecture for which Nablus and its villages are known. On its own terms, the book is a stunning articulation of the experience of violence over time; it gives Young Adult readers the imaginative vocabulary to talk about how they feel about structures of social policing that begin with the Israeli military and extend to family networks.[5] Reading the work in translation, even in a "the conflict"–styled classroom, students would have to pause to think about what Nakba really means—what it is to live displacement and occupation for generations—or to see the complexity and violence behind a "stuck" political process.

At the heart of *Trees for the Absentees* is the construction of a life that carries the weight of centuries of violence. This is beautifully expressed through the language of a child's imagination, a child for whom "Reality was my imagination, and my imagination was reality" (4). Through the description of her world of "real imagination," the reader learns and easily absorbs that the young woman lives side by side with a ghost from the Ottoman era, the specter of newborn baby souls carrying torches into a dark world (that her grandmother the midwife delivers), and the memory of her grandmother (who was both the village midwife and corpse washer). The protagonist lives alongside, carries the legacies of, and interacts with all of these otherworldly/imaginative beings, bringing them into her work as a body scrubber at the city's hammam (public bath/spa). Indeed, it is in the hammam that these elements come together. Nestled above Roman-era arches, Nablus's hammam was built in the 1600s. The ghost that the protagonist falls in love with worked there near the end of the Ottoman era. He has a Turkish name, Bayrakdar, meaning standard bearer, because his grandfather (whom he is named after) fought the Turks during the Ottoman era and held the flag for his people's liberation. It is through the stories the younger Bayrakdar tells the protagonist (who lives in the present of the 2010s) that the reader learns about the long legacies of violence that the people of Nablus endured. This was, the protagonist reflected, "a reality that wrote its own script, and there was nothing we could do but believe in it, even if it contradicted all standard measures of what was real" (83).

Linking the Palestinian present even further back into a history of violence, the name of the young woman narrator Philistia (*Filistia*) links her to the *Filsta*, the Philistines—the first recorded people to inhabit parts of Palestine. This marks her out as a character who carries the past. So Bayrakdar finds Philistia across time, while the young woman wonders: "Was it the similarity of our lives that had brought us together: my dad imprisoned by the Israeli occupation, and his father who was imprisoned during the British mandate?" (40) or even the boy's grandfather, nearly executed by the Ottoman officials. Or, she thinks, perhaps it was because the two had both worked at the hammam "at different times in history" (40)—Bayrakdar during the 1920s and Philistia in the 2010s. The stories the two tell each other catalogue the torture and starvation of the Seferberlik—a mobilization campaign that saw the grandfather Bayrakdar "Conscripted into the ranks of the Ottoman army . . . [where he was] forced to run away from his posting in Libya and the intolerable conditions. Half-starved he fled and managed to cross Egypt" (41). The Ottoman Empire had sought to maintain its rule as Europe, during World War I, extended battles for territory into North Africa. But conditions were harsh, thousands defected, and many of these were shot if apprehended. The suffering inflicted by the Seferberlik echoes across time; not only for Bayrakdar's father who (like the first Bayrakdar facing the Turks) organized against the British and was imprisoned for the crime, but in the experience of Philistia's father, who is in an Israeli prison hours away in the Negev, and who has previously been imprisoned by the Palestinian Authority "during the Intifada" (29). While one of the young woman's friends connects the experiences of Philistia's father—"There are Palestinian prisons and Israeli prisons, but what's the difference? The prisoners are *all Palestinians*" (29; emphasis added)—what the reader sees through the story of the protagonist and her ghost is much wider. The reader can see that *all Palestinians* trace a history of injustice not only to the PA or Israel, but to British and Ottoman rule as well. All of them imprisoned Palestinians. The ramifications of this legacy extend well beyond the walls of any institution or administration. This story of reverberation, of the sum total of violence on the life of a teenage girl; this is the story that *Trees for the Absentees* tells.

Bsharat's novel devastatingly shows how generations of imprisonment have left a mark on even the most mundane aspects of Philistia's life. As she writes to her father: "Dad, everyone in the entire village thinks they can poke their nose into our business and have an opinion about everything, just because you're in prison" (55). What this looks like for Philistia is paternal aunts who disapprove of her going to university, who disapprove of her going to work (especially at the hammam), and who resent every penny of financial support that comes from their side of the family. Life itself becomes a struggle, at the level of the household. "Dad," Philistia writes, "what are we supposed to do, just stop living?" (55). And while she remains deeply connected to her father through letters, his role in her life, their family, and broader social existence is not at all stable. Because the figure of the prisoner is so ubiquitous in Palestinian society (more than half of all men have been in prison at one point or another),[6] the young woman reflects, "When I see my father behind bars it's like a portrait of a man in prison, and we have some kind of connection to him but it's not clear what it is. Is the connection just the act of visiting him now and then?" (13). Philistia feels reduced to a role, a character type, the "child of the prisoner," and she does not know either what that means in the moment of the visit, or what it will mean if and when he is released. As she wonders, "And then what? When he gets out, and he comes over to play with us and we play with him, will our relationship still be based on the verb 'to visit'? Then our house will become a prison too" (13). With this reality of imprisonment dictating so much of her life, Philistia hopes that the legacy won't continue to shape her relationship with her father forever.

Finally, the image of the tree, which emerges about halfway through the story, gives young adults an imaginative and productive figuration for living with all this loss. The idea is built through several interlinked references—to Philistia's friend's crush who rejects her, to her father who is far away, to Bayrakdar who is only in her imagination, and to the olive trees of the village, ripped up one afternoon by Israeli settlers. Bringing these losses together, Philistia forges a vocabulary by asking her friend about the "Tree that's been growing in your heart" (69). For her friend, this tree of loss represents her crush, her first love, who chose another. Giving counsel to her friend, Philistia wisely explains that loss and love are the same, and that "Just because he's gone, it doesn't mean you can't plant him in your heart." She goes on:

Replant [him] in the garden at the very back of your soul. So [he] can grow there for the rest of your life without you being aware of [his] presence. You won't need to water [him]; in fact [he] will quench your thirst. Many people we love are planted there at the end of the garden, including our loved ones who have died—that's what Grandma Zahia says. (71)

Philistia instructs her friend and the reader about the legacy of the Nakba, the impact of the "conflict," and the insistence of communities to read onto reality their own version of events. Teaching *Trees for the Absentees*, even structuring a syllabus around Philistia's representation of the "conflict" and its layers would render an entirely different narrative arc, and indeed a different definition of "conflict" itself.

The Survey—the Problem of a Single Text

After courses on "the conflict," Palestinian literature appears most frequently on syllabi that promise the world. These survey a subject, anything from "Arabic Literature" to "The Short Story," to general courses on world or postcolonial literature. Here, Palestinian texts appear to be at once tasked with representing Palestine *and* its literary contribution to whatever horizon the course hopes to explore (be it the history of literature or the short story). Obviously, no survey course is going to dig into any one literary or political history sufficiently, nor are they meant to. The problem, however, is that Palestine is represented in this genre of course—across this huge variety of themes and ideas—by a single author: Ghassan Kanafani. The revolutionary writer, assassinated by Israeli intelligence in Beirut in 1972, is the single most-taught Palestinian writer in Anglophone classrooms, bar none. The Open Syllabus (OS) project offers some staggering numbers here that illustrate the point. The OS has compiled more than 7 million syllabi and has a searchable database indicating where and how often texts are taught.[7] Kanafani's works are read across 366 syllabi (of the 7 million-plus).[8] Compare this to the other canonical authors Mahmoud Darwish (read on 135 course lists), Sahar Khalifeh (125), or Emile Habibi (6). More contemporary Palestinian writers hardly blip. Adania Shibli is on three syllabi, and International Prize for Arabic Fiction–winning author Ibrahim Nasrallah is read on one course list. Ahlam Bsharat, an award-winning writer herself, appears on zero course lists. Kanafani is the only Palestinian fiction writer (who writes in Arabic) to show up on the Open Syllabus galaxy, which visually represents the top million-plus most-assigned texts from the project's 7,292,573 syllabi.[9]

Not only is Kanafani the most taught, but he is also represented on all of these reading lists by just two books: the novellas *Men in the Sun* (which is read on 264 course lists) and *Return to Haifa* (93).[10] This means that, really, *Men in the Sun* is tasked with representing everything that Palestine could possibly represent, from the history of the novel to the Palestinian contribution to postcolonial literature. *Men in the Sun* is about the experience of four Palestinian men (a teenager, a 20-something, a 30-something, and a 60-plus) from different corners of exile and displacement seeking life and livelihood as stateless refugees. Spoiler alert. Three of them die and are tossed on a rubbish heap by the fourth, who only wonders why they didn't (futilely, he acknowledges) try to save their own lives by banging on the sides of the water tanker they suffocated in. The book is a call to action, a call to politics, a call to arms. It is also, at least if we are to believe all the syllabi it is on, almost everything else. Kanafani's *Men in the Sun* is taught as the paradigmatic text of the refugee, of the experience of the Palestinian Nakba, of migration, of resistance, of capital flows and migration, of the experimental novel. It is the paradigmatic text on gender roles and the nation, on global literary modernism, on political film adaptation (the story was made into a film in 1972),[11] and countless other topics. This is not to say that *Men in the Sun* is not a fine example of all these things. It is just that we explore the novel based almost exclusively on our own priorities—or, even more accurately, the priorities of our institutions. Worse, Kanafani gets slotted in simply because he is the most taught, and therefore the most accessible for teaching.

So while I hesitate to urge us away from Kanafani—he is a master at his craft—there are a few considerations which suggest that teaching politically means doing just that. First, when we teach only one author's works, Palestine is represented, almost in blanket form, as the Palestine of the revolutionary period of the late '60s. This was, and remains (partially because of Kanafani's fame, but also because it was just an inspiring time), what Palestine is known for. This is the time of collective organization, of the formation of Palestinian political organizations, of mass transnational solidarity. Kanafani and his political compatriots hosted everyone from the Japanese Red Army filmmakers to Jean Genet, who authored his *Prisoner of Love* as a sort of elegy to the ethos of the era after spending six months in Beirut in the '70s.[12] This was, to quote a scholar of Palestinian fiction quoting Genet, "the moment when Palestinians, as Genet put it, 'were dangerous for a thousandth of a second': when the political horizon of social and political transformation was open, and Arab revolutionary potentialities were on the cusp of realization."[13] But just as important when teaching Palestine is that this moment was not realized. This possibility for "something else" in the world order—so much championed by leftist intellectuals, then as now—glimpsed through Palestinian fiction (as exhilarating as it is to read and teach) is an era long past. Any "something else" on the horizon will have to come through new vocabularies. The good news, however, is that these also exist in and through other more contemporary Palestinian writings.

We, collectively, need a different vocabulary to understand Palestine. So, when we teach Kanafani (and we will), we must put him in context and not let the format of our survey courses allow his works to carry the weight of contemporary Palestine as well. This might involve teaching him and his vision—of refugees, displacement, resistance, the modernist novel, and so on—as revolutionary and emblematic of a special moment. This, in fact, opens some room for useful discussion about the topics he is asked to teach. Let's take as an example his portrayal of refugees. Yes, sure, he "humanizes" them by giving a personality and story and life experience to each (hardly surprising), allowing readers a glimpse into the personal toll of displacement—but he also portrays refugees in a way totally at odds with his contemporary discourse. To the world, and even in much of the Arab-world, Palestinian refugees at the time he was writing were discussed in terms of the "Arab refugee problem."[14] This seems to have been an almost seamless transition of language from Europe's discourse on the Jewish "refugee problem,"[15] and indeed seems to have taken on basically the same understanding of the nature of the "problem" and the possibilities for solution.[16] (The problem was that people were not under the control/protection/authority of a state and the solution was finding a state that could control/protect/exercise legitimate authority over the populations.[17]) Kanafani was different.

Of course, Kanafani's writing was depicting the actual lives of actual refugees in a world where he himself was a refugee. But he was not writing what Arab literary critics of the day called "sentimental documentation"[18] spurred on by a false political commitment and "mercurial affection."[19] This is perhaps because Kanafani was writing *to* refugees and not about them. Whatever the reasons that separated Kanafani from his peers, he was radical. Kanafani's work was not performative, it was not sentimental, and it certainly did not view refugees as a problem. Kanafani flipped the script; in his works it was displacement that was the problem, it was a world order that saw Palestinians shut out of a world of states. As one British commentator precisely observed in 1946, "before the [First World] War refugee problems were avoided because frontiers were open," but "since the War frontiers have been closed and nobody can cross them."[20] Kanafani was writing to refugees in a call to overturn that new world order, and its violent limitations, which they could uniquely—horrifically—see.

Kanafani did not just "humanize" or make real the lives of his characters (as his texts are asked to show on so many reading lists) but depicted Palestinians and refugees as being on the cusp of something different. Having come together from their disparate refugee camps, or locations of displacement, the titular *Men in the Sun* see the injustice of their forced roles and repeatedly *almost* say something. Their silences ring loud in the text, even before the famous final invocation from the lorry driver, who finds them suffocated in the drum they had been hidden in: "Why didn't you knock on the sides of the tank?" Because at that point in world politics, what was there to say? As Assad, the young man, looked into the metal container that was to smuggle him to Kuwait, "He seemed to want to say something but couldn't" (44). The same sentiment is expressed by the youngest, Marwan, who, at the second border stop, after knowing the heat of the tank, "looked at his watch and nodded. He tried to say something but it was beyond him" (48). The men know there is something wrong with what they are being pushed into by the world—life in a refugee camp, migrant labor in the Gulf, a life under the radar, escaping the systems of state that actively exclude them. Kanafani described this world through his characters' view of the tank: a "cursed" "hell" that the men sensed was incompatible with life.

It is, then, this cursed system, the prison of the closed frontier, that kills the men. It is this that the driver, the fourth Palestinian (who is also refused a stable existence in the wake of the Nakba) of the story, asks the corpses: "Why didn't you knock on the sides of the tank? Why didn't you bang the sides of the tank? Why? Why? Why?" (56). Because in practice there was nothing to do. Had they simply ridden through the borders they would have been arrested. Had they stayed in their camps they would have languished—with no ability to make a living, to organize politically (at the time), or to shape their own futures. Life as Kanafani penned *Men in the Sun* was one of waiting, of nostalgia, of big words and little action from Arab World leaders. And the most powerful thing about the novella was that it worked. The Palestinian resistance that Kanafani called for in *Men in the Sun* would materialize, and this resistance was able (for a time) to shake the walls of the tank and the walls of the world it traveled through. Just as important, however, is the fact that the tank didn't crumble. The "hell" of closed borders persists—as so many narratives of boat crossings attest. What we can reflect on, perhaps, in reading this radical moment that passed, is that what it takes to shake the tank is a new way of thinking, of writing about refugees that has less to do with political discourse, and more to do with action that would change the devastating outcomes of displaced lives. So, if a single text is asked to carry all of Palestine and Palestinian literature, addressing its political moment at least leaves room for a discussion of the world that stymied its passionate call for change, and a space to think about what the forces were that prevented the men from living, and what it might take to think about a different world today.

The Theme—the Problem of Imposing Cultural Constructs

It is much, much harder to trace the use of Palestinian texts across thematic syllabi—the themes vary so widely and are usually dependent on either lecturer research fields or departmental priorities. I can thus offer only anecdotal evidence of this syllabus type, but early insights seem compelling. In the syllabi compiled for this project, Palestinian texts served to illuminate class explorations of conflict, solidarity and human rights, the Arab Spring, cities in focus (Beirut, Cairo, etc.), forced migration, the nation, transnationalism, gender, religion, and disability. Again, this is only a tiny selection of what I imagine Palestinian texts are mobilized to teach. This "theme course" tends to be structured along the lines of the survey, where reading lists represent diverse locations and experiences, but centrally, in order to explore different aspects of the theme at hand. Returning to the anecdote that opened this chapter, on Coetzee's reading of Adania Shibli's text and ascribing an autism diagnosis to her protagonist, I want to explore what might happen if the colleague who proposed the text for her disability studies syllabus went ahead and taught it. I suggest that teaching Palestinian literature might most productively be read to challenge, expand, or show the problems of moving the terms we explore in our themed courses across contexts. As with "conflict" or indeed "refugees," the terms developed to critically examine the world in which the Western academy is embedded are not always the same as those that inform Palestinian writing.

Teaching Shibli's *Minor Detail* through the lens of a misdiagnosis very neatly raises the question of using Euro-American diagnostic criteria. Following years of increasingly loud criticism, it is now standard practice in Palestinian psychology and mental health for "disorders," in particular those related to cultural practice like cognition, development, and mental health—at the minimum—to go through a process of linguistic and cultural translation before they are deployed.[21] This has certainly been the case for autism.[22] Even these processes of translation/adaptation, however, are not always sufficient to address the needs of individuals in a context of ongoing harm, or adequately "diagnose" what brains and bodies are doing to cope with various levels and durations of violence in a Palestinian cultural setting.[23] Many researchers and practitioners have criticized the diagnoses of "disorders" (in cognition, in mental health, and so on) in Palestine as pathologizing the individual when in fact their behavior is a perfectly reasonable response to the realistic expectation of further violence. One mental health practitioner working in Gaza gave the example of children startling at loud noises—usually part of the diagnostic criteria for PTSD.[24] As he explained it, however, in an area habitually bombed, a quick reaction is not merely normal, but potentially lifesaving.²⁵ We might say the same for the awkward and reserved behavior of Shibli's protagonist. Not only does such misdiagnosis not serve the individual, others have commented, but it puts responsibility for fixing the ills of decades, sometimes centuries, of violence on the individual (or their immediate caregivers). As Dr. Samah Jabr so succinctly put it, in Palestine, it is often "the situation that is sick, not the individual."²⁶

So, it is not that Shibli's protagonist is cognitively unable to process the correct/"normal" social response to her surroundings—it's that there is no "correct" way to smoothly interact across generations of violence and inequality. Reading into the novel, the absurdity of an expectation of "normal" or "ordered" action "in a place dominated by the roar of occupation and ceaseless killing" (64) becomes readily apparent. This section takes on two slightly arbitrary "symptoms" that are attributes of *Minor Detail*'s protagonist, and are also listed as symptoms of autism in the Mayo Clinic's diagnostic criteria. A first "symptom" relates to the very premise of the novel, when (in the words of the Mayo Clinic) a person "fixates on an object or activity with abnormal intensity or focus." A second "symptom" is when a person "develops specific routines or rituals and becomes disturbed at the slightest change."²⁷ Both "symptoms" are very much apparent in the behaviors of the protagonist, but on analysis, seem to have rather more to do with politics than brain function.

Much of the action of the novel is about routines: making them or being anxious about breaking them. These are described in detail. For example, the protagonist's habit of sitting at the large table in her front window to drink her morning coffee, read the paper, and quite often to work—when she does not need to go into the office. This routine has been set up in excruciating detail. The curtains have been hung on all windows and are only open by the big table; the protagonist will "sit at the table; nowhere else" (58), all in an effort to exercise some control over who sees her, how, and when. This sort of routine, she writes, "grants a person a sense of serenity, despite everything else" (57). She also takes a certain route to and from the house every day, and only when a soldier points a gun at her does she take another path (60).

It turns out, however, that these routines are created almost by force. The route to work, we learn, is chosen because going anywhere else is either dangerous or prohibited. The protagonist explains in agonizing detail the different reasons that she cannot go from one city to another. This has to do with the division of the West Bank into different lettered "zones," which are each administered politically and militarily by different authorities—some by the Palestinian Authority government, others by the Israeli military, others by the Israeli civilian government, others by the Israeli border police.²⁸ Palestinians in different areas are given color-coded identity cards, and the color (or sometimes the listed place of residence) indicates which areas they are allowed to access. There are only rarely signs to indicate to a person what "zone" they are in, and they either have to know through experience, or—as in the case of the protagonist— simply stick to the safe route where they know they can go. As the protagonist puts it, "the longest trip I can embark on with my green identity card, which shows I'm from Area A, is from my house to my new job" (66–67), and while "legally" she could go to "Area B," barring exceptional circumstances, "nowadays such exceptional circumstances are in fact the norm and many people from Area A don't even consider going to Area B" (67). The protagonist adopts her behavior to cope with a political disorder, not a cognitive one.

There is no map, no plan for movement that adequately prepares an individual to navigate "so many borders, military ones, geographical ones, physical ones, psychological ones, mental ones" (75). To physically navigate between zones—from Ramallah to Jerusalem, to Yaffa, to the Negev, in search of a historic Israeli settlement and a cleared-out Bedouin encampment—the protagonist takes several maps, one "produced by centers for research and political studies," which shows permanent Israeli military infrastructure; "another map [that] shows Palestine as it was until the year 1948"; and one "produced by the Israeli ministry of tourism, [that] shows streets and residential areas according to the Israeli government" (75). None of the maps, however, "indicate the locations of flying checkpoints" (75) or indeed the battalion blocking the road near Rafah preparing for a Gaza invasion. There is no way to know about these, other than to anticipate their possibility constantly, and either live with the risk or avoid the possibility entirely. The geography is so ever-changing that the only safe space (itself hardly that) is a habitually taken corridor between home and office, or a seat in the same place by the window so that neighbors at once miss you if you are gone, but don't intrude too much on your personal affairs (65). And so, the protagonist very logically reasons, "all I can do without risking calamitous consequences is work in the office or sit in my house at my table in front of the big window" (62).

Next, the fixation. For *Minor Detail*, it is obsession with finding out what happened to a young woman in 1948, "twenty-five years to the day before I was born" (65). All she knows from the newspaper article she had been reading is that "a group of soldiers capture a girl, rape her, then kill her" near an outpost in the Negev. Understanding who that girl was and how what happened is the driving force of narrative. To find the answer, the protagonist risks leaving her safe corridors. She comes across the information "one morning" when "reading the newspaper," stumbling onto "an article on a certain incident" (a detention, bombing, shooting, or confiscation—she doesn't say).

She goes on: "It naturally wasn't the incident itself that began to haunt me. Incidents like that aren't out of the ordinary, or, let us say, they happen in contexts like this" (61). Rather than the "incident," she fixates on the "minor detail"—the story of a woman who was killed. "This minor detail, which others might not give a second thought, will stay with me forever; in spite of myself and how hard I will try to forget it, the truth of it will never stop chasing me" (65). Even as she gets annoyed when her colleague opens a window to prevent it from shattering when a nearby home is bombed, then more annoyed by the dust that the explosion leaves on her papers, it is still the story of the woman that takes the spotlight of her attention. In the "roar of occupation and ceaseless killing" (64), this detail allows her to see and feel the horror of her situation.

The protagonist draws a parallel between fixating on finding the story of the Bedouin girl and the stylistic analysis of art. It is the attention to detail, she relates, that can determine if something is a real or a fake. Forgers, she relates, "barely pay attention to little details like earlobes or fingernails or toenails, which is why they ultimately fail to perfectly replicate the painting" (63). She relates a folktale about three brothers, who with Sherlock Holmes-ian attention discover the whereabouts of their stolen camel, "simply by noticing various little details which everyone else finds to be insignificant" (63–64). Indeed, it is the attention to detail in the writing that links the first half of *Minor Detail*—the story of the rape and murder of the Bedouin woman, told in excruciating detail by the perpetrator—to the second, the story of our protagonist. The story of the woman cannot be found in any archive, and "there aren't many people alive today who remember little details about what life was like before all this" (60). What eventually remains of her story is the description of a gray uniform, the kind of gun the soldier used, the shape of the hut where the girl was kept, the smell of petrol, the barking of a dog. It is in attention to details that we see again a diagnosis of a horrific political context, the inability to narrate it without it becoming simply a "roar." Fixation on one small thing that is, in this new perspective, not so small at all, generates a new perspective on the problem of disability diagnoses across contexts and opens opportunities for students to think critically about where disorder resides, if not in the individual.

Notes

1. Coetzee also diagnoses an Israeli protagonist in the novel as a "psychopath," which commentators have also noted as highly problematic. The blurb appears on the back of the US edition of *Minor Detail*, from New Directions publishers in New

York. References to Shibli's work are to the original translation, Adania Shibli, *Minor Detail*, trans. Elisabeth Jaquette (London: Fitzcarraldo, 2020.) For referencing, I have stuck to the most commonly available translations of the works, and made reference to the Arabic text where relevant.

2. Edward W. Said, "Permission to Narrate," *Journal of Palestine Studies* 13, no. 3 (1984): 27–48; and Said, *Orientalism* (New York: Vintage, 1978), i.

3. For an excellent discussion on the politics of knowledge creation on Palestine outside the classroom, see Yara Hawari, Sharri Plonski, and Elian Weizman, "Seeing Israel through Palestine: Knowledge Production as Anti-colonial Praxis," *Settler Colonial Studies* 9, no. 1 (2019): 155–75.

4. See Elias Khoury , "Finding a New Idiom: Language ,Moral Decay, and the Ongoing Nakba," *Journal of Palestine Studies* 51, no. 1 (2022): 50–57.

5. *Trees for the Absentees* (2013) was written for and marketed as a work of Young Adult fiction by its Arabic publishers, the Tamer Institute (Ramallah); English translation by Ruth Ahmedzai Kemp and Sue Copeland (London: Neem Tree Press, 2019).

6. See https://www.addameer.org/statistics.

7. https://opensyllabus.org.

8. Note that interpreting the numbers generated by the site's database is somewhat complicated, as syllabi occasionally use Arabic texts and transliterate or transcribe the title of works, or even authors. So, looking up Ghassan Kanafani, one must look for and compile references to any combination of Ghasan Kanafany, Ghasān Kanafānī, and غسان كنفاني, etc.

9. https://opensyllabus.org.

10. Though scientifically this is hard to say, as the OSP logs only book title. The English translations of both *Men in the Sun* (trans. Hilary Kilpatrick [Boulder, CO: Lynne Rienner, 1999]) and *Return to Haifa* contain the titular novellas, and a handful of short stories and short story excerpts. Note also that a smattering of courses teach the novella *All That's Left to You* (7).

11. The novel was made into a film in 1972 by Egyptian director Tawfiq Saleh, titled *al-makhdū'ūn* (The Dupes).

12. Edward W. Said, "On Jean Genet's Late Works," in *Imperialism and Theatre* (London: Routledge, 2003). 232–43.

13. Bashir Abu-Manneh, *The Palestinian Novel: From 1948 to the Present* (Cambridge: Cambridge University Press, 2016), 146.

14. 'Amr Halīq, "Daw' 'ālami 'ala mushkilat al-lāji'īn al-'arab" *Al-risāla*, no. 819 (March 1949): 310–20.

15. John Hope Simpson, "The Refugee Problem," *International Affairs (Royal Institute of International Affairs 1931–1939)* 17, no. 5 (1938): 607–28. The report, the earliest on record to use the term "The Jewish Refugee Problem," was written by a British colonial official who was appointed to the League of Nations in the late 1930s as an expert on refugees.

16. By the summer of 1948, discussion of global refugee issues included what was newly identified as the "Arab refugee problem." See "[Chronology, 23 July 1948–5 August 1948]," *Chronology of International Events and Documents* 4, no. 15 (1948): 513–40.

17. As John Hope Simpson put it: "When they went to Greece it was both a refugee movement and a movement of sons of the soil coming back to the soil to which they really belonged." Simpson, "Refugee Problem," 607.

18. Ibrahim Jabra Jabra, "Letter to the Editor," *al-Ufuq al-Jadīd* 4, no. 1 (January 1965): 3.

19. Amīn Shunnār, "What Is Nakba Literature?," *al-Ufuq al-Jadīd* 4, no. 1 (January 1965): 1.

20. Simpson, "Refugee Problem," 607.

21. See, for example, on the development of a new set of criteria on PTSD, Mohamed Altawil, "The Effect of Chronic Traumatic Experience on Palestinian Children in the Gaza Strip" (PhD diss., University of Hertfordshire, 2008); and on measures of "insecurity," Weeam Hammoudeh, Dennis Hogan, and Rita Giacaman, "Quality of Life, Human Insecurity, and Distress among Palestinians in the Gaza Strip before and after the Winter 2008–2009 Israeli War," *Quality of Life Research: An International Journal of Quality of Life Aspects of Treatment, Care and Rehabilitation* 22, no. 9 (2013): 2371–79.

22. Ramzi Shawahna, "Palestine and Autism," in *Encyclopedia of Autism Spectrum Disorders*, ed. F. Volkmar (New York: Springer, 2017), accessed October 7, 2022, https://doi.org/10.1007/978-1-4614-6435-8_102180-1.

23. Lena Meari, "Reconsidering Trauma: Towards a Palestinian Community Psychology," *Journal of Community Psychology* 43, no. 1 (2015): 76–86; Samah Jabr and Elizabeth Berger, "The Trauma of Humiliation in the Occupied Palestinian Territory," *Arab Journal of Psychiatry* 28, no. 2 (2017): 154–59.

24. For an audio recording of this conference, and the comments from Marwan Diab from the Gaza Community Mental Health Programme, see "Palestinian Childhoods: Human Rights, Mental Health and Resistance," accessed June 2023, https://backdoorbroadcasting.net/2019/04/palestinian-childhoods-human-rights-mental-health-and-resistance.

25. Diab (mark 36.32).

26. Jabr and Berger, "Trauma of Humiliation."

27. "Autism Spectrum Disorder," Mayo Clinic, January 6, 2018, https://www.mayoclinic.org/diseases-conditions/autism-spectrum-disorder/symptoms-causes/syc-20352928.

28. "Greater Jerusalem Access, Movement, and Restrictions in OCHA Maps," *Jerusalem Quarterly*, no. 63/64 (Autumn/Winter 2015): 142.

"Don't Speak or Laugh! Greece Is in Danger!"

Censoring Dissident Discourse on So-Called National Issues in Greece

Dimitris Christopoulos and Dimitri Dimoulis

To Swallow or Not to Swallow the Dictionary?

The *Dictionary of the Modern Greek Language* (*Lexiko tis Néas Ellinikis Glossas*), edited by Professor Georgios Babiniotis of the University of Athens, was first published in 1988.[1] The entry for "Βούλγαρος [Voulgaros]" (Bulgarian), reads:

1. A national of Bulgaria, or a person of Bulgarian descent.
2. (offensive-impolite): a fan or player of a Thessaloniki sports team (primarily PAOK).

Before the Balkan wars (1912–13), Macedonian Orthodox Christians who spoke Bulgarian and identified themselves ethnically as Bulgarians made up 10 percent of the population of the present-day Greek region. They were known as "Exarchians" (followers of the Bulgarian autonomous Orthodox Church, or the "Bulgarian Exarchate"). Another 10 percent of the Macedonian population who also were Orthodox Christians and also spoke Bulgarian identified themselves as Greeks. During and after the Balkan wars, the Exarchians were exterminated or expelled to Bulgaria by the Greek army and various armed militia groups, while the majority of those who spoke the same language but without professing a Bulgarian national consciousness remained in Greece.[2] Because of this ethnic cleansing there is no longer a Bulgarian ethnic minority in Greece. Therefore, it is inappropriate to call the inhabitants of the current Greek region of Macedonia "Bulgarians." However, in the Greek nationalist imagination, "Bulgarian" symbolizes the enemy that committed atrocities against Greeks. To call the inhabitants of areas that had a strong Bulgarian presence in the past "Bulgarians" is a form of nationalist insult. "You, residents of Greek Macedonia and fans of Macedonian soccer teams, are antinational elements, you are detestable and suspect, you are 'Bulgarians.'" We have here an insult of an almost racist nature.

Professor Babiniotis, who included this pejorative meaning of the word "Bulgarian" in his *Dictionary*, is a public figure of solid reputation. In the 2012 coalition government led by the right-wing party Nea Dimokratia he was even put forward for the post of minister of education. He has often made clear (not least in the foreword to the same *Dictionary*) his strong views about the uninterrupted longevity of the "Greek Nation" and the Greek language since antiquity, and has advocated for the "superiority" of both Greek culture and language. He is also an officer of the Orthodox Patriarchate in Constantinople. But even Babiniotis's right-wing, nationalist opinions weren't enough to save him from an outcry. He soon faced a court trial, as well as vehement popular criticism, for the dictionary entry, with the accusation that he had insulted the identity of Greek Macedonians in general, and the supporters and players of the PAOK soccer team in particular.

The use of the term is, of course, widespread. No native speaker of Greek could be unfamiliar with such usage. The backlash was as unwarranted as criticizing a doctor for correctly diagnosing an illness.[3]

The First Instance Court of Thessaloniki found in favor of the complainants, opining that a dictionary should serve a pedagogical role and must not contain meanings of words that do not contribute to the cultivation of its readers. It ordered that the entry in question should be deleted (decision 18.134/1998).[4] The censorial stance taken by the judiciary not only indicated to the lexicographers how they should do their job, but also outlined specifically how their pedagogical purpose had to "serve the nation." Those the court had found wanting did not lodge an appeal, and the reference to the meaning of "Bulgarian" in a Greek footballing context was removed from the next edition of the *Dictionary*. The Superior Court (Areios Pagos) did, however, accept an appeal lodged by the public prosecutor, and eventually judged the decision to be in error, since it overlooked the nature of scientific research and publishing as well as the right to academic freedom.[5]

Professor Babiniotis had, then, slipped on a *national issue*.

How can public opinion be so immersed in a very short dictionary entry or protest so strongly against recording a very common use of a Greek word? This is, however, a prime example of how the idea of the "national" is created. In Greece, there is a special category called "national issues" which causes political controversy. Describing certain things as "national issues" elicits two contradictory if related responses: the first is that these issues are particularly important to public opinion and the political scene; the second is that they are, consequently, taboo, and risk criticism, backlash, sanctions, and accusations of antipatriotism for those who challenge them. And, of course, the idea of pedagogy itself is used as a reason to both inculcate and disseminate these national issues. The controversy over a dictionary entry turns into a discussion about, among other things, national education.

Becoming a "National Issue"

"National issues" might be defined as issues that relate to the interests of the "nation" as a whole, and not to the ambitions of a particular group, class, or political party, and for this precise reason, it is not permitted, especially for members of ethnic communities, to disagree with them. The ideal situation that seems to be advocated for the ideal citizen here is silence. If the more citizens speak, the more they doubt, then the less they speak, the better. Citizens may disagree on a wide range of issues, but it is not permissible to disagree on what concerns the existence and continuity of the national whole, something considered superior to individual interests and party politics.

There seem to be no criteria to identify what makes issues "national"—they have no scientific basis, after all. What makes unemployment, public health, or environmental degradation public issues (that can be discussed by everyone) and genocide of the Greek-speaking minority in the Pontus region of the Ottoman Empire in the early twentieth century a national issue (that cannot be discussed at all)? A list of issues that have become "national issues" at a given historical moment in the public space seem to have in common (1) a negative determination and (2) a criterion.

1. *National issues have no substance,* no common core that imbues some cases or conflicts with national importance. Rather, they are undeclared historical constructs brought into being by the action of state organs, assisted by intellectuals and the media. Efforts are made to conceal this lack of substance behind hyperbolic statements such as "we have been Greeks since time immemorial" or "Macedonia is Greek."
2. Issues become "national issues" through a process of four distinct stages: consolidation, dissemination, censorship, and depoliticization, all of which are strongly related to educational practices.

The first stage involves consolidating an opinion. Historical events, political relationships, and situations are reconstructed and interpreted on the basis of what is nationally "correct."[6] Popular memory is consolidated into an official version, expressed by public intellectuals, conservative politicians, and orthodox priests acting as "guardians of the nation."

The second stage, and the one most strictly tied to educational institutions, consists in the *dissemination* of these views as a kind of *credo* that everyone has to learn by heart and reproduce. Schools and the mass media play a crucial role here. The ideological mechanisms disseminate both the "national significance" of a certain subject and the correct interpretation of that subject.

An easy example is the idea, commonly disseminated in public education, that there is "no Turkish minority" in Greece. This is a "national issue." Faced with the reality that there are over 130,000 people born and living in Greece for whom Turkish is their mother tongue, who are Muslims (or at least grew up in Muslim families), and who share a Turkish national consciousness, the "nationally correct" interpretation is that the members of this minority are Muslim with an extremely heterogeneous or even nonexistent national consciousness. The members of this minority may be of "Turkish descent". But they are not Turkish, even though they believe it and often claim to have Turkish national consciousness.

The Greek public is exposed constantly to such national issues,[7] which can be reduced to "a single national truth."[8] As overstated or simplistic as the phrase sounds, this peculiar type of "knowledge" is reproduced along intentionally simple lines, and disseminated in the public sphere with associative emotion, without requiring or even pretending to require the assimilation of rational discourse, historical rigor, or detailed political analysis.

Discussions about "national issues" become suspect simply because they take place. National correctness is learned by heart as a kind of self-indoctrination. Almost all Greeks are certain there was a genocide of the Greek speaking population of Pontus, not because they have researched the history of the Ottoman Empire, but simply and only because they are Greeks and Greeks (should) know and believe that such a genocide took place. That they are almost alone in the world in holding this belief does not seem to matter. In short, "national issues" are those about which we are always right and everyone else is always wrong.

The third stage (which we distinguish from the second stage for analytical reasons, although both coincide) consists in forbidding national correctness to be called into question. This is where mechanisms of *censoring* are introduced. National issues are bound into a united front, pitted against the Others, the Foreigners, and all potential enemies of the Nation. Anyone who casts doubt is then symbolically expelled from the national community, and accused of being a traitor allied with "foreign entities" or "centers." Differences of opinion on national matters exceed the limits of political pluralism or intellectual freedom. This means they are not examined in terms of freedom of speech, academic research, or political preference: they are examined in terms of compulsion, as political blasphemy or crime.

The fourth stage concerns the legacy or societal effect when an issue becomes "national," and this is *depoliticization*. While liberal democracies safeguard debate on political issues, "national issues," ironically and strategically, lose their political nature, that is, their openness to debate. Disagreement about them is acceptable only on the grounds of relegating them to the status of views outside the nation ("That's what the Turks say").

When people see an issue as political, they often make an effort to persuade others to come round to their opinions and their interests, but "national issues" are marked by nondecision, that is, as something that *must not* be (presented as) a political issue. The result is that crucial issues—particularly, as we shall set out below, about the nation's purity, its history of atrocities, and the situation of minorities—remain inaccessible to public deliberation and decision. They are settled through decisions which, along with the factors motivating them, cannot be made public. The "nondecision" determines the unseen and unheard, the opinion that does not exist. In this context, depoliticization means that a crucial political development ceases to be debated because repression and violence have played a prominent role in handling it. This marks the overwhelming victory of a political viewpoint that has crushed all the rest: it has rescinded certain discussions from public debate, and, as a result, has stopped them from acquiring the usual paradigms of political communication or engagement.

Perhaps one of the key "national issues" at the heart of the making of modern Greece is the location of Greek antiquity in public consciousness: that is, the univocal connection fostered between the identity of the modern Greek state and population, on the one hand, and Greek antiquity, on the other, and by extension the construction of the three-thousand-year continuity of "Greek" consciousness, language, and culture, which includes the notion of Greek superiority in comparison with other peoples. This insistence on creating a long history as uninterruptedly Greek has been a way to legitimize the Greek state, founded in the nineteenth century, and its demands for territorial expansion, by taking ancient Greek civilization as a model for modern Greece. From this ideological perspective, the Greeks of today share the mystic essence of the ancient thinkers, poets, philosophers, Olympic champions, and democrats; and, as a chosen people, they demand that this fact be recognized.

But this can happen only if their historical pedigree is not called into question: and following from this, the nation's free discussion, as we said before, of its history of atrocities, its minorities, and the formation of its identity. As such, prohibitions on a counter-discourse to this—such as that the Greek national identity is grounded in elements from the present (language, customs, way of life), as well as elements from the past, which are necessarily subject to multiple readings—are many and severe. Critical intellectuals consider the tendency to represent present-day "Hellenism" as an (improved) version of ancient Greece to be "vampiric."[9]

This allows us to formulate a rule. *The more wide-ranging the "national issues" are at a given moment, the more rigorous the bans on politics will be, and the more intense the pressure to conform in thought and action.* As bans on political disagreement, "national issues" reduce freedom of speech and the possibility of democratic debate and thereby constitute a powerful form of censorship.[10] Over the long term this has immense consequences.

Of course, Greek political debate is characterized by freedom and pluralism. The spectrum of parties which operate freely is as broad as possible; the views they express are diametrically opposed; and acerbic exchanges are tolerated, even verbal violence that would be condemned or prosecuted in other countries. Greek political culture considers it legitimate for members of Parliament to exchange insults. One example is the 2019 debate in the Greek Parliament during which a member of the right-wing Nea Dimokratia party called deputies of the right-wing SYRIZA party "fascists" and the Speaker of the Parliament, a SYRIZA member, in turn called the MP a "Nazi."[11] Nobody thought to call for prosecution. It is also common for citizens to refer to government bodies publicly and on television in a disparaging or even insulting manner.

But at the same time, in a way that reveals the power of censorial enforcement, the Greek political scene requires unanimity on "national" issues, and imposes this on everyone (though a few far-left political groups and a fistful of university teachers and researchers resist). The situation of censorship is compounded by a deep state in Greece whose actions are continuous and coherent, irrespective of any changes in government. The deep state produces and imposes authoritarian ideological practices that are processed and implemented by the Orthodox Church, the army, the police, political parties of the (far) right, and the judiciary. These mechanisms produce perceptions and practices based on doctrines of nationhood, history, and correctness.[12] The state remains associated, in its lawmaking and its practices, with Orthodox religiosity and nationalism. It is intolerant of pluralism and liberalism, even in matters that the vast majority of European countries have long since consigned to the realm of the strictly private.

The consistency in manipulating censorship is easy to see when we consider the trivial nature of offending opinions, which may range from simply making a political statement, to views held by a small group of citizens, a scholar's publication, the founding of an association, or even, as described previously, a phrase in a dictionary. The insignificance of the pretexts theoretically belies the severity and thoroughness by which state compulsion works to eradicate any rift in unanimity on issues that have been placed on the pedestal of nondebate. Yet the impetus to crack down on the smallest of events comes from the need to reaffirm national correctness in the face of all and every "scandal." Toward this end, censorship of speech is consistently and constantly necessary. The result of the imposition of such paternalistic control over the long term is that academic and pedagogical freedom, and public deliberation, contract.[13]

How Censorship Works in Media and Education

Greece became a consolidated constitutional state with the end of the military dictatorship in 1974. The rule of law includes the respect for a constitutionally enshrined freedom of expression. How can we reconcile this fundamentally undemocratic idiom of "don't speak of national issues" with the Greek Constitution? How, in other words, does censorship work, and what is its relation to educational institutions?

There are two kinds of censorship. *Socio-structural censorship* determines what can be said and done by whom and under what circumstances. This form of censorship operates diffusely without the explicit formulation of rules and without fixed penalties. Meanwhile, *state-legal censorship* imposes restrictions on speech and actions explicitly and usually carries with it legal sanctions for noncompliance.[14] It is one thing for an atheist to be criticized and not be invited to family gatherings, quite another for them to face dismissal or imprisonment because of their beliefs.

The untouchability of "national issues" is an exemplary case of how these two types of censorship work together. On the one hand, national correctness is imposed via educational mechanisms and processes as a form of preventive censorship. On the other, the pressure for national correctness leads to self-censorship that seeks to avoid the unpleasant consequences outcasts can expect to suffer.

In a democratic setting, state-legal censorship intervenes more rarely and less easily because of the legal guarantees in place for freedom of speech, not least academic freedom, as well as the other rules pertaining to democratic expression and personal freedom. Preventive censorship by means of a compulsory state decision is prohibited under the Greek Constitution of 1975. Article 14 guarantees freedom of expression and bans censorship.[15] Similar provisions are contained in the European Convention on Human Rights and other international treaties.¹⁶ Yet this does not rule out entirely state-legal censorship on "national issues," which serves to encourage social, and hence self-, censorship, since the acting subject knows there will be unpleasant consequences if they express anything that is not nationally correct. So while it may be generally impossible to forbid researchers to publish works on a "national issue," a wide range of disparate structural pressures can be brought to bear to stop them from doing so. Journalists, media personalities, or even politicians who express antinational, "nonexistent" views can be marginalized.

Thus, an observer of the Greek scene will note that views contrary to what is nationally correct are seldom expressed in the media. The situation has changed somewhat from decades in the past, when the Greek state still had a monopoly on television stations. Even today, however, such cases stir up a storm of reactions, with the "antinational culprit" either repenting or being marginalized, sometimes to the extent of being banished from the political sphere altogether. Journalists tend to hush up bad "national" news or cover it up with a nationally "correct" belief. There are no studies which investigate whether this is a spontaneous civic attitude, willing self-censorship, or (and in what circumstances) direct censorship by the directors and owners of mass media. Whatever the case, the result is the same. Most media outlets align themselves with national correctness both at the level of terminology and at the level of opinions, repeating the national catechism on a daily basis.¹⁷

Even in cases when the guarantees of freedom of opinion impede the direct suppression of views that diverge from national correctness, the Greek prosecutorial/judicial practice finds indirect ways to use criminal law to repress those who think differently. One way, particularly related to the media, is by using the provisions relating to spreading fake news and disturbing the public peace (Articles 191 and 192 of the Greek Criminal Code). Expressing one's opinion on historical issues or matters of foreign policy is not "fake news" or "lies." It is true as a genuine expression of a personal opinion, irrespective of what other people or state officials believe about it and of the extent to which it can be shown to be mistaken on the basis of proof. Similarly, the public peace is not threatened by someone making an utterance or publishing articles that are contrary to the opinion of the government or of the majority, including the tenets of national correctness. The peace may well be threatened by extreme nationalist mobs who protest violently (with riots, vandalism, threats, beatings, or otherwise). In that case, it is those who resort to violence who should be penalized, rather than those who peacefully express an academic view. Predictably, the criminal courts that penalize the "dissidents" for spreading fake news and disturbing the public peace declare the reason to be that there is but one truth in "national matters."

In light of this, in recent years, Article 2 of Law 4285/2014 has been added to offer an indirect way for criminal courts to be used for indirect censorship. The article criminalizes the denial of genocides, war crimes, crimes against humanity, the Holocaust, and Nazi crimes that have been recognized by international courts or by the Hellenic Parliament. And of course this route to criminalization of knowledge is problematic, not only because it limits freedom of expression in the name of the nationally sacrosanct "truth," but also because it reduces something resolved by a collective body (usually by a majority of that body) to something divinely ordained. To give an example, the judge or the academic historian who may have disagreed on classifying certain events as crimes against humanity or genocide and who had freely expressed their opinions would probably find themselves facing a prison sentence if they repeated the same view after the adoption of this statute.

In 2015, Heinz Richter, a German history professor and researcher specializing in twentieth-century Greek history, was prosecuted for denying Nazi crimes against the Cretan people. Professor Richter's books have been translated into Greek, and he has been awarded an honorary doctorate from the University of Crete for his important research work. The historian presented his version of events from the Second World War in academic publications. He stated, *inter alia*, that the population of Crete resisted the German aggression during World War II in ways that contravened the law of war, with especial brutality, and that this, in some way, justified the Germans' acts of retaliation. Many considered these views not only academically inaccurate, but also offensive to the memory of heroes of the Greek Resistance, and hence prosecutable.

As a result, Professor Richter was prosecuted on the basis of the aforementioned Article 2 of Law 4285, criminalizing the denial of genocides, war crimes, crimes against humanity, the Holocaust, and those Nazi crimes which have been recognized by international courts or by the Hellenic Parliament. In this case, an extremely broad interpretation of the legislation led to the charge of "denying" Nazi war crimes. Professor Richter was acquitted by the Single-Member Court of First Instance of the city of Rethymno (Decision 2383 of 2015), which considered Article 2 of Law 4285 to be unconstitutional on the grounds that it violates academic and research freedom. The decision is pending appeal.

The issue set the mechanisms of national psychodrama in motion, with recriminations and insults as well as the initiation of a process to revoke the honorary doctorate from the University of Crete in the light of Richter's "nationally inappropriate" arguments.[18] The doctorate was revoked in 2018 and an appeal is pending before the Superior Administrative Court to annul the revocation.[19] The lesson is that questioning national truths such as the just and heroic resistance of the Greeks against the "barbarian" Germans cannot be discussed even in scholarly writings; otherwise the researcher will face persecution and sanctions.

There are similarities with the case of Nikos Filis, who as minister of education caused an uproar in 2015 when he declared in the press that the Pontic Greeks were victims of "bloody ethnic cleansing" but not of a "genocide" in Kemal's Turkey.[20] His view was considered both a betrayal of the nation and indicative of an "ignorance of history," given that the Hellenic Parliament had resolved that a Pontic genocide had indeed taken place. It was also considered scandalous that a Greek politician, and a minister at that, could not say what he believes and had to promote national truths instead. The numerous protests were one of the reasons Nikos Filis was ousted from the Ministry of Education; they also prompted formal complaints relating to the denial of a recognized genocide,[21] which are still pending.

When it comes to the educational or informational material produced by the state, direct censorship is allowed. This is the case with schoolbooks used in primary and secondary education, which represent an ongoing form of state-legal censorship. Law 3966 of 2011 provides for the mandatory adoption in all public schools of textbooks compiled under the supervision of the Ministry of Education; previous legislation included an identical provision.[22] Authors whose views diverge from national correctness are not chosen by the consultants and senior ministry officials charged with commissioning schoolbooks. And if they are chosen, their work is subject to interventions that are clearly censorial in nature.[23] Even after the textbooks have been distributed to schools, some books elicit a reaction from the media and nationalist public opinion and are either corrected or withdrawn. In this case, preventive control is supplemented by repressive censorship, invoking the government prerogative to publish and teach anything it likes. This censorship relates mainly to history schoolbooks, in particular, which can be presumed to relate to national issues.

Yet the best-known example that links preventive with repressive censorship is probably the history textbook for the sixth grade of primary school, which was withdrawn in 2008 after just one year in use. In a wide-ranging and intense public clash, those opposed to the book referred to errors and omissions, but the underlying tone of the criticism was that it was unacceptable for "young Greeks" not to be taught about the existence of "secret schools" under Ottoman rule and other similar items which help maintain the Greek national myth, regardless of the facts brought to light by historical research.[24]

Thus, for example, even the Academy of Athens, which does not undertake studies of schoolbooks, presented a series of criticisms, which included the fact that the history textbook in question "makes no mention of the smooth running of democracy after the fall of the dictatorship, and the need for national unity."[25]

Under this "national" perspective, history courses become a medium for national indoctrination with the blessing of the Greek Constitution, which states, "Education constitutes a basic mission for the State and shall aim at the moral, intellectual, professional and physical training of Greeks, the development of national and religious consciousness and their formation as free and responsible citizens" (Article 16, 2).

Of course, for the Greek national narrative, cultural homogeneity is the ideal. Languages other than Greek, religions other than Orthodoxy, and cultural traditions other than "Greek" (whatever that may mean) have the potential to undermine national unity and are met with suspicion, which often turns into censorship. The reality we encounter on the streets of Greece is that it is far from homogeneous, given that over one million foreigners live in the country. The number of Greek nationals who have a different religion (or no religion at all), who speak foreign languages with their family or follow specific cultural traditions, runs into millions—many of whom do not consider themselves Greek in their national consciousness. How are these realities dealt with?

Usually, by setting to one side the dictates of individual freedom and equal treatment, and seeking by various means to have these facts hushed up. Sociostructural censorship requires that references to such groups be made using special codes. The Greek state, through statutes and decrees, changed the names of people, villages, and regions so that they conformed with the ideal of ethnic homogeneity ("Hellenization").[26] Journalists will use the term "fellow Greeks" (*homogenis*) to refer to people with Greek grandparents who were born or who live in the USA or Australia, for instance, and who do not speak a word of Greek. Bizarrely, however, and even though it comes to sound normal with repetition, they will use "Turkish-born citizens of Thrace" rather than "Greek-born citizens of Thrace" to refer to those born and living in the mainland. But all this has culminated in the past two decades most strongly in two issues: the attitude of the Greek state to the neighboring state of Macedonia and to the minority groups of Thrace.

Macedonia declared its independence (and was generally recognized as a sovereign state) in 1991 after the breakup of Yugoslavia. The Greek authorities and the nationalist section of public opinion reacted strongly to the independence and the name of the country, considering that it was attempting to usurp "Greek" history and cultural tradition by claiming continuity with ancient Macedonia.

Behind the controversy was the issue that in the northern part of Greece, which also bears the name Macedonia, there were over 160,000 people (a so-called nonminority) living after the First World War who spoke the Macedonian language and had a different ethnic consciousness from the Greek or Bulgarian consciousness. A large part of this Macedonian-speaking population was expelled from Greece or forced to be "Hellenized." The use of the Macedonian language was persecuted and only Greek was taught in schools.[27] The Greek state has always denied the existence of a Macedonian minority and language.[28] And the reactions to the name of the newly created state were linked to the (imaginary) fear of claims for the annexation of part of Greek Macedonia to that state.[29]

Since the 1990s there have been frantic media campaigns to show that Greece is justified in refusing to recognize Macedonia unless it changes its name and also admits that there is no Macedonian minority and language in Greece.[30] This very real crusade had made the Macedonian question a dominant "national issue" that provokes strong reactions against anyone who dares to disagree with it.

Linguistic censorship appears very easily when reference is required to such nonrecognized entities in Greece. Banishing "nationally blasphemous terms"[31] allows censorship to clearly reveal its re-creative nature, for not only does it prohibit dissent, but it also reproduces practices of national correctness. Not only does it deny names, but it creates new ones. The real geopolitical problem of Macedonia became the "Macedonian" Issue. And then it became the "Skopian" Issue, using the Greek name of the capital of Macedonia. (Imagine German politicians and journalists calling Italy "Rome.")

State-legal censorship is then utilized when individuals or groups do not simply submit to socio-structural censorship, perhaps by accusing the Greek state of oppressing a minority or preventing its linguistic, religious, or cultural reproduction, or when a political movement demands rights for minorities.

In the 1990s, apart from political and journalistic reactions to "national dissidents," activists were prosecuted for spreading fake news in order to disturb the public peace and for jeopardizing relations with foreign countries (Articles 191 and 192 of the Greek Criminal Code). In some cases, the defendants were sentenced to prison, with the courts also following the rationale of national correctness.[32]

Meanwhile, acts of violence were also committed in 1995 against the political party "Rainbow," which represents the Macedonian "nonminority," by Greek nationalist groups with the indirect encouragement of the authorities.[33] Subsequently, it was the victims (members of the Rainbow party) who were prosecuted for disturbing the public peace. The European Court of Human Rights found against Greece in 1998 and 2015 for stopping a Macedonian minority association from operating,[34] and in 2005 for failing to protect legitimate political activities of the Rainbow party.[35] The court's main argument hinged on the principle of pluralism in a democratic society requiring that disagreements and tension be defused through dialogue and tolerance, rather than through the repression of those who think differently from the majority.[36]

The second issue that reached a peak in the past two decades concerns the minority of Western Thrace in Greece. There are 130,000 people today with Greek citizenship who speak Turkish and have a Turkish national consciousness. The Greek state and its propaganda mechanisms have always tried to deny or downplay this fact, referring to a "Muslim" minority or denying the Turkish national consciousness of those belonging to this minority. This is also linked to state actions and policies aimed at marginalizing the Turkish minority and suppressing protests and political demands.[37]

The multiple prosecutions of Ahmet Sadik represent a textbook case of repressive censorship. Sadik was a politician and deputy in the Greek Parliament from the Turkish minority in Thrace, which occupied the Greek courts for many years. He was also prosecuted and condemned for spreading fake news and disturbing the public peace and international relations over national matters (Articles 191 and 192 of the Greek Criminal Code). But less well-known are the cases relating to recognizing the collective bodies of the Turkish minority in Thrace, which were pending through the courts for decades. The Greek courts refused to recognize them, essentially on the grounds that the operating of an association which sought to promote the interests of people who consider themselves to belong to a Turkish minority, either because the associations include the word "Turkish" in their title or because this was inferred from the evidence, was contrary to the legal order. The courts reached their decisions by repeating the nationally correct view (there is a "Muslim minority" in Thrace, not a Turkish one) and taking the stand that any other view is illegal. And this occurred despite the Strasbourg Court finding Greece guilty repeatedly of breaching the provisions of the European Convention on Human Rights concerning the freedom of association irrespective of the views and identities of the individuals associating or assembling.[38]

To top it all off, in November 2017, it was revealed that an order had been issued by a Public Prosecutor's Office to attorneys and the police to list the names of academics studying issues relating to the Turkish minority (a term which was quarantined in quotation marks in the documents). This investigation took place after a member of the far-right and extreme nationalist party Golden Dawn brought a lawsuit in 2016 against those who used the term "Turkish minority" in Greece, accusing them of spreading fake news and "betraying the country." The Public Prosecutor's Office was sympathetic to the request. After the case was publicized and the minister of education criticized, invoking free speech and free research, the investigation order was revoked.[39] For every inch of the way, then, education and pedagogy in schools, universities, and the media are imbricated within the state and its practices of censorship, as well as the praxis of democracy.

Concluding Thoughts

Imperatives of national correctness are implemented in Greece by a dual process of socio-structural and state-legal censorship, making it clear that in Greece some things are simply not said. And while one would expect society's overall progress to reduce the scope of national correctness, there are indications that the opposite is true. Nevertheless, it would be somewhat superficial to attribute the resilience of Greece's national "red lines" and "no-go zones" to "culture lag." Rather, the mechanism for enforcing correct views on national issues and censoring divergent ones achieves three things: the national issue is cordoned off behind red lines; it is rendered a no-go zone; and, as a result, foreign policy is depoliticized and history hyperpoliticized.[40]

The cases we have cited shed light on the productive nature of censorship. It concurrently exists within, alongside, and is often carried through educational praxis, eventually molding, imposing, and reinforcing ideological practices that can withstand time and establishing continuities in the practice of censorship itself. The "peculiarity" of the democratic setting, with Greece as a case in point, is the coexistence of unconstrained freedom of speech in almost everything except "national issues," which are those in which censorship is the norm, in opposition to every other issue, where censorship is now the exception. Ultimately, "national issues" are probably those in relation to which the freedom to contradict does not exist.

Notes

1. Review in Dionysis Goutsos, "Lexiko tes neas Hellenikes glossas," *Journal of Modern Greek Studies* 17, no. 1 (1999): 163–70.

2. Tasos Kostopoulos, *Polemos kai ethnokatharsi (1912–1922)* (Athens: Bibliorama, 2007), 25–27, 48–59.

3. For a detailed discussion of the Babiniotis case, see Akis Gavriilidis, "Lexiko Babinioti" (Babiniotis Dictionary), in *Lexiko logokrisias stin Ellada: Kachektiki dimokratia, diktatoria, metapolitefsi* (Dictionary of censorship in Greece: Weak

democracy, dictatorship, regime change), ed. Pinelopi Petsini and Dimitris Christopoulos (Athens: Kastaniotis, 2018), 404–5.

4. First Instance Court of Thessaloniki, Decision 18.134 of 1998, *Armenopoulos* (law journal) (1998): 1330 (in Greek).

5. Areios Pagos (plenary composition), Decision n. 13 of 1999, http://www.cylaw.org/cgi-bin/open.pl?file=/areiospagos/2/1999/1999_2_0013.html (in Greek).

6. Konstantinos Tsitselikis, "Ethniki orthotita: Ena agkathi sto ypogastrio tis dimokratias mas?" (National correctness: A thorn in the belly of our democracy?), in *I logokrisia stin Ellada* (Censorship in Greece), ed. Pinelopi Petsini and Dimitris Christopoulos (Athens: Rosa Luxemburg Foundation, 2016), 222.

7. Maria Repousi, "Ta orizontia politika revmata tis symmorfosis stin ethniki orthotita" (Horizontal political currents of compliance with national correctness), in Petsini and Christopoulos, *I logokrisia stin Ellada*, 234–42.

8. Tsitselikis, "Ethniki orthotita," 221.

9. Akis Gavriilidis, *I atherapefti nekrofilia tou rizospastikou patriotismou: Ritsos, Elytis, Theodorakis, Svoronos* (The incurable necrophilia of radical patriotism: Ritsos, Elytis, Theodorakis, Svoronos) (Athens: Futura, 2007); Álvaro García Marín, "The Origin Is Already Haunted: Greece as the Uncanny of Modernity," *Modern Greek Studies Online* 1 (2015): 1–22.

10. Tsitselikis, "Ethniki orthotita," 220–22.

11. See tanea.gr/2019/01/09/politics/parliament/epeisodio-anamesa-se-georgiadi-xristodoulopoulou-xaraktirismoi-gia-fasistes-kai-nazistes.

12. For theoretical and empirical analyses, see Dimitris Christopoulos, ed., *To 'vathy kratos' sti simerini Ellada kai i Akrodexia: Astynomia, dikaiosyni, stratos, Ekklisia* (The "deep state" in modern-day Greece and the Far Right: Police, justice, army, Church) (Athens: Nisos, 2014).

13. See also Tsitselikis, "Ethniki orthotita," 221–24.

14. On this distinction, see Pinelopi Petsini and Dimitris Christopoulos, "Eisagogi: Giati i logokrisia" (Introduction: Why censorship), in Petsini and Christopoulos, *I logokrisia stin Ellada* (*Censorship in Greece*), 13.

15. Greek Consititution of 1975, Article 14.1. Every person may express and propagate his thoughts orally, in writing and through the press in compliance with the laws of the State.

16. European Convention on HumanRights, Article 10.1. Everyone has the right to freedom of expression. This right shall include freedom to hold opinions and to receive and impart information and ideas without interference by public authority and regardless of frontiers.

17. The groundbreaking study by Tasos Kostopoulos reports cases of opinions being suppressed in the press for reasons of "national correctness": "'Ethnika themata' kai aftologokrisia ton MME." ("National issues" and self-censorship in the media), in *Opseis logokrisias stin Ellada* (Aspects of censorship in Greece), ed. G. Ziogas et al. (Athens: Nefeli, 2008), 40–56.

18. See tvxs website, May 19, 2016, http://tvxs.gr/news/ellada/kriti-pairnoyn-piso-ton-titlo-toy-epitimoy-apo-ton-rixter.

19. Anna-Maria Droubouki, "Richter Heinz," in *Lexiko logokrisias stin Ellada: Kachektiki dimokratia, diktatoria, metapolitefsi* (Dictionary of censorship in Greece: Weak democracy, dictatorship, regime change), ed. Pinelopi Petsini and Dimitris Christopoulos (Athens: Kastaniotis, 2018), 477–79.

20. Kostis Papaioannou, "Genoktonia Pontion" (Pontic genocide), in Petsini and Christopoulos, *Lexiko logokrisias stin Ellada*, 329–32.

21. Dimosthenis Papadatos-Anagnostopoulos, "Oi filoi 'ethnokatharsi,' oi echthroi 'enoktonia': I ypothesi Fili kai i epanacharaxi tou synorou Aristeras-Dexias os anaviosi tis dekaetias tou '90" ("Ethnic cleansing" for friends, "genocide" for enemies: The Filis case and the redemarcation of Left and Right as a revival of the '90s), in Petsini and Christopoulos, *I logokrisia stin Ellada*, 225–26.

22. See https://www.lawspot.gr/nomikes-plirofories/nomothesia/nomos-3966-2011.

23. Repousi, "Horizontal Political Currents of Compliance," 234–40. The author calls the consultants at the Greek Ministry of Education who monitor the content of school textbooks "censors" (236).

For details on the textbooks that have been withdrawn for "national" reasons, see Charis Athanassiadis, *Ta aposyrthenta vivlia: Ethnos kai scholiki istoria stin Ellada, 1858–2008* (Withdrawn books: Nation and school history in Greece) (Athens: Alexandria, 2015).

24. Dimosthenis Papadatos-Anagnostopoulos, "Istoria Ektis Dimotikou" (Sixth-grade history), in Petsini and Christopoulos, *Lexiko logokrisias stin Ellada*, 373–76.

25. Academy of Athens, "Kritikes paratiriseis sto vivlio tis istorias tis ektis dimotikou" (A critique of the sixth-grade history textbook), *Antivaro blog*, March 22, 2007, http://palio.antibaro.gr/society/akadhmia_teliko.php.

26. Examples and legislation in Eleni Kyramargiou, "Kainouria onomata, kainourios hartis: Zitimata metonomasion ton oikismon tis Elladas 1909–1928" (Change of toponyms in Greece, 1909–1928), *Ta Istorika* 52 (2010): 3–26.

27. Tasos Kostopoulos, *I apagorevmeni gloss:. Kratiki katastoli ton slavikon dialekton stin elliniki Makedonia* (The forbidden language: State persecution of Slavic dialects in Greek Macedonia) (Athens: Vivliorama, 2008), 29 and passim.

28. Anastasia Karakasidou, "Cultural Illegitimacy in Greece: The Slavo-Macedonian 'Non-minority,'" in *Minorities in Greece: Aspects of Plural Society*, ed. Richard Clogg (London: Hurst, 2002), 122–64.

29. Historical and political overview in Dimitris Christopoulos and Kostis Karpozilos, *10 +1 Questions & Answers on the Macedonian Question* (Athens: Rosa-Luxemburg-Stiftung Office in Greece, 2018); Alexis Heraclides, *The Macedonian Question and the Macedonians: A History* (London: Routledge, 2020).

30. Athéna Skoulariki, "Au nom de la nation: Le discours public en Grèce sur la question macédonienne et le rôle des médias (1991–1995)" (PhD diss., Université Paris-II, 2005).

31. Tsitselikis, "Ethniki orthotita," 220.

32. Cases and commentaries in Kostas Papastergiou, "Makedoniko zitima—Dikes" (Macedonian questions—Trials), in Petsini and Christopoulos, *Lexiko logokrisias stin Ellada*, 418–19.

33. See the facts in the ECtHR, Ouranio Toxo and Others v. Greece, October 20, 2005, http://hudoc.echr.coe.int/webservices/content/pdf/001-70720.

34. ECtHR, Sidiropoulos and Others v. Greece, July 10, 1998, http://hudoc.echr.coe.int/webservices/content/pdf/001-58205?TID=ihgdqbxnfi; for an analysis, see Dimitri Christopoulos, "'I pliris ensomatosi ton meionotikon sta anthropina dikaiomata': Scholio stin apofasi Sidiropoulos kai loipoi kata Ellados" ("Full integration of minority rights into human rights": A comment on the decision in Siridopoulos and others v. Greece), *To Syntagma* 2 (1999): 307–24. For a similar verdict against Greece in the ECtHR decision, see Maison de la Civilisation Macédonienne et autres c. Grèce, July 9, 2015, http://hudoc.echr.coe.int/eng?i=001-155822.

35. ECtHR, Ouranio Toxo and Others v. Greece, October 20, 2005, http://hudoc.echr.coe.int/webservices/content/pdf/001-70720.

36. See the unbearably nationalist reasoning of the Greek courts mentioned in the judgment of the ECtHR, Maison de la Civilisation Macédonienne et autres c. Grèce, July 9, 2015, http://hudoc.echr.coe.int/eng?i=001-155822.

37. Konstantinos Tsitselikis, *Old and New Islam in Greece: From Historical Minorities to Immigrant Newcomers* (Leiden: Brill, 2007); Olga Demetriou, *Capricious Borders: Minority, Population, and Counter-conduct between Greece and Turkey* (New York: Berghahn Books, 2013).

38. ECtHR, Bekir Ousta and Others v. Greece, October 11, 2007; Emin and Others v. Greece, March 27, 2008; Tourkiki Enosi Xanthis and Others v. Greece, March 27, 2008. For an analysis see Tsitselikis, *Old and New Islam in Greece*, 227–58 and 273–87.

39. "Anakrisi kathigiton gia ton oro 'tourkiki meionotita'" (Teachers interrogated over the term "Turkish minority"), newspaper *Ta Nea*, December 13, 2017; Anta Psarra, "Ora na spasei to apostima" (Time to lance the abscess), newspaper *Efimerida ton Syntakton*, December 16, 2017.

40. See also Papadatos-Anagnostopoulos, "Oi filoi 'ethnokatharsi,' oi echthroi 'genoktonia,'" 231.

The Politics of Mentorship
May Hawas

Childhood

As a schoolchild, Arabic was never my strongest subject. It's a difficult language, even for native speakers, and its teachers always seemed to act as if they were guarding a treasure chest which, if opened, would only reveal a golden affirmation of the teacher's own profundity. Speakers of other difficult languages like German or Chinese might feel the same, perhaps. In all cases, I didn't dislike Arabic as a child; I just felt there was too much fuss being made about the grammar. Really, I thought. If you could read the text without it, what was the *point* of knowing where to place the *tashkil*, or the vowels?

The men of the family, the tradition went, were always much better at Arabic grammar, and the towering pedagogue in the family was my late grandfather: a crusty and intimidating old man who looked crusty, intimidating, and old even as a young man. When the children of the family spent summer with the grandparents, the holidays would inevitably be interspersed with a strong dose of grammar teaching.

After sunset, he would call us into his room, one by one, or a couple at a time, take out the appropriate Arabic schoolbook, and give us a lesson. The lessons would start with my grandmother bringing in Turkish coffee, and the smell would filter lazily into the heavy wood furniture. I would leave the room on a warm summer evening, made drowsy by the delicious smell of coffee and wood, my grandfather's low drone, and the monotonous buzz of a belligerent mosquito—only to find some other cousin outside the door, waiting resignedly for their own lesson.

Beyond these fine sensory details, and my less fine disgruntlement at the impromptu lessons, I remember very little—almost nothing, alas—of the actual content. It's only now, years after, that I realize my grandfather can't have been overjoyed to spend this much time drilling Arabic grammar into reluctant children as payment for his sins of being able to actually appreciate the complex language. I don't even know if any of our parents had asked him to do it. The point was that he had knowledge, and therefore he felt obliged to share it. It became a family duty, even if self-imposed.

Years after my grandfather had passed away, my mother, who had spent much of her youth trying to drill French school grammar into my head, was roped into spending some of her middle age doing the same for a friend. She was asked by a fellow mum at my brother's school to help out her youngest daughter. This was in Egypt, where private home lessons are the norm, from primary school to university. Yet, the logic went, if there was a friend who could do it . . . well, better the teacher you know. Thus, the timid little girl came to our house for some weeks during term for a few years, and I could hear Mum *bravo*-ing and *excellent*-ing her through French grammar. And every one of those same years, festive holidays would find us awash with gifts sent by the girl's mother. Easter biscuits, homemade birthday cakes chantillyed and compoted to perfection, crates of seasonal fruits from their fruit trees: dates and pomegranates in autumn, navel oranges in winter, persimmons in spring . . . For the price of a couple of these gifts, the woman could have paid for private lessons for the year. But someone who was a family friend knew French, and that was an infinitely better scenario. They wouldn't be a paid teacher. They would be an old-fashioned *mentor*, and would take a personal interest. Pedagogy, in Arab societies, quickly becomes personal.

Through my PhD years, I realized that I felt gratitude more keenly for my mentors than my fellow students did, but I didn't know why. The Americans told me: your doctorate gives you a network. The Europeans and the British didn't speak much about mentorship beyond issues of signing supervisory forms. Meanwhile the Egyptians described it with some melodrama, drawing on a popular proverb (currently inscribed on the backs of schoolbooks issued by the Ministry of Education): you owe your life to the person who teaches you a single letter. I connected the dots only after I moved from public to private academic institutions and encountered international student bodies whose politics and values I didn't necessarily empathize or agree with. It had been instilled in me that pedagogy had a societal and communal value and purpose, but in the international professional sphere, pedagogy was a service—certainly a much-better-regulated one, but not necessarily the stuff of legacy.

Mentorship

The vocation of pedagogy in Arabic is deeply societal and sometimes communal. At its heart lies an understanding of the power of mentorship. This understanding is infiltrative in society and inherent in all social bonds. It operates at all levels, in all transactions, between neighbors, in families, within institutions, and across trades and professions. The value of mentorship does not just refer to the formative rule of some gowned or turbaned demagogue, but also manifests in a synchronized form of simultaneous passing down and receiving of value that helps validate social mobility. In other words, the individual cult of hard work only works if contextualized (idealistically!) within a support system of mentorship. To rise alone, by your own doing, in this world? Nothing could sound more like individual genius, which smacks less of meritocracy and more of self-aggrandizement and social alienation. Rather, and however fallacious in practical terms this might be, one's social rise is interrelated with the mentorship one might receive. It is, ultimately, mentorship that propels and sustains whatever self-initiative the individual may have.

Successful public figures have invariably emphasized this. The late Egyptian-American scientist Ahmed Zewail, for instance, received the Nobel Prize for Chemistry in 1999. Zewail, who had moved to the United States shortly after his graduation, suddenly found himself one of the most important public figures in Egypt. Asked about his success in one interview after another, he soon became famous for his modesty and dedication to teamwork. Yet after the spurt of celebratory fame had fizzled, his most famous saying among the Egyptian public remained: "Westerners aren't geniuses, and we aren't stupid. But they support those who fail until they succeed, and we fight those who succeed until they fail." Today, years after his passing, no one knows if Zewail actually said this. But even if it is only a popular interpretation of his work ethic, it indicates a collective understanding on the part of the Egyptian public that to achieve the kind of success indicated by, say, the Nobel Prize didn't mean being blessed with a kind of individual genius, but rather it meant having a support system. Without such support, hard work, even genius, wouldn't get you far.

As in science, so in sport. Compare the Zeweil scenario to that of British-Egyptian world squash champion Mohamed El Shorbagy, who, unlike Zeweil, lived most of his life in Egypt. El Shorbagy came under heavy fire in 2022 for choosing to switch his allegiance from Egypt to England. Gently batting the guns away, he explained that at his particular age and position, he now needed support more than ever: a team, a doctor, or even a coach. Egypt had not, he explained, ever given him this.

El Shorbagy's case drew attention because a large number of the world's men and women squash champions come from Egypt, which has not dominated other sports. As the international media cottoned on to this rogue phenomenon of Egyptian excellence, a discourse began to circulate, often generated by the players themselves, that their strength came from having to play by their wits, outside of any orthodox support or coaching line.[1] The players' theory was that they started battling freestyle at a young age, battled their fellow world champions on the "neighborhood" courts, and kept battling their way to the top. The popular ethos among players became, we "attack" the game, we break the mold, and so we beat the game.

It is understandable why few players ever mentioned support. President Hosni Mubarak (1981–2011), a big squash player himself, had certainly placed the sport in the public limelight, but if state support during his presidency was scant, after his time, it only decreased. Yet the number of Egyptian champions keeps rising. Breaking the mold may have initially been a sign of the sport's vigor and youth. By the time El Shorbagy (currently the longest-reigning international squash player) was speaking of his lack of support and his current need for what England was offering, he was addressing mature generations of squash players, and touching upon a breaking point understood by all highly competitive people. If, for lack of support, breaking the mold had once seemed the goal, *retaining* a mold and creating a legacy without support would be impossible. If El Shorbagy had risen up the ranks freestyle, he would now lose his position without mentorship.

As such, the English Squash Federation had barely announced El Shorbagy's new affiliation when the player started emphasizing the long support he had received from British coaches and the wider England squash team, articulating his excitement at the prospect of training a younger generation of English players. El Shorbagy's new discursive challenge, then, was not to break a mold, but rather to retain and pass down a legacy. In finding a support system in England, El Shorbagy could finally be free to adopt Egypt's most traditional understanding of mentorship. The Egyptian media so aghast at El Shorbagy's turncoat moment had, as is characteristic of the Egyptian media, got the wrong end of the stick. With El Shorbagy's departure, Egypt hadn't just lost an athlete. It had lost a mentor: both a model champion and a model coach for future squash players.

If athletes and scientists speak of support, scholars speak of teaching. We are trained, as Arabs, to respect teaching as a profession, even if we laugh at the over-scholarly; and if there is one class of teacher that is respected above all (though that repute has become tarnished of late), it is the university academic.

There is, predictably, a hyperbolic number of synonyms for the word "teacher" in Arabic. The word "professor," for instance, translates into Arabic as *"al-ustadh"* (the most famous *ustadh* historically having been Alberonius). Yet *ustadh* is also a master of knowledge in general, as well as a polite form of address. So a local teacher might be called *"ustadh,"* a religious scholar might be called *"ustadh,"* a university professor might be called *"ustadh,"* but also, informally, *"ustadh"* is a commendable epithet for anyone who is a master of their game: a *boss*.[2]

Teachers are specifically respected, however, because education is a communal vocation with the intended purpose of social mobility for its students. Pedagogy is a two-way process that repeats endlessly to create larger societal cohesion. A verb like *"tatalmadth"* sums it up. "Being a student" is turned into an active verb. *Tatalmadth* means simultaneously to have been a student at the hands of a mentor, and to have made oneself a student of a mentor. Double responsibility, then: some placed on the mentor, and some placed on the student. In making sure everyone feels stressed about their various responsibilities, it's all very Arab.

No wonder then that at the university, the last stage and perhaps pinnacle of the educational process, which targets students who are legally adults and on the brink of vocational utility, pedagogy exists on the edge of the relation between the state and its body politic. No wonder, too, that the most famous pedagogues and the leading Arab literary critics, from the nineteenth century to the present, have all been social reformers, if growing steadily more impoverished as time has passed. Few may have made such a personal comment, at least in writing, but the most emphatically "Arab" part of Edward Said's writing voice always seemed his very recognizable high moral ground, anger, and occasional didacticism. The voice seemed to stand outside his European and American training and erudition, especially when his work was read in Arabic-speaking countries. In tone (though certainly neither in knowledge nor in content), you might as well have been hearing all your former university teachers at your back telling you why you were wrong in all the ways that counted and some of the ways that didn't.

I can't think of any modern Arab literary critic who achieved the global status of Edward Said, but I can think of many who were towering figures in their local societies and notable international ones elsewhere. In the first half of the twentieth century, their academic work was most notably infused with journalism, and many of their debates filtered into all the institutions of political life, from parliamentary debate to the judicial courts. I mention here the public intellectuals of the modern renaissance—Taha Hussein, Ahmed Lutfi al-Sayyid, Ali Abdel Raziq, Abbas Mahmoud al-Aqqad, Jurji Zaydan, Abdallah

Al-Nadim, and the women public intellectuals who still tend be sequestered from the men in intellectual history: Nabawiyya Musa, Doria Shafik, Malak Hifny Nassif, Mai Ziadeh (a sort of quieter, Arab Madame de Staël). Nor is it a coincidence that almost all of them were trained in letters. Like *paideia* or *Bildung*, literature (*adab*) in Arabic has a definitive pedagogical component. The work of such intellectuals took the form of literary reviews and social commentary, and they found a lot to preoccupy them in Egypt's modern state.

From midcentury onward, it was state security that seemed to be more preoccupied with the academics. As such, a fragile history of twentieth-century diasporic Arab criticism moves in parallel to the one in the home countries. It may begin in the early twentieth century with the likes of Khalil Gibran and Mikhail Naimy in the United States, through to the less famous Ahmed Zaki Abu Shadi, but explodes in numbers in the middle of the century, with the installation of military governments in the Arabic-speaking world. Those who live long lives (i.e., don't get imprisoned, or assassinated), who write criticism *as* criticism, are often dispersed and unhistoricized, sometimes writing in many languages: Sadiq Jalal al-Azm, Nasr Hamid Abu Zaid, Adonis, and many others. What do they all have in common? The vocation of the intellectual: the belief, partly pedagogical, that they have a responsibility to voice, to critique, to lead by example, and to edify the public. While "public intellectual" may sound more exciting than "educator," in Arab societies, the two conflate easily.

Of course, this might stem from the status of the Arab university itself, which has traditionally been a public endeavor. A history of public education in the Arabic-speaking world might even be traced, if one desires, to past centuries when learning took place in, and was inherently tied to the practices of, the public. This was the case if the education process was organized by more formal institutions in libraries and Islamic universities like Al-Azhar (founded 970 C.E. in Cairo) or Al-Zaytuna (traced back to the seventh century, but formally described in the fourteenth century in Tunis). It was also the case, however, when education took place in mosques, churches, and Jewish temples; in the greater, informal public areas, such as the marketplace; in public lectures; or in other public spaces at the hands of storytellers, copyeditors, auditors, check-readers, and scribes. Education, both before and after the institution of the modern state, almost always entailed, if not some sort of employment, then a means to livelihood, and sometimes, for the enslaved, a road to emancipation.

Before the modern state it is of course impossible to verify quantitatively what having an "education" referred to. What we do know, however, is that being educated was not restricted to or conditioned by an elite status, and that the practicalities of pedagogy did not take place in a closed circle or in a club of the learned (who might, say, interpret the religious codes for you, and buy your ticket to heaven), but often in the public eye—if not between the vegetable sellers, then in the public squares where the lectures were given: among the booksellers, in mosques, and even in the form of entertainment, by the storytellers and poets.

It was, in fact, with the institution of the secular state university at the cusp of the twentieth century in the Arab world that pedagogy first came to be seen as a rich man's club (though scholarships were available and sponsored by endowment). Still, even then, and very quickly, in the span of a few decades, higher education was made open to all, with the university becoming free. The proper support of university education, in the Arabic-speaking world, then, has predominantly been seen to come from the state, and university education has largely been a subsidized endeavor.[3]

Nonetheless, throughout its history, and regardless of who was in charge of the finances, the state university has *always* had a tenuous relationship with the state. Calls to free the university space from political intervention seemed to start almost as soon as the university itself did (and have continued till the present). Arab higher education often takes place in this strangely hostile climate of fear, built on social hierarchy and authoritarianism, walled in and cemented down by fear of the state, and resisted by teachers' insistent practice of their vocation as well as the movements of a student body that is politicized in the way only *public* students can be: coming together as a mixture of all classes in society, and a vital representative of the body politic.

With fear—and this is what concerns me here, though it has taken some time to come to it—politics comes to mean something very different from the expected practices of citizenship, which may range from voting to campaigning. Such practices and obvious activism have existed, of course, manifesting (every time political restrictions are relaxed) in student protests, organizations, and unions, with different groups (as, in Egypt, the Leftists and the Muslim Brotherhood) rising to prominence in different decades. Outside of these organizations, however, politics more commonly becomes something much more muted and less tangible. To be Arab and political at a state university doesn't necessarily mean to practice politics: it can also mean to have any kind of voice at all about any given situation, from what to call or include in a department program (should it be "Arabic and Islamic Literature" or "Arabic and Eastern Literatures"?) to whether or not to acquiesce to a demand from administration that *Moll Flanders* or *Sons and Lovers* should be taken off a syllabus.

In the highly censored areas of the Middle East, when the threat of not toeing the line could rob you of your employment, dignity, and even freedom, does that make the general state educator brave or complacent? There are no easy answers to that question. There are many, of course, who choose to steer clear of any decisions, fading into the background as they choose to walk "by the wall," as the Arabic expression goes. Yet for most of the student body, such teachers are never regarded as powerhouse figures. They remain in the background of the faculty, where indeed they are very happy to locate themselves.

Cultures of fear and authoritarianism never create healthy pedagogical practices, though they may produce startlingly brilliant students, and overpoweringly empathetic academics. The paternalistic, patriarchal structure of mentorship, after all, resonates with similar discourses in Arab political leadership and, even on a nuclear level, in the popular, sociological dynamics of the family. The discursive roles of leader, teacher, parent can overlap. This can be a good thing and a bad thing. When mentorship is far more than the relationship between a student and a teacher, it becomes part of the love that binds a community; but if it turns into a discourse that helps prop up and defend unquestioned authoritarianism and hierarchies, the evils are obvious.

Still, despite the authoritarianism and the hierarchy; despite the lack of entitlements, and the sheer fear within the institution; despite the intense corruption and need for connections to get employed and get ahead outside the institution; and despite the technological advances and the new, incredibly successful, entrepreneur-influencer models who seem to have skipped the long waiting times required by the traditional work-hard-and-keep-at-it ethos of old; despite, in short, the real world and a world order that indicate otherwise, the societally binding value of mentorship has never, in the Arabic-speaking world, been completely defeated.[4]

Easy to see, then, why the Arab pedagogue and intellectual loses their sense of vocation when they lose their public. Said had managed to make of exile a mantra, merging the trauma of being Palestinian with the philosophical history of exile and the diaspora. Still, exile is a very lonely place. An exile has lost their mentors, and often lacks a public to mentor. What gets lost in exile is the body politic. Without this public, without the understanding that you mentor to increase your value as a teacher as well as to "raise" generations, pedagogy itself becomes meaningless. And, if fear was the reason for the departure of such intellectuals from their home countries, the fear never quite ends. Their exile, whatever they make of it, often turns into something of a spectacle for their host societies.

Activist, journalist, philosopher, and writer Yassin al-Haj Saleh, who spent sixteen years in Assad's jails and currently lives in Germany, argues that freedom means never to be satisfied with homeliness. His long essay "Freedom: Home, Prison, Exile . . . and the World" posits a simple premise: that freedom leads either to culture or to war. He defines culture as the process of transforming the outside into an inside and a home. The freedom to create culture, then, beyond tradition, place, self, prison, or any other regulative or societal norm, is simply the ability to transform what is unknown into something known. This process enables us to transform the exilic into the homely, because exile is, like imprisonment, ostensibly, the opposite of freedom. "Culture," he writes, "is the science that turns the unknown/uncharted universe into a charted world." Yet with this comes a caveat. Once charted and fixed, the world turns into a prison, so the only way to stop being imprisoned is to constantly "come out of" the world, even by revolution.[5]

The section on exile is the most pertinent. Al-Haj Saleh writes:

> The exiled have no society with traditions that they are trying to resist or abandon. Their actual problem is that they have been stripped of such traditions, of customs and habits. They are more in need of a reference point, or a home, rather than "freedom," because they have much of the latter, but they don't know what to do with it, or whom to relinquish it for. We need freedom only to dedicate ourselves to a cause, or to renounce it for the sake of someone else. (al-Haj Saleh, my translation)

What, then, is the point of freedom offered by these host societies for someone who is a publicly conscious citizen of another state? The exiled, after all, have no home; no past and no history to return to; and no present to come out of, rebel against, or engage with. They have no cause to adopt. What al-Haj Saleh doesn't say, but perhaps should, is that they also have no one to teach, and no one to lead.

Al-Haj Saleh's solution is, characteristically, active. The only way to overcome exile is to let go of one's old soul. He writes provocatively: "Loyalty to the nation is true treason." The only way for exile to be liberating is to affiliate with a global society of strangers, but also to accept exile's own independent state. In this kind of free fall scenario, the potential transformative scope for the non-free ceases to be individual (i.e., the ability to act freely), and the definitions of freedom itself transcend definitions of "home" or the "nation." Rather, the exiled aim to change the world at large, even if they risk losing the ability to live:

> We need to change the world in the world, because the world is a global benefit, that is, it is for the benefit of all and each: societies, groups, and individuals.
>
> With all disrespect intended to all nations. (al-Haj Saleh, my translation)

The mission of the free, then, is immanent utopia: the transformation of this world as they are in the world. Al-Haj Saleh speaks of very different stakes, both in suffering and in aspiration, than most of us do

Translated pedagogically, when deprived of a normative body politic, the Arab intellectual seems to cease entirely to become a voice for mentorship, at least as it is traditionally understood. This leaves two possibilities: either to be a professional teacher, devoid of the societal role of mentorship; or to be a critic, writing for worlds of publics and intellectuals at large. Since you cannot be a pedagogue in the Arab sense *without* being a vital part of the body politic, then you can "just" be a critic in exile. Al-Haj Saleh describes this as the move from devotion to the nation to devotion to transforming the world. It's a tall order. It seems, however, that it's sometimes easier to transform the world, theoretically, in the diaspora than to change the nation in dictatorship.

Traveling Pedagogy

I will admit I often choose novels I like when putting together a syllabus. No coincidence then that Amitav Ghosh's work has often found its way into my courses, and I have discussed his novels, whether as a researcher or as a teacher, in Egypt, Belgium, and England. Two instances stand out. For two consecutive years, I taught *In an Antique Land* (1992), first at Alexandria University, then at the American University in Cairo.

The choice for the undergraduate world literature course in Cairo was easy. I was already a fan of the book, and have written on it and followed in its Arabic footnotes, which prompted me to read some of the classics of tenth-century Arabic geography. This particular run of the course was cotaught by Gaurav Desai, who was on a formal academic visit to Cairo from Ann Arbor, Michigan, at the time, and whose own gateway into Ghosh had been via the Asian footnotes. Meanwhile, the stars had aligned to bring into our sessions Mark Muehlhaeusler, at the time the director of the Center of Excellence for the Middle East and Arab Cultures at the American University in Cairo. With a degree in Arabic and Hebrew, Mark had been, in a previous life, head librarian at the Cambridge University Library, and knew more about the Geniza documents than anyone. The die was cast, and the entire class went to visit the empty Ben Ezra Synagogue and the Hanging Church nearby, where the ancient world of Cairo beckoned to us. One of my students wrote to me after the course ended, and that note, perhaps, across all my teaching, has made me think most gratifyingly about what I had wanted to do: "Thank you for encouraging us to be *worldlier* versions of ourselves." I have not forgotten that note.

Yet at the heart of the class lay the ambivalence of the novel. Filled with anthropological observations and empathetic humor, eked out through faded calligraphies, and caked with the mud of the Egyptian village, Amitav Ghosh's novel of old and new Egypt, and old and new India, and old and new scholarship is, quite obviously, political, and Egyptian students, cosmopolitan as students in the Third World are, recognized this. The ideology at the heart of the novel is a call for unity, especially Third World unity, a belief in mobility for all and hybridity of all, and a respect for the ancient as well as the modern. This is, of course, the voice of a very young and idealistic Ghosh: tentative, questioning, wondering, exploring, and listening to the voice of history. For the Egyptian public (even for the generally sheltered groups at the American University), it was easy to listen to the voice of history, which is present everywhere on Egypt's decrepit streets. It is *political*, however, to see this history as important to Egypt's present: to the way people lived, and the world we wanted to create. In the novel's idealistic political aspirations, read by scholars with a startling harmony of reading interests, who did not happen to be at that moment thinking of deadlines, administrative duties, and exams, we could all find opportunities to consider being worldlier versions of ourselves. While being worldly is not necessarily to be political, it can be a first political step, because being worldly is to *dream* of being political, to learn to work through innuendo and implication, with and against the archives, and to learn to listen "to the street."

I have taught Amitav Ghosh elsewhere in Egypt, namely in the public university in Alexandria—the same university, in fact, that Ghosh speaks of with some familiarity before heading off to the Egyptian village. This was also for a world literature course, though at a more advanced level. The much less privileged students of the public university in Alexandria initially found Ghosh's narrative too idealistic, too full of "history": a history, they insisted, that they knew already. (For the private university students elsewhere, all this focus on Egypt's past was quite new.) Why do we need this touch of the exotic?, the Alexandria students seemed to ask. Caught in the flux of their own disappeared history and aging minorities, devoid of the ability to dream big, the cynical Alexandrians saw no relation in their own lives to the aging monuments of Cairo, the labor of the villagers, or the political hope of modern, worldly India in Ghosh's persona. Speaking about being worldly here sounded to them like engaging in the most traditional political cliches of cosmopolitan Egyptian history: the "we are all one" trope of comforting liberal secularism that had become, unfortunately, too hackneyed, and seemingly too bourgeois, for them to see in it a reflection of themselves. In this case, Ghosh's cosmopolitanism—though itself conceived out of his practical experience—resounded too much of *theory*, of the "we are all one" political rhetoric thrown about in Egypt after major sectarian incidents, during the few celebrated Christian holidays, or even as hard-line Islamists won major elections. In short, for these public university students, the historical cosmopolitan discourse stood too much at a distance from reality. It meant looking *back* at history, and, in seeking only to listen and wonder, the discourse became apolitical.

Not a little of this may have also been because of the Alexandrians' own inherent political predilections. The worlds of Cairo and the Delta remain specifically suspect to the Alexandrian public. The first, over-polluted and reeking of officialdom, the second, oversimplified and reeking of impoverishment, have formed political symbols and lobbies far louder than their own seacoast community. As such, the glory that was once Cairo, spoken of with such awe by Ghosh, was immediately more suspect to them, just on principle alone, than it had been to the Cairenes. Rather than dream, what *Antique Land* eventually enabled us to do at the public university was to dig deeper into the contradictions of the local: to speak of broken dreams and failed action, of conflict between secular and sacral literature, and of spiritual faith and political disunity. In the end, to be worldly was to help *reinstate* a dream by listening to the street, though the street this time didn't require students to venture out of the classroom to explore monuments, just to articulate in public terms the frustrations, failures, and grievances that they already experienced in the community.

Of all the institutional opportunities to teach this novel that came later, I couldn't bring myself to assign it to Italian, American, or even British students. The Italians, inheritors of an ancient civilization and its bureaucracies, caught at the crux of the trade routes of the Mediterranean, would certainly understand; the latter two I was more skeptical of. Above all, what I did not want to do was to turn the novel, Egypt, or India, or the voice of the idealist anthropologist, or even my own voice, into a spectacle: a window not so much onto the worlds that we want to create, but onto the exotic.

This is especially true in England. The fear that the criticism of Cambridge scholarship or the acquisitions in its libraries, for instance, or of colonialism in Ghosh would pass unnoticed by students rather than eliciting recognizable self-questioning, shock, rage, or sorrow—that it would, in other words, turn into something distant and foreign rather than personal—felt like a betrayal of the novel's political agenda. It would become *moralistic* rather than actionable, even as the Geniza documents lay in Cambridge's vaults. Without a body politic, even the wonderful Ghosh is, at best, entertainment.

To dream of being political, after all, there must be something stronger than assent; than "we have done this, let's move on." For pedagogy to be meaningful, it must have a different purpose than to seem to say: "Look what you have done." Instead, a public pedagogy is "Look what *we* have done." Not didacticism, but empathy. This is where the public comes in, and this is the founding condition for pedagogy to become political. Teaching politically requires, first and foremost, the assumption of a public of which the teacher is part. For those of us who are not diasporic, it means, if one is to be really effective, revisiting constantly the old question of the relation between the university and the state. For those of us who are distant, it means revisiting constantly what pedagogy itself means, or might mean, for lack of a public, even if that will always necessarily require losing a large part of ourselves: the part that believes in free, public education, and the importance of listening to the voice of the street. Cut off from the body politic (whether this results from physical exile or from alienation in your own society of fear), a pedagogue, in the Arab sense, stops foregrounding pedagogy, even unintentionally, and starts foregrounding theory: whatever can be made historical, distant, philosophical, absolute, or even, as al-Haj Saleh put it, utopian.

It took years of primary school and three years of undergraduate English literature to instill in me an initial, questionable admiration of all things English. It took postcolonial theory and a particular kind of comparative literature to make me realize I had different things to say. As the institutions changed, so did the name of what I was supposed to be doing. Because it included Arabic and French in Egypt, it was called comparative literature. Because it included Arabic in multilingual Europe, it was called world literature. Because it included "foreign languages" in largely monolingual England, it stumbled and fell many times, until, inevitably, we settled on criticism.

Reform

> Never do I want to give the impression that I am against Islam. Far from it. Nor do I want to give the impression that I am a new Salman Rushdie. I am not. One of my worst fears is that Westerners will consider me only as a critic of Islam. That's not the whole picture at all. I am a teacher, a scholar, an intellectual, and a researcher. (Abu Zaid, 11)[6]

> I am at liberty to write what I think. But look at the downside. I'm free to say and write whatever I want outside the university, but where freedom of thought is absolutely essential, I have been silenced. I can write all the books I want to, even propagate what some folks call heresy, but under no circumstances am I permitted to teach. That's considered much too dangerous. What kind of freedom is it that doesn't allow me to transform my ideas into any sort of power? Silenc-

ing is at the heart of my case. Expelling me from the university is a
way of silencing me. (Abu Zaid, 11)

The case of the late Nasr Hamid Abu Zaid was probably the best-known case in Egypt of a contemporary academic persecuted by the Islamists. A scholar of Islamic studies at Cairo University, Abu Zaid became the target of a campaign against him when he applied for promotion to professorship. An Islamist colleague on the committee rejected Abu Zaid's promotion, then escalated the case within the Islamist network in Egypt. Eventually Abu Zaid found himself being charged with and found guilty of apostasy by the Egyptian court. The Islamists declared his marriage null and void (since a Muslim woman cannot marry an "apostate"), and he faced public humiliation and slander in the press. Abu Zaid soon moved to the Netherlands, taking up a professorship at Leiden University, and lived the rest of his life in exile.

Abu Zaid's autobiography, *Voice of an Exile: Reflections on Islam*, was published in 2004, almost twenty years after he left Egypt. He begins the narrative by explaining who, or rather what, he was. "I am a teacher, a scholar, an intellectual, and a researcher" (11). Admitting that he found in the Netherlands the freedom that he had been denied in his home country, he follows up with the same question that al-Haj Saleh has asked: What was the point of freedom in exile if he could not transform his ideas into power in the educational institutions of his home country?

Abu Zaid's autobiography covers a good forty years, starting with his childhood and ending on the cusp of his first visit back to Egypt. It contains several chapters on contentious issues in Islam, but the most space by far is given to the dilemma of an Arab educator who has been deprived of his public. For a book that ostensibly tells the much-publicized story of a much-maligned life, its overarching theme remains the philosophy of pedagogy.

For Abu Zaid, this philosophy starts from his childhood in a small village in rural Egypt. His first "teachers" are his father's friends and neighbors. They teach him about Egyptian history and contemporary politics, and spur the desire for social justice that becomes his pedagogical calling. This calling reaches its peak in his academic experience in Egypt's largest university. A later research visit to the United States launches his interest in hermeneutics, giving him the tools with which to approach texts and to engage with academic discourse on an international level, but his life experiences remain the single drive to articulate his vocational purpose. Abu Zaid is unrelenting on this point: pedagogy must have a purpose, but finding this purpose comes from having a sense of home. Finding purpose, of course, is the supreme reflection of the political act.

By now, a clear pattern of Arab pedagogy appears. Paradigms of home give you an understanding of societal need and your role within society. *Citoyenneté* empowers pedagogy at the university level, which manifests in the process of mentorship between teacher and student, but this kind of citizenship can only happen meaningfully in contexts of freedom. Abu Zaid is distinctive in articulating not just how organic the relationship of mentorship to social momentum is supposed to be, but how systematic it is as a process. Pedagogy, according to Abu Zaid, is a two-way journey of teaching and learning undertaken by teachers as well as students. The journey, however, is also a historical process. By teaching, mentors enter into the process of developing human thought, and the students continue to undertake this process after the mentors have passed. As such, the lecture hall is not just a "lab" where ideas are born, nurtured, tested, and developed, but also a "microcosm of society at large." A pedagogue, then, and especially a university pedagogue, was not just part of social momentum, but an agent of political progress.

It sounds, of course, eminently political, yet Abu Zaid's philosophy is entirely personal. His description of the time he spends with his students is always emotive. These students aren't numbers or dissertation titles; they are characters with families, time pressures, and problems. They tremble with fear, wait hesitantly by the doorways, linger in the hallways, ask for time to reconsider, adopt him as a father, and introduce him to their parents. Abu Zaid's passion is obvious: his excitement that he reaches a consensus with one student; his delight that he manages to shock another; his pride that he doesn't lecture and hector like other teachers in Cairo but depends on discussion and free exchange; his intense pleasure in being challenged; his recurrent paternal analogy about his "hundreds" of sons and daughters worldwide; and his gratitude that all one hundred of the students that he taught across four years in Japan surprise him with a send-off at the airport.

It takes a conversation with eminent Islamic philosopher Mohammed Arkoun to show Abu Zaid how the value of theory might travel but the value of pedagogy does not. Arkoun tells Abu Zaid at a conference that he deals with outdated issues. Abu Zaid defends his work: these issues may be old in the Sorbonne, and you can speak about them in your ivory tower, but where I come from, people die because they cannot speak about these issues. One lesson is not to mess with an exiled Arab scholar at a conference. The point, however, is that the validity and credibility of scholarship is the degree to which it ultimately engages with the voice "on the street" and brings that reformative voice into the academy. Otherwise, scholarship ends up being the sum of its critical footnotes.

For someone who had faced physical danger, separation from his spouse, and a near lifetime of physical exile, it is remarkable that Abu Zaid's biggest sense of loss seems to be the chance to teach at the Egyptian university. It is also telling that Abu Zaid reads his entire case as an intentional and structural method used by his opponents to cut off any connection he might have to the students, ultimately disabling him from participating in the country's social momentum. Preventing him from teaching becomes the most politically damaging, and personally painful, action his opponents take, because it dismembers him from society and deletes him from societal history.

> When I was prevented from teaching, I felt that an essential part of me had been cut. Teaching Egyptian students gave me energy and life. I tried in my work to teach them to think critically and rationally. Without this kind of thinking, the efforts to improve society disappear. A society that is based on principles of freedom and justice. Gone with the wind. I didn't become a teacher to try and convince students of my point of view. But to feel part of the development of human thought, which would continue developing after me, with my students. This is why it hurt me truly and deeply that I am not longer part of this process in Egypt: the country that I love and whose future I care about. (Abu Zaid, 137)

Of course, to form such an opinion, that preventing someone from teaching cuts them off from the root of society, you need to already have an understanding of how political the vocation *is*. After all, Abu Zaid retained his tenure as professor at Cairo University after the court ruling of apostasy. He could, perhaps, enter campus. He may, perhaps, even have an office. He might, perhaps, sit on committees. What he was explicitly forbidden to do was *teach*. When, years later, he finds out that his books have been removed from the university library (even though they are available in Egypt's bookshops), he understands how comprehensive the move has been to erase him from the students' sphere of consciousness. He never forgets the pain of effacement.

After societal effacement comes theory. In the last few chapters Abu Zaid reflects on issues in Islam within contexts like 9/11 and the war on Iraq. Finding himself writing at a time of intense global scrutiny of Islam, this scholar soon comes up with a new intellectual purpose in exile: "My goal, through my writing, has been to impact the Arab world with a new perspective, a perspective that ultimately will bring about reform of Islamic religious thought" (191). Cut off from the body politic, then, it is a new perspective, in other words, theory, that will transform the world. Yet even this ceases to satisfy. He begins to feel that his writing is like firefighting, that he writes on exigency, not by vocation: to put out a fire here or there, but not, as with his previous scholarly preoccupation with the Quran, to produce knowledge.

> Being critical has become increasingly difficult. I often get the sense that I am respected in many places in the world because I have been so critical of Islamic thought. I'm not looked upon favorably when folks perceive that I am critical of certain things within their particular culture. (Abu Zaid, 193)

Abu Zaid then, is considered a critic when he criticizes Islam, but not when he criticizes, say, Israel, or anti-Muslim sentiment. The dread that his critical work would be a spectacle, not a reformative power in society, ends the book.

At the peak of his professional prowess, celebrated worldwide, awarded with prizes that most intellectuals could only dream of, this once poor man from a small village who became the Egyptian Islamists' biggest villain but lived to tell the tale could only feel critical dissatisfaction with his now alienated work. Of course, in light of his legacy, both locally and internationally, Abu Zaid was too harsh on himself. Like al-Haj Saleh, he simply spoke of aspirations and stakes higher than most.

Freedom and a Caveat

Even mentors, then, need a support system to enable them to fulfil the role of mentorship, whether at home or elsewhere. If an initial, individual brilliance flourishes by existing despite the system, continued development requires support. It requires freedom, and for freedom to flourish, there has to be a democratic law that enshrines the right to question both the purpose of pedagogy within a given institution and the institution itself.

Since the kind of public mentorship enshrined culturally in Arab societies isn't given the institutional opportunity to flourish, in the democratic societies of exile, criticism flourishes in the freedom to question, critique, and change the law.

What law? The first is that of knowledge itself: its bounds and boundaries, its implicit assumptions, and its representational quality. The history of diasporic criticism and its estranged pedagogies isn't the history of those who challenge the nation-state, but of those who, like the philosophers, look upward to challenge the gods.

The second law is that of the institution. If, in authoritarian countries, it is relatively easy to find individual mentors, it is almost impossible to find a law, or a structure that, democratically, by right, you can question. Yet the last course of credibility for the tuitioned, corporatized Western institution lies in the freedom to question the university system, through voting bodies and through unions. Meanwhile, for students, the freedom to critique flourishes in the centrality of discussion to the institution.

There are, of course, caveats to this freedom. For those whose bodies, color, or affiliations stand in the margins of the institution, one caveat is the (at worst) racism or (at best) implicit bias inherent to the Western institution. This is evident in its curricula and disciplinary divisions. It is also, however, culturally systemic in the casual exoticization of foreign entrants (in whatever contextual sense "foreign" might mean). Normative responses by its members, for instance, run the gamut from the "feel good" moment expressed by even those most welcoming to a complete dismissal of the foreign entrant by the less gracious as a necessarily bureaucratic checkmark. At best, then, a Black, female, or international hire is "really needed" and hailed as a savior figure to save the academy from its own worst sins and to shoulder the burden of liberal-minded representation; at worst, they're a diversity hire, a checkmark for affirmative action, quota, or REF score. In both cases, these perceived foreign entrants are something much more and much less than, or bottom line, just different from any other working scholar or pedagogue. Abu Zaid and al-Haj Saleh had both questioned the use of freedom in new host societies if exile deprives you of a public. Relatedly, what sense of home can a host give you if they keep reminding you that they are the host?

So undoubtedly the caveats—everywhere—are many. Is it part of being an Arab pedagogue to find the institutional caveats? Not really. The Arab understanding of mentorship assumes consent, not conflict. It assumes that the system is both working and supportive of the mentoring process. Criticism assumes the opposite. And in that division lies the divergent fate of Arab pedagogy and exilic criticism.

Notes

1. Philip Sopher, "Why Egypt Crushes at Squash," *The Atlantic*, November 22, 2014, https://www.theatlantic.com/international/archive/2014/11/why-egypt-crushes-at-squash/383062/. David Segal, "A Squash Mystery in Egypt: Is There Something in the Nile?," *New York Times*, November 1, 2019, https://www.nytimes.com/2019/11/01/sports/a-squash-mystery-in-egypt-is-there-something-in-the-nile.html. Daniel Gallan, "Why Egypt Dominates at Squash," *New Frame*, January 21, 2023, https://www.newframe.com/why-egypt-dominates-at-squash/.

2. This isn't only a hangup in Egyptian Arabic. In Shami dialect (Lebanese, Palestinian, Jordanian, Syrian), the more popular version is *maʿallim* (also a teacher, though equally connected to vocational professions).

3. This is changing. Current governments have chosen to step away gradually from this model by slowly increasing university fees, and, insidiously, by creating two parallel programs, one with large fees for "private" students and another for "public" students, which have differently sized classes and different access to resources on the same campuses.

4. This sense of mentorship is threatened, of course. Within the cultural ecosystem, dictatorial systems undermine the platform on which freedom of speech and therefore critical thinking can be encouraged. Within the technical realm, impoverished societal conditions mean that opportunities for employment come from having connections more often than from getting an education. The digital age has also undermined the slowness required by mentorship. New generations have, rightly, new idols. It is thus all the more remarkable that mentorship still retains its value in the hearts of Arabic-speaking communities, even if it does resemble a raging against the dying of the light.

5. Yassin al-Haj Saleh, "Al-hurriyya: al-bayt, al-sijn, al-manfā . . . al-ʿālam" (Freedom: Home, Prison, Exile . . . and the World), *al-Jumhuriyya* online, March 25, 2016, https://aljumhuriya.net/ar/2016/03/25/34733/.

6. Nasr Abu Zaid with Esther R. Nelson, *Voice of an Exile: Reflections on Islam* (Westport, CT: Praeger, 2004).

Teaching Literature Politically
Some Examples
Bruce Robbins

The righteous thing to say on the subject of teaching literature politically, or maybe teaching *anything* politically, would be this: rather than teaching my students, I have learned from them. Rather than providing strong guidance, I have felt myself guided. Ideally, I would like to acknowledge that I have been exposed to political lessons that astonished me, enriching my vision of the world's travails, of its social collectivities and of their unsuspected (by me) aspirations for shared as well as individual improvement. I wish I could say that. It would sound a lot better than what I am about to say. But on reflection, I don't think it would be true. Or it would not be true often enough. My experience of teaching literature politically has most often been an experience of trying, probably without much success, to impose political considerations on students who have very different things on their mind. Most often, students don't come to literature classes looking for politics. If they're interested in politics, they know they can find it elsewhere, and probably in a more expert and enlightened packaging. They may not be unpleasantly surprised to be told that politics can also be found in the novel they've been assigned. But if so, they are likely to take it as a sort of morally significant extra. What they expect from novels, grossly speaking, is a refreshment to their sense of life and life's possibilities, some new ideas about how it would be possible for them to live their lives, what it would be possible (and fun, and meaningful, and fun because meaningful) for them to be. In my experience, talking about the politics of a given novel very likely means confronting and trying to overcome a certain student resistance. It can be a bit of a downer.

Why I nonetheless have always felt compelled to impose such a downer, and why I have persisted, are personal questions, and the court is going to disallow them. But perhaps a less personal answer will show at least what I think I get out of doing so. What follows is a series of examples.

Example #1: Milan Kundera's *The Unbearable Lightness of Being*

The politics of *The Unbearable Lightness of Being* seems so self-evident as not to invite much if any class discussion.[1] Like many other Czechs, Tomas, the protagonist, leaves the country for Switzerland in horror at the Soviet invasion of 1968. When he decides to return (for love), he gets in trouble over his refusal to recant a brief allegorical article he's published about the pro-Soviet regime; he is thrown out of his job as a doctor and has to work as a window cleaner. He and the novel are both antitotalitarian. What else *could* they be? What else is there to say? Quite a lot, as I somewhat stridently insist in the course of two lectures. For one thing, his sex life, as it appears to his younger lover Tereza, is ideologically identical to the totalitarianism of the regime. Its essence is the denial of the individuality of his many sexual conquests, their absorption into a common anonymity that is also (in her dreams, at least) fatal to them. Tomas presents his sexual adventures as just the opposite, a connoisseurship of female individuality. And Kundera presents the regime as Tomas's puritanical antithesis. And yet from Tereza's perspective, and it is an important perspective for the novel, the political truth of Tomas is perfectly aligned with the totalitarian regime.

That is one political perspective I push hard on. The other is a bit subtler. It takes off from the meditation on Nietzsche and time with which the novel begins. "The idea of eternal return is a mysterious one," Kundera writes on the first page, "and Nietzsche has often perplexed other philosophers with it: to think that everything recurs as we once experienced it, and that the recurrence itself recurs ad infinitum! What does this mad myth signify?" Kundera's interpretation puts the emphasis not on Nietzsche's myth itself—the almost incomprehensible idea that everything that happens, happens again and again—but on what the thought experiment reveals about life *without* eternal recurrence. "Putting it negatively," Kundera goes on, "the myth of eternal return states that a life which disappears once and for all, which does not return, is like a shadow, without weight, dead in advance" (3). The key effect he underlines is an *ethical* effect: the passage of time empties ethical judgments of their supposed meaning. That which is transitory "prevents us from coming to a verdict. For how can we condemn something that is ephemeral, in transit?" (4). It is this ethical effect of ephemeral, transitory life, this effect of life without eternal return, that Kundera seems most interested in when he refers to lightness. The title of his novel declares that lightness is unbearable. But as I tell the students, it seems to me (to put this crudely) that, unbearable or not, Kundera is *in favor* of lightness. If everything we did recurred eternally, he writes, explaining his title, our lives would be heavy—we would have to live with our actions forever, like bickering spouses in a world without divorce. As it is, however, we are painlessly divorced from the meaning of our deeds and misdeeds by the simple passage of time. This is lightness. Kundera *likes* lightness. A schematic but not unfair summary of *The Unbearable Lightness of Being* would say that it's the story of a man who tries (with his mistress) the bold experiment of living light—living without traditional commitments, whether conjugal or political—and who is dragged down and destroyed by the combined weight of love (with his wife) and politics, two things he has tried hard to avoid. What makes lightness unbearable is the commitments of politics and love. Kundera sees politics and love as triumphing over the ravages of time. That's what he dislikes about them. Ethically speaking, Kundera prefers time, despite its ravages.

I cannot resist telling the students that, as far as love and politics are concerned, I'm not on Kundera's side. Are they? They seem more likely to take the vision of ethically subversive time that Kundera derives from Nietzsche as intriguing. I lay it out like this. On the one hand, lightness is the object of a bold experiment in which a few noble and adventurous souls try to live without the burden of commitments, traditions, conventions. These characters suffer under Soviet totalitarianism, but the pursuit of lightness also sets them apart from their allies, the *opponents* of totalitarianism. Politics of any kind, even antitotalitarian politics, belongs to the realm of the weighty, the realm of kitsch. Lightness, the antithesis of kitsch, means refusing to be weighed down. This antigravity experiment is one large thing many students continue to be excited by, and I can see why. On the other hand, lightness is also a term for things as they are, time as ordinary people already experience it, with no boldness or experimentation required. It's a description of what we call linear irreversible time. Linear irreversible time is usually held to be characteristically Western or European, one side of a binary that supposedly divides the world between modern and premodern, developed and underdeveloped, us and them. But Kundera sees it as subversive of moral judgment. Where does time's subversion of moral judgment fit into time's political mapping of the world? *Does* it fit? Is the subversiveness or relativizing of moral judgment also characteristically European? Or, I ask, perhaps not? Heaviness can certainly be read as the antithesis of European modernity: as tradition, convention, repetition. But the heaviness that results from Nietzsche's thought experiment with eternal return can also be understood as a rewriting in temporal terms of Kant's categorical imperative: that is, as an address to the free will. As Kant challenges us to do nothing that we would not be ready to posit as a universal rule, so Nietzsche, seen from this angle, would be using eternal return to challenge us to perform no action that we would not be ready to repeat over and over again to infinity. Nothing could be more characteristically European than this imperative to unending self-scrutiny. It is precisely this refusal of the unexamined life that the anthropologist Talal Asad accuses Western imperialism of and indignantly rejects in his answer to the question "What is critique?"[2] If self-scrutiny is a means to self-improvement or progress, then Kundera would certainly be unenthusiastic about it. So if Kundera is invoking eternal return only in order to decide that we should be grateful that there *is* no eternal return, as I'm suggesting, then it's unclear how he might be positioning Europe in the world, what he might be saying about the divide between the "civilized" West and the "barbarous" rest.

Why do I assume he's interested in civilization and barbarism? Because the account of eternal return on the first page explains how we should face life that is "like a shadow, without weight" by using the following figure: "We need take no more note of [such a life] than of a war between two African kingdoms in the fourteenth century, a war that altered nothing in the destiny of the world, even if a hundred thousand blacks perished in excruciating torment" (3). It is difficult to read this last sentence in front of a classroom without pausing on Kundera's unembarrassed racism. He takes for granted that "we," understood as Europeans, need take no note of what the non-Europeans were up to, even if a hundred thousand of them perished in excruciating torment. I have to say, though it pains me to say it, that in more than twenty years of teaching this novel I have yet to receive any comment about this racism from a student.

At the same time, it's unclear how important the racism is to the point Kundera is trying to make. Can the African war be ignored because those who died in torment were Africans, hence unimportant per se as well as geographically debarred from having any impact on "the destiny of the world," the world understood as not African? Or can they be ignored because they died in the fourteenth century, seven hundred years ago—in other words, because a great deal of time has passed? Is this about race, or about time?

Kundera's purpose does not seem to be Orientalist in Edward Said's sense—that is, it does not seem committed to underlining a supposed ontological divide between Europe and non-Europe. I say this in my lecture because the racist hint is left hanging; he does not follow it up with an explicit argument that European history is meaningful while history outside Europe is not. On the contrary, he goes on to suggest on the next page that *all* history is meaningless, Europe's included, and this is so whether or not the historical actors and events in question had an impact on the destiny of the world. His next example of light or weightless history is European: "If the French Revolution were to recur eternally, French historians would be less proud of Robespierre" (4). The logic seems to be the following: it is because things happen only once and then are carried off by time that we can permit ourselves the illusion that historical actors like Robespierre deserve our admiration. If we were forced to live with their deeds forever, we would be more critical of those deeds. As it is, events recede into the past, and thus the act of criticizing them becomes irrelevant, however atrocious the actions may have been. As an example, he says that portraits of Hitler have begun to remind him of his childhood, overwhelming him with "the memories of a lost period in my life, a period that would never return." He admits to a sort of reconciliation with Hitler. "This reconciliation with Hitler reveals the profound moral perversity of a world that rests essentially on the nonexistence of return, for in this world everything is pardoned in advance and therefore everything [is] cynically permitted" (4).

Kundera doesn't much like Robespierre, and at first glance he might seem attracted by eternal recurrence as a way of securing tighter ethical accountability for our supposed heroes, in particular political heroes. But to repeat myself (in the lecture, I do, shamelessly): I think he is much *more* attracted by life *without* eternal recurrence, the irreversibly linear time in which events vanish forever and are therefore weightless. Does he really *want* a stricter ethical accountability? It may seem unbearable that things succeed each other in linear fashion and are inevitably lost from view, hence are "dead in advance," without weight, without meaning. But lightness has its advantages. Kundera says that, being light, "everything is pardoned in advance and therefore cynically permitted." A cynical reading would suggest that in his eyes the anticipated permissiveness is not so very unpleasant a prospect. Anyone who had been on the receiving end of ordinary blaming (as we can assume Kundera had—from the Communist Party, from women, from the Western left) would have reason to welcome the assurance that he inhabited a zone beyond blame. This was a roundabout way of suggesting that such blame emanated from unphilosophical souls who had not yet recognized the true evanescence of things. Lightness lets us off the hook.

As a then-citizen of what used to be called the Second World, Kundera did not seem eager, I tell the students, to embrace a postcolonial identity within Europe, whether as a Czech victim of the Soviets (the most obvious temptation, at least in this novel) or, looking further back, as representative of a people incorporated into and subordinated by previous empires. His assumption may be a characteristically European or at least un-American one: that if you go far enough back in time, everyone of whatever nationality has both suffered and committed unspeakable wrongs. In the interest of present peace, therefore, it is better to forget than to remember. In this sense, one could say again that, appearances to the contrary, Kundera actually favors the "cynical permissiveness" that comes with making the passage of time fast-acting and morally relativizing.

This is neither antitotalitarian nor totalitarian. It's antipolitical.

At the end of the course on world fiction since 1965 in which I lecture on Kundera, I always ask which novel or novels should be voted off the island and by which novel or novels they might be replaced. Kundera is almost never volunteered for expulsion, and the final papers make it clear why: his essayistic style of self-conscious narration, with its philosophical excurses, is experienced by students as liberating, sometimes just as liberating as his nonjudgmental frankness about sexual life. I'm not sure whether that liberation ought to count as a politics, or rather as an antipolitics. I'm not sure whether I look totalitarian to my students when I try so hard to enforce a more critical view.

Example #2: The Literary Representation of Atrocity

Everyone is against atrocity. Why should such a course even exist? And how can it be an example of teaching literature politically? How can there be a politics of something that everyone without exception is already against? One answer is: literature was not always against it. In fact, literature didn't always recognize that such a thing as atrocity existed. In order for the existence of atrocity to be recognized, mass violence against noncombatants had to be seen as a moral scandal. In order for that to happen, the noncombatant had to be recognized as a class of persons who should not be subjected to violence. In the prolonged premodern period when the sacking and burning of besieged cities was normal procedure, along with the indiscriminate rape and massacre of inhabitants by the invaders, it seems safe to say that the category of the noncombatant was not recognized. To begin with, then, there is a historical question: When did atrocities themselves become visible as something that anyone *could* be against? And then a subsidiary question, which as the course developed grew gradually in importance: When did it become possible for the people of country X to accuse their own country of committing an atrocity against the people of country Y? When and how did national self-scrutiny in the name of foreign victims arise as a potential moral practice?

I illustrate this practice in class by telling an anecdote which explains, at least in part, my personal interest in atrocity. My father was an American bomber pilot during the Second World War. The targets of his B-17 squadron were German cities; the list of targets is on the wall of my office. Many, no doubt most, of the victims of those missions were noncombatants. Did Americans see the 500,000 to 600,000 civilian casualties of the Allied bombers as the victims of an atrocity? Was my father the perpetrator of an atrocity? Or did the context of the bombing—"they started it," "they were Nazis," "it was a just war"—absolve the perpetrators of their guilt vis-à-vis the noncombatants? I confessed to some moral and emotional turmoil on the subject of these questions. Whatever else this confession was, it also seemed to be a successful pedagogical gambit. It drew teacher and students into a common project.

Everyone is against atrocities, but not everyone agrees about whether the context of the atrocity ought to matter, morally speaking. (And thus not everyone agrees that X, or the Allied bombing of the German cities, is indeed an atrocity.) I framed the issue for the students by laying out what I called the "human rights paradigm" for atrocities. The human rights paradigm, I told them, assumes that the only thing that matters is establishing with certainty who did what to whom. In that way, you maximize the chances that the perpetrators can be held accountable. Context would blur the picture, so context is ruled out. To pay attention to the train of actions and events that brought the victims and perpetrators together would risk justifying at least to some extent the violence the perpetrators had committed, allowing indignation at the suffering and death of the noncombatant victims to be softened by historical explanation, letting the perpetrators off the hook. I confessed to the students that I had mixed feelings about this question. Pedagogically speaking, telling them that I really didn't know where I stood again seemed to work.

It was tempting for students to feel that uncertainty or indeterminacy was not merely our shared premise at the outset, but also the ultimate conclusion toward which a course on atrocity was inevitably tugged. Primo Levi's *If This Is a Man / Survival in Auschwitz*, one of our first readings, gives memorable expression to this judgment when a Nazi guard tells Levi, "There is no why here."[3] Toward the end of the semester, Kurt Vonnegut's *Slaughterhouse-Five* repeats this sentence omitting only the last word, thereby generalizing the deduction that Vonnegut took from his prisoner-of-war experience of the Allied firebombing of Dresden: "There is no why."[4] Chronologically speaking, this bafflement goes all the way back to Bartolomé de las Casas: "the Spaniards were prepared to hack them to pieces for absolutely no reason whatever."[5] But the unintelligibility of mass violence was not the moral I wanted the class to draw, and it took a reimposition of would-be authoritative knowledge and its accompanying political vision to make sure that was not where we ended up. I added outside framings, taking advantage of the same gesture in some of the texts I had assigned. Was the unintelligibility of atrocity the moral to draw from the dropping of the atomic bomb on Hiroshima? Not according to Kenzaburō Ōe I told the class. It took the Japanese Nobel Prize winner some decades after his first interviews with the inhabitants of Hiroshima in order to change his mind, but look at how, gradually adopting what he called an Asian perspective, he came to hold Japanese militarism in Asia responsible for Hiroshima, as well as the Americans.[6] In much the same spirit, Charlotte Delbo pauses in the midst of a description of the Nazis executing members of the French Resistance in order to mention the execution in the early 1960s, by her fellow Frenchmen, of an Algerian member of the resistance to French colonialism.[7]

Comparison is one form of context. It introduces at least a minimum of intelligibility where there might otherwise seem to be only absolute evil, beyond any possibility of human comprehension.

The greatest benefit of intelligibility, I told the class, is that understanding, even very partially, brings with it the possibility of a politics aimed at preventing future atrocities. An ethical perspective that limited itself to judging the action and trying to hold the guilty accountable would not necessarily work in the same direction as a political perspective, which factors context in, stretching from how this happened to consider what could be done to stop it from happening again. If you call someone a monster—say, Vladimir Putin after the atrocities committed by Russian troops in Ukraine—you give yourself a certain moral satisfaction, but you also render that person illegitimate as a possible interlocutor in a political negotiation to end the hostilities. You make it harder to understand how and why these atrocities happened, and you make it harder to end the situation in which atrocities continue to be committed.

One of the most memorable moments in that course—actually, a series of moments—came when I got a palpably positive response to the discovery that some scruples about the killing of noncombatants were expressed even in antiquity, in this case in the Bible (the ethnic cleansing of the Midianites in Numbers) and in Julius Caesar's *The Gallic War*. These moments belonged to an argument about when it had become possible for someone to accuse their own country of atrocities against the inhabitants of another country. The evidence seemed overwhelmingly against. Over and over again, the paradigm seems to have been set by the Crusades: killing pagans and even Christians of the wrong denomination is doing God's work. It seemed plausible, then, that national self-accusation of atrocity only became possible after World War II, with knowledge of the Holocaust and the sudden audibility in Europe of anticolonial voices, reminding a reluctant world about European atrocities that were all too normal outside Europe. It may be a particularity of Columbia University, where students are put through the boot camp of Great Books and are primed to detect and dismiss any lack of respect for the writers of the past, but the idea that for hundreds and hundreds of years, the Western tradition had been completely blind to atrocity ran into some student resistance. Evidence that at least some scruples had been registered (for example, when the Israelites who have killed all the Midianite men have to be rebuked by Moses for *not* killing the children and married women—they have not assumed in advance that *everyone* was to be killed) was welcomed.

There was some heavy lifting involved, therefore, in getting students to acknowledge that in the domain of atrocity, there has been something like moral progress. Favoritism to the present was severely frowned upon. The students wanted to be as critical of themselves, and of their own time, as it was possible to be. This desire collided head-on with the perception that moral norms against the killing of noncombatants had, if you will pardon the expression, developed over time, thereby making a real difference at least to the literature, and most likely also beyond it. My pedagogical gambit here was to quote the final lines of C. P. Cavafy's poem "Waiting for the Barbarians": "And now what will become of us without barbarians? / These people were a kind of solution." Did the students agree with Cavafy, I asked, that the concept of the barbarian was what we now call a construct? Yes, they did. Did they agree that "barbarian" was not an accurate or acceptable label to attach to any social collectivity? Yes, they did. But if so, wasn't their own commonsense on the subject of the barbarian evidence of moral progress? Did their parents' generation believe the same thing? Their grandparents'?

It's possible that in carrying out this forceful interrogation of student beliefs, I was abusing my pedagogical authority. If so, the justification I offer for it is political. It's much easier to talk people into trying to change the world for the better if you can make them see that, thanks to the efforts and sufferings of people in the past, the world has already *been* changed for the better, at least sometimes and in some ways.

I have confessed to a certain unease about my application of pedagogical authority to political ends. Of course, I can remind myself that I have not been practicing advocacy; I have not been making specific calls to activism. By that standard, my pedagogy could look quite apolitical. It's possible that my own standard is too severe. Asked in the past about the meaning of what I get paid to do, I have found myself falling back on a rough version of Kantian aesthetics, adapted to the classroom situation. What happens in my classroom, I have said, is something like what, according to Kant, happens in the act of making an aesthetic judgment. You say what it is you like, but you appeal to others to like it too. You say what it is you like without assuming there exists a universally valid standard for your judgment. You are acting freely in saying what it is that you like. Acting freely is more pleasurable than obeying rules, and you are respecting the same freedom in the others, and thus offering them the same pleasure. Yet you do appeal to them. You want them to agree. The assumption is not that we have checked our differences of background and identity at the door—that would be neither possible nor desirable—but that, out of respect for the backgrounds and identities of others, we will not insist that our different identities give us access to the final truth about the matters we are discussing. Because identities are indeed different, no one can be authoritative. Everyone has to be listened to. It's a sort of model of democratic community—so much so that it has been suggested that Kant's Third Critique doubles as the work of political theory he never wrote, his last and best answer to the question of how a just society might be achieved given that the twisted timber of humanity seems unwilling or unable to submit to the dictates of Reason. This still sounds good to me, but I'm afraid it corresponds only imperfectly to what actually happens when I teach, especially where politics is concerned. When I teach, I preach. I may not mean to, but I do.

As briefer examples, I will take two novels that are student favorites, Elena Ferrante's *My Brilliant Friend* (2012) and Chimimanda Ngozi Adichie's *Americanah* (2013). In the case of *Americanah*, I am trying to spoil their pleasure. Both white and nonwhite students are eager to identify with the nonwhite narrator and with the narrator's perspective. A critical perspective on that perspective is hard to come by. And the last thing they are thinking about their beloved underdog is her class. To spoil all this (well, not all of it), I push hard on the moment when the Nigerian heroine drops her African American boyfriend, a young and successful academic. The boyfriend, who seems both to her and to the reader close to perfect, has organized a demonstration in support of an elderly African American man, an employee of the university who has been the victim of an injustice. The boyfriend would like our heroine to come along. She doesn't go. She lies to him about why she doesn't go, and instead attends a party attended by a powerful older man who can perhaps help her obtain a prestigious fellowship. She gets the fellowship and leaves the boyfriend. My point is that, throughout the novel and despite the highly engaging voice that keeps my students enthralled, this is who she *is*: someone who is climbing a ladder and who cares about no one but herself. It should surprise no one, then, or so I say, that in the ending (spoiler alert) the man she chooses is not merely the first man she had made love with, but a man who has embraced and benefited hugely from exactly that Nigerian corruption of which the first part of the novel seemed so relentlessly critical. He has become rich at the expense of the Nigerians around him. That is what she chooses over, for example, solidarity with the victims of racism in America. It would of course be possible to give the novel credit for showing all this with self-conscious irony. But where, I ask the students, do they see any actual evidence of such irony? The moral of the story, pedagogically speaking, is that, faced with a novel which is so much about race and gender, race and gender are the only things the students will see. They will not see, for example, class.

In the case of *My Brilliant Friend*, I am not trying to spoil anyone's pleasure, only to redirect it. The students have tended to be dazzled, and rightly so, by Ferrante's account of competitive female friendship, an account in which men fade into the deep background, and by the perceptiveness of the double coming-of-age story, ending so artfully (another spoiler alert) in a wedding that is also a betrayal. One thing Ferrante gives teachers of literature in her Neapolitan tetralogy is the gift of a sustained work of fiction in which the center is the friendship of two women, and not, as so often, women's relations with fathers, lovers, husbands—with men. For my students, at least half of them women, a first encounter with the tetralogy's first and most teachable novel, *My Brilliant Friend*, will often feature the excitement of a fresh and insightful exploration of female subjectivity, a girl's "coming of age," and the way female friendship mediates the crucial relations of daughters with mothers. Into this I forcibly and predictably inject the element of politics—to begin with, via the novel's astonishing concept of "the before." The phrase "the before" comes to stand for the history of neighborhood complicity with fascism, monarchism, and the Mafia which accounts for who has money and who does not. The before, which fills in the landscape of mysterious social powers in which the two girls grow up, is the content of an education that is both unofficial—it doesn't get taught at school—and also distinctly political. In both senses, it contrasts with the education that Elena receives at school, which is quite conservative, even though it eventually leads Elena into political involvement. Knowledge of the before comes through Lila and the working-class boys of the neighborhood who, unlike Elena, will not pursue or receive an official education. On the other hand, the before marks a parallel track, leading the neighborhood kids to some of the same knowledge of the world that, thanks to the left-wing teachers who take her under their wing, Elena will also obtain. Like Lila herself, it grounds Elena's story of emerging female creativity and subjectivity, which might otherwise seem on an independent course, in a wider and deeper social history. This is a political dimension to the novel that, in my experience, students will tend to skip over as inessential and even distracting, even though it somewhat evens out the educational trajectories of the two friends. It won't speak for itself. In my experience, it has to be selected and underlined.

At the same time, a male teacher's insistence on the novel's political dimension creates a disturbing resonance with the novel's episode of sexual initiation and sexual assault, a pedagogical challenge that in the #MeToo era can hardly be passed over in silence, much as both teacher and students may want to avoid it. It is reverence for literature that makes Elena vulnerable to the sexual advances of a man who takes advantage of her youth, a man she does not desire. No one intending to offer political lessons can afford to ignore that one. On the other hand, the largest political lesson in that situation may come from the generosity of the (largely female) students, who have tended not to identify uncritically with the victimhood option, which was certainly open to them, but rather to seek out other dimensions of the episode, including those that offer the protagonist (and themselves) more agency.

In my pedagogical experience, generosity has also been a hallmark of student response to classroom discussions of J. M. Coetzee's *Disgrace* (1999), where sexual and racial politics mix confusingly. A white man exploits and then stalks a nonwhite sex worker. The same man has an affair with a female student, possibly a woman of color. It is through his eyes that the story is told, and told with some charm. The novel plays with fire, in other words, forcing the reader to identify (to keep the vocabulary nontechnical) with a highly literate subjectivity that, like Humbert Humbert's, will likely seem monstrous even to those who might also find it charismatic. There is some question as to whether students will keep reading long enough to see him punished, in the second half of the novel, when his daughter is raped by Black South Africans and he is almost murdered. There is some question as to whether his victimization will be enough to make a difference. Without endorsing Coetzee's jaundiced vision of postapartheid South Africa, I have tried to teach the novel as politically interesting because it imposes on the characters a sequence of distinct political criteria. First come the politics of gender and sexuality, then the politics of race. In the conclusion, the novel arrives at a politics of species, when the protagonist, divesting himself of one privilege after another, comes to identify with his fellow animals, and does so without the condescending bitterness that has arguably characterized him thus far. I explicitly asked the students to find in *Disgrace* exactly the kind of irony at the expense of the seemingly charismatic protagonist that I challenged them to find in *Americanah*. And I have to say that, whatever their initial suspicions, they seemed on the whole willing to recognize, in the novel's second half, a harsh reeducation of that privileged male desire that Coetzee seems earlier to be ready to defend to the death.

These pedagogical examples would seem to assume that there is indeed politics in the novel. Depending on one's understanding of what politics is, that assumption might also be questioned. After several years of coteaching (with the novelist Orhan Pamuk) an undergraduate seminar entitled "The

Political Novel," I was obliged to consider the possibility that what many of the most famous examples of the genre seemed to want more than anything was to *escape* from politics. Politics, yes or no, is of course a very different question than *which* politics, left, right, or center, where some position on that set of coordinates is taken for granted. Yet in Turgenev's *Fathers and Sons* (1862) and Camus's *The Plague* (1947), to take two classic texts understood as political, the novel is arguably structured around the question of whether private persons should get involved in public matters or stay well clear of them, going about their business and seeking personal happiness. Bazarov, the most memorable and most political character in *Fathers and Sons*, did not seem to many of the students very "relatable." It's his friend, not Bazarov, who is relatable. He finds love and happiness in the end, and he does so by withdrawing from his political aspirations. Not liking Bazarov very much, the students found it all too natural that his offer of love to Mme Odinskaya should be refused. It was a struggle to make them see that the refusal was not just the decisive moment in the novel, but the decisive *political* moment: the moment when Russia itself, as Turgenev sees it, and even Russia at its best, is unwilling to try to renew itself. National allegory is not the go-to move for students whose assumption—not an unreasonable one—is that novels are about the quest for private happiness. But if allegory can be successfully introduced into the classroom's toolkit, there is good critical work to be done with it. For example, in Turgenev, by noticing how the presence of a servant, representing the alien outsider, helps mediate a surprising reconciliation between the two duelists, the "nihilist" Bazarov and the aristocrat Pavel Kirsanov, who have just been shooting at each other. It is by reference to the class Other that their own social and political differences, which a moment ago had been a matter of life and death, suddenly come to seem almost negligible.

In Camus's *The Plague*, an inevitable choice of text for a course on the political novel in a time of pandemic, there is no trouble getting the students to think allegorically. But there is a large step between the allegorical and the political. Politics asks characters to take sides within a society that is internally divided. The infected society of Camus's Oran is not divided. The Arabs of Oran are excised from the novel, along with the issues of colonialism that had not quite come to a head yet in the immediate aftermath of World War II. But if there is no split between native inhabitants and colonizers, neither is there any other split. No other meaningful social divisions are on display. The plague itself is assigned no social or environmental origin. Thus the residents of Oran cannot choose sides. They are offered only the choice of being in or out, engaging themselves in helping the victims of the plague, which might come with some risk to themselves and their personal happiness, or keeping themselves as safe as possible. This is not politics; it is humanitarianism's problematic of indifference. Some readers have seen Camus as allegorizing the dilemma of French citizens under the still recent German occupation: Sartre's *engagement*. A collaborationist profiteer does make an appearance. But otherwise the analogy doesn't hold up. French society *was* divided, and not just between pragmatic collaborationists and principled resistants; fascism was a well-articulated force within it. Unlike fascism, Camus's plague comes from nowhere. The novel offers, and resoundingly rejects, the option of seeing the plague as a punishment for the sins of humankind. It does not offer the political option that seems the most desirable alternative: working against the return of the plague. Which Camus warns, very plausibly, will happen one day.

The ideology of private happiness being as powerful and as pervasive as it is in the US, the would-be teacher of politics-in-literature lessons will have to do extra work in order to establish that politics is really there, and not just a personal fetish of the instructor. One way in which I have tried and failed to put this lesson across is by getting personal. In a society structured the way ours is structured, I told a theory class, it is impossible for a would-be progressive person to avoid living in a state of contradiction. Trying to encourage students to apply this hypothesis to themselves, I offered myself up as an example. I told the students that I don't believe structuring a society so that everyone is in competition with everyone else is a good idea. I'm in favor of an equal distribution of society's goods and services. From each according to their ability to each according to their need. Call it what you will. But as an academic, I have never failed to enter each of my publications onto my individual CV. There was and is a ladder, and it would be disingenuous of me to pretend that I was not climbing it along with everyone else. Maybe not stepping on the fingers of those climbing behind me, but certainly climbing. Whether the students understood what I was saying or not, no one else volunteered any examples. Economic egalitarianism has always been harder to put across than issues of identity.

A final anecdote, this time not located in a classroom. Once upon a time, I was denied a promotion, and one senior faculty member voting on my case (so it was leaked to me) argued that I didn't deserve the promotion because I failed students who were supporters of Israel. After some time had gone by, I managed to have lunch with the faculty member in question. I told him that I had not taught any subjects related to the politics of the Middle East (that has changed since), so I didn't know any students' opinions on that subject. Nor, as it happened, had I failed any student for any reason. So what had he been thinking of? After some insistence, I got to the substance: one Israeli student had complained to this faculty member that "it made him uncomfortable" merely to know that, outside the classroom, I was critical of Israel. I got the promotion the following year, but I hesitate to draw any conclusions from that fact about the power of the Zionist lobby or the idiocy of some of the scholars who do its bidding. In any case, making students uncomfortable is one traditional way of describing our discipline's pedagogical goal. The student in question was not in any of my courses, so I can't say my teaching was in fact responsible for what I hope ended up as a productive feeling of discomfort on his part. Of course, to see discomfort as a desirable end-product of teaching is to decide that a certain form and degree of top-down coerciveness is, after all, not merely acceptable but even to be sought.

For some years, I have asked students in more than one course, during the first week of classes, to memorize a famous line from George Eliot's *Middlemarch*: "If we had a keen vision and feeling of all ordinary human life, it would be like hearing the grass grow, and the squirrel's heartbeat, and we should die of that roar that lies on the other side of silence." Memorization seems like the most old-fashioned of pedagogies, but used in moderation it provides a sense of accomplishment, and followed up (for example, by making reference to Zadie Smith's "The Embassy of Cambodia," another of my pedagogical staples), it reminds students, in any number of diverse situations, that there is a great deal going on in the world outside themselves, however difficult it may be even to understand, let alone fulfill, one's responsibilities to the world.

Notes

1. Milan Kundera, *The Incredible Lightness of Being*, trans. Michael Henry Heim (New York: Harper, 1984).

2. Talad Asad, "Free Speech, Blasphemy, and Secular Criticism," in *Is Critique Secular? Blasphemy, Injury, and Free Speech*, by Talal Asad, Wendy Brown, Judith P. Butler, and Saba Mahmood (New York: Fordham University Press, 2013).

3. Primo Levi, *If This Is a Man / Survival in Auschwitz*, trans. Stuart Woolf (New York: Orion, 1959).

4. Kurt Vonnegut, *Slaughterhouse Five* (New York: Delacorte, 1969).

5. Bartolomé de las Casas, *A Short Account of the Destruction of the Indies*, trans. Nigel Griffin (New York: Penguin Classics, 1992).

6. Kenzaburō Ōe, *Hiroshima Notes* (Tokyo, 1965), trans. David L. Swain and Toshi Yonezawa (New York: Marion Boyars, 1995).

7. Charlotte Delbo, *Auschwitz and After* (1965), trans. Rosette C. Lamont (New Haven, CT: Yale University Press, 2014).

Baking and Breaking Bread, or Daniel Defoe and the Catastrophic Imagination
Rishi Goyal

"How has the pandemic changed the world? Or, more narrowly, can you point to a new social, political or cultural formation that gained traction during the pandemic and will outlast it?" I posed those questions to my students in the first class I taught over Zoom. The responses ranged from dystopic figures of surveillance technologies and healthcare rationing to the restructuring of everyday life in terms of work-from-home models and the rise of "podding." We engaged in an extended discussion of cottagecore (a mostly online pastoral aesthetic), which eventually led us to breadmaking. In the early days of the pandemic, alongside the roll calls of the dead and the silencing of urban life, we witnessed the rise of a different, more quotidian, but still viral phenomenon: the cultivation of sourdough starters. Everyone, we agreed, seemed to be baking their own bread. But why? Legacy media and internet outlets recounted the recovered pleasures of home breadmaking. People shared recipes and pictures online, of both successes and failures. But few people shared their bread or broke bread with others or even ate the bread themselves. People baked bread for different reasons. Because of real or perceived food shortages, baking bread appeared to be a way to provide yourself or your family with food independent of grocery stores and supply chains. Many people did not want to leave their homes to shop for fear of contracting Covid-19. For some it seemed to give a sense of control in an upside-down world. Perhaps it reminded people of the idea of simpler times. Others were just stuck at home and bored. Regardless of the reasons, home bread bakers participated in survivalist fantasies of a premodern way of life that in contemporary America is only available to those farthest from the precarious margins. Home breadmaking is more modest than other forms of survivalist prepping like outfitting a bunker, stockpiling years' worth of food and ammunition, or setting human traps. But home breadmakers share with survivalist preppers the fantasy of self-reliance and self-containment. Home bread bakers (at least until they ran out of flour and yeast) were imagining a life without society where they were not intimately entangled with and dependent on others. Like so many other transitory sociopolitical formations during the recent pandemic, this proved to be a fantasy, one also shared by another famous survivalist, Robinson Crusoe.

The fantasy that we do not need other people might arise from a fear of other people, though not exactly in a Hobbesian sense. During the early days of the pandemic, especially when the mode of transmission of the coronavirus was incompletely characterized, we were taught to fear contact. It would be an exaggeration to say that other people's looks could kill, but the same could not be said about their breath or their touch. Lockdowns, quarantines, and curfews reinforced the dangers presented by other humans. Given the highly contagious nature of the coronavirus, many such measures were rational and warranted. But others, like wiping down surfaces or cleaning inanimate fomites were probably not. The biological effects of the coronavirus resulted in significant disease and death, but global political and social choices greatly exacerbated (and in some fewer cases ameliorated) the catastrophic loss of life. Sociopolitical analyses have confirmed that we were slow to recognize the threat posed by the widespread coronavirus, that our public health system was underprepared to respond to the pandemic, and that we lacked a coherent and effective governmental strategy to contain the virus or mitigate its effects.

But analyses of the present, especially when they engage with biological processes and systems, can by blinkered by the nearness of the event and a disregard for ideological structures. To ward against these blind spots, I turn to literary texts, historical documents, and political philosophy. During the first year of the pandemic, while working in a busy urban emergency room treating acute cases of Covid-19, I taught an undergraduate comparative literature class, "Utopia and the Pandemic," in Columbia University's newly christened Medical Humanities major. The unaccountable deaths, immiseration, and cynicism of the moment needed a rebuttal in Utopian hope and desire, and teaching literature appeared as the pathway to offer it. The students and I built a shared framework of politics and literature where our utopian longings stretched toward an always out-of-reach horizon. While we read classic and contemporary political theory, public health theory, and novels, we spent the first half of the semester on two works by Daniel Defoe: *Robinson Crusoe* and *A Journal of the Plague Year*. Reading these novels in the time of our global viral emergency enabled us to collectively envision possibilities for and alternatives to our narrative, imaginative, and sociopolitical structures.

Defoe's two novels present alternative responses to catastrophe. *Robinson Crusoe* presents a fantastic vision of *Homo economicus* who through individual self-will and self-sufficiency is able to overcome all obstacles. This is not just man on an island but man as an island. *A Journal of the Plague Year* offers a more variegated, contextual, and historically sensitive account of catastrophe on the societal level but one that is mediated through a rich, fictive consciousness. Both books present differing visions of how individuals or societies respond to catastrophe and cataclysm. Teaching these novels in tandem during the Covid-19 pandemic illuminated contradictions in the political responses to the epidemic as the narrative form and literary sensibilities presented individualistic and collective accounts.

I will not rehearse the many justifications for the singularity of the novel genre but I will reflect that in its creative form, the novel, especially Defoe's brand of empirically realistic fiction centered on the perceptions and responses to experience, foregrounds the fiction of fiction sustaining the fiction of reality. To put it another way, reality itself is another fiction, ideologically constructed after the fact. One particular value of teaching fictional texts and narrative structures as responses to the "real" world and historical pressures is to demonstrate that the "real" world is not a natural or predetermined world but is socially and politically constructed. It is one of many possible worlds ("like the metaverse," one of my students remarked) and is the result of human choices, values, and structures of power and difference. By recognizing the fictional conventions of "reality," we learn to recognize that many of the failures of the pandemic response were not inevitable features of the biology of the virus or the unfortunate human. They were the result of political and social choices and ideological structures: the underfunding of public health departments; the privatization of emergency response systems; the LEAN model of manufacturing as applied to health readiness; limited nursing homes offering such poor wages that employees shuttled between multiple jobs at multiple facilities; cramped housing with poor ventilation; the differential spatial distribution of pollution that disproportionally affects the poor and communities of color. The list is endless.

Between *Robinson Crusoe* and *A Journal of the Plague Year*, we have two very different responses to catastrophe. In a review of a novel by Margaret Atwood, Frederic Jameson suggested that "the post-catastrophe situation in reality constitutes the preparation for the emergence of Utopia itself." Both Defoe novels offer utopic longings and transformations in the face of catastrophe, but where *Robinson Crusoe* presents the fantasy of the self-contained and fully complete solitary individual, *A Journal of the Plague Year* presents a more circumstantial, contingent, and contextual reordering of society on communal and collectivist principles.

* * *

The students and I were drawn to bread baking because it is such a potent and recurring scene and symbol in the Western tradition. It has biblical undertones, from the Lord's prayer ("Give us this day our daily bread") to the body of Christ, and has an association with the "birth of civilization." It also figures prominently as allegory in *Robinson Crusoe*. The novel's plot may be familiar to readers. Robinson is the third son of a German immigrant. Despite his father's admonitions to stay home and pursue the "middle station" in life, he risks all and puts out to sea. His first voyage is a disaster, ending in a swoon and a shipwreck. His subsequent voyages are no better. Establishing himself as a "Guiney trader" despite the initial shipwreck, he sails toward the Canary Islands, where he is taken prisoner by a Turkish rover of Sallee and enslaved for two years. He escapes with the help of a local boy, Xury, whom he sells to establish himself in Brazil. After some success as a plantation owner, Crusoe sets sail again, now as a slaver intent on bringing back human capital from the Guinea coast to work on the plantations. Crusoe's early sea trips and disasters foreshadow his later travails. On the trip to the Guinea coast, his ship and its crew are wracked by storm upon storm. They abandon the vessel, escaping in a lifeboat. This too is destroyed by a raging, mountainous sea. Gasping for breath, taking in water, Robinson endures twenty- and thirty-foot waves, to find himself as the sole survivor of this shipwreck, resting on the sandy shore of the island he will inhabit, mostly alone, for eight and twenty years.

Throughout the first part and the opening days on the island, Crusoe's narration of his inner dialogue sets the story apart from a mere adventure tale. His self-reflection, recriminations, and moralizing suggest an intelligence bedeviled with self-doubt but still eager to be the agent of his own fortunes (and miseries). Battered as he is by circumstance and storm, he still actively perceives himself as a prime mover. Determining that he is unlikely to escape the island or to be rescued, Crusoe settles in. But to do so in the face of absolute calamity is not an easy task. He has washed ashore, alone, in a remote corner of the globe, practically naked, with no possessions. That he not only survives, but thrives, spotlights the myth of self-sufficiency which buttresses the rational, liberal, Western post-Enlightenment subject. The island provides Crusoe with the freedom to demonstrate "the autonomy of the individual," as he is free to imagine his own social and political order. He is, as Edward Said noted, "the founder of a new world" (*CI*, 70).

Crusoe establishes dominion over the entire island as "king and lord of all this country indefeasibly, and had a right of possession" (*RC*, 114). While he inherits his right to free trade and passage on the seas from Grotius, he takes ownership of property as his right from Locke. Where Crusoe seems either an indifferent or perhaps just an unlucky sailor, his management and improvement of life on the island is truly astounding, if not downright fantastic. He is a mariner, a renegade, and a castaway but he is also a tailor, carpenter, shipbuilder, baker, farmer, goat herder, trapper, milliner, *and* breadmaker. He builds two separate homes and many fortifications; plants and rotates crops; weaves a series of baskets; makes a kiln, oven, and mill; domesticates a herd of goats; stitches himself a goatskin hat, breeches, and coat; constructs an umbrella and tobacco-pipe; makes goat cheese; and bakes bread. Crusoe is the very picture of ingenuity, resourcefulness, and labor.

While he asserts that he is "king and lord of all the country," he establishes this right through enclosure, labor, and improvement. Despite being alone on the island, he spends much of his free time building fences and enclosures around his bower and country seat and his seacoast house. Even though the island is uninhabited, he supports his claim to ownership by removing fields and lands and gardens from the commons and working on them. As Locke would have us believe, Crusoe establishes his property rights by removing the land from the natural common state through enclosure and then adding to it his labor. The natural land of the island becomes private property through this mysterious alchemical process. But private property is not just a right established through labor and enclosure; it is a kind of miracle of augmentation, for "he who appropriates land to himself by his labour, does not lessen but increase the common stock of mankind: for the provisions serving to the support of human life, produced by one acre of inclosed and cultivated land, are (to speak much within compass) ten times more than those which are yielded by an acre of land of an equal richness lying waste in common" (*Second Treatise*, 23). For Locke (and Crusoe) this becomes a principle for colonialist appropriation and accumulation. A man may claim as much land as he can improve, and he can claim the land of indigenous natives if they are not improving it.

Crusoe derives his sense of ownership and mastery of the island from rational scientific cultivation and the augmentation of yield. For Crusoe both the value of the land and his dominion over it are dependent on improvement. The natural world has no value on its own, but is valuable only if improved by scientific management and a Baconian mastery. Locke's justification here, however, is paramount: "For whatever bread is worth more than acorns, wine than water, and clothes or silk than leaves, skins or moss, that is wholly owing to labour and industry" (*Second Treatise*, 26). Which brings me back to breadmaking. Crusoe tells us that he worked for his bread: he made a spade and shovel to sow and plow; a kiln to make earthenware pots; a mortar and pestle to beat the grain; a sieve to separate the chaff; and an oven to bake the bread. He mowed, reaped, cured, thrashed, separated, ground, and baked his meal and made the instruments to suit these tasks. But what seems like fantastic ingenuity really rested on an error, luck, and like much else, items salvaged from the shipwreck.

Soon after landing on the island, Crusoe finds that his old ship had come up near shore. He makes thirteen dangerous trips to the wrecked vessel and recovers, among other things, ammunition, arms, clothes, shoes, a carpenter's chest, nails, hatchets, saws, an axe, a hammer, scissors, a shovel and tongs, kettles, rigging, rope, pins, thread, needles, and the rucksack with barley and rice seeds. His breadmaking actually begins when he inadvertently comes across stalks of barley and rice growing on the island. He sees this as a miracle and sign of God's divine grace. But ever the rationalist, he acknowledges that they were byproducts from a rucksack he had recovered from the shipwreck which he had inadvertently emptied in the right place and the right time. The seeds from the ship, mixed with the rain, soil, and sun of the natural world, provided the bounty.

I want to make a brief but final point regarding society as I conclude the section on *Robinson Crusoe*. Crusoe spends much of his time on the island regretting his lack of companions. But about midway through the novel, he is thunderstruck. He sees a footprint in the sand. Rather, though, than embracing this sign as an act of salvation, he is terrified. The idea or possibility of another human as represented by the print strikes him with abject fear and horror. The entire timbre and tone of the novel changes at this point. We have truly entered a new world. We experience a frenzied dread and paranoia as Crusoe makes more fortifications, traps, and automatic-firing weapons riggings. He dreams of cannibals and violence and imagines that the only way to keep safe is to kill anyone who comes to his island. It will be another decade, though, before he sees another human and two more years after that before he engages them. It is around this moment, with the naming and enslavement of Friday, that his fantasies of independence and self-reliance are finally jettisoned. Crusoe names Friday for the day he saves him and teaches Friday to call him Master. He makes him useful and converts him to Christianity. He teaches him to cook, bake, cultivate the land, and perform all the labors that increased the value of his property and that seemed to define his freedom. With

Friday performing all the work and creating all the value, Crusoe can finally be lord of his island.

Robinson Crusoe projects the perfect picture of a rugged individualist who masters his surroundings through industry and diligence, but he is also inheritor of all the spoils of the Western world and amasses wealth and capital through an instrumental plantation economy and settler colonialism. The mythical Crusoe seems completely self-made, and his successes are meant to be seen as a product of his ingenuity and hard work. But the truth of his success stems from the natural abundance of the island and the congealed labor of the many objects he recovers from the shipwreck. His liberalism is the myth of economic, social, and political independence. The persistence of this myth and the fantasy of individual autonomy impede our engagement with existential crises like pandemics and the climate emergency that require interdependence, cooperative coalitions, and sympathetic care and aid for those most affected.

* * *

If Crusoe is the prototypical imaginary white European male who is an organ of power and self-determination, HF, the narrator-protagonist of *The Journal of the Plague Year*, is a quieter, more diffuse consciousness. A *Journal of the Plague Year* presents a fictionalized account of the Great Plague of 1665 in London that is said to have killed more than a quarter of the population. The text was written as a kind of premonitory fictive political response to an outbreak of bubonic plague in Marseilles in 1720 and purports, like *Robinson Crusoe*, to be a true firsthand account. The book opens by developing the character and voice of the narrator as well as the context in which the plague comes to London. HF, despite many admonitions, remains in the city in the face of the ongoing epidemic even when those who can are fleeing. While the structure of the novel depends on his presence during the plague, it also depends on his presence from a moral perspective. By putting himself in harm's way, he appears more credible as a narrator and validates the experiences of the poor who had to stay. HF chronicles the effects of the last great plague on the city of London, its people, its laws, its institutions, and its government.

This is the same field described by Michel Foucault. In the widely read "Panopticism" chapter from *Discipline and Punish*, Foucault describes and analyzes actions to be taken to limit the effects of the plague on a town at the end of the seventeenth century. Houses are locked, everyone is ordered to stay inside, watchmen are set. Against the earlier model of the leper who was rejected and exiled from the town, the plague calls for an individualization, differentiation, and visible organization of bodies. Everyone and everything is catalogued and maintained in its "proper" place. The disciplinary power that he describes is one of spatial partitioning, segmentation, and surveillance: "The plague-stricken town, traversed throughout with hierarchy, surveillance, observation, writing; the town immobilized by the functioning of an extensive power that bears in a distinct way over all individual bodies." Foucault presents the ramification of power in the seventeenth-century city affected by a pandemic plague as the political dream of absolute order in the "utopia of a perfectly governed city" (*DP*, 198). In *A Journal of the Plague Year*, HF chronicles many of the same procedures, orders, and practices that Foucault relates (he reprints the entire "Orders Conceived and Published by the Lord Mayor and Alderman of the City of London concerning the Infection of the Plague, 1665" [*Journal*, 36]), from the posting of the orders of the Mayor, to the shutting up of houses and sequestration of the sick, to the appointment of watchmen in front of homes and the systems of surveillance and order. But where Foucault presents a frozen and immobile partitioning, Defoe presents a much more porous and fluid circulation of bodies, objects, and ideas.

Of all the orders, HF most strikingly condemns the shutting up of houses, or what the Covid world recognized as the lockdown: "The shutting up houses by Force, and restraining, or rather imprisoning People in their own Houses, as is said above, was of little or no Service in the Whole; nay, I am of the Opinion, it was rather hurtful" (*Journal*, 61). He also reports that many people simply circumvented the orders and the watchmen altogether. While Foucault suggested that the political dream of immobilization and imprisonment of the plague city was complete, HF instead chronicles the countless ways in which citizens got around the orders: "it would fill a little volume, to set down the arts us'd by the People of such Houses, to shut the Eyes of the Watchman, who were employ'd, to deceive them, and to escape, or break out from then: in which frequent scuffles, and some Mischief happened" (*Journal*, 44). They jumped through windows, forged extra keys, dug holes through neighbors' houses, bribed or attacked watchmen, disguised themselves, and made their houses appear to be locked up when they weren't. These were acts of radical disobedience that HF describes with sympathy, and they are compounded by failures of the administration and the simple arithmetic of too few watchmen, given the extent of the plague.

In addition to these Orders, Defoe presents weekly bills of mortality throughout the text. In a counterpoint to these official documents, Defoe's narrator HF wanders the city witnessing stories of survival and affliction. He describes mostly sympathetic portraits of individual fictional lives under the pressures of the plague. He talks to a waterman living by the seawall who supplies families living on the river with food and necessities in exchange for money for his wife and child, who are locked up with the plague. He relays the oracular predictions of doom of eccentric characters like Solomon Eagle, an itinerant half-naked street-dwelling prophet who wore a pot of burning coals on his head. He witnesses parentless children and many made insane by infection and loneliness. He watches and listens as one man jumps into the dead carts after his family while another, a piper, is accidentally placed in one after drinking too much ale. He individualizes the countless lives of the multitude that inhabited the infected city.

Our class discussions could not avoid the transhistorical parallels. We were struck by the many startling similarities to our own pandemic response. Every illness was assumed to be the plague or Covid; the rich left the city while the poor were overrepresented in the death tolls; there was profiteering based on false treatments and widespread misinformation; the poor, because of their working conditions, often spread the disease; the essential workers kept working despite facing the gravest dangers; people avoided each other; the number of dead were undercounted and, at the height of the plague and our pandemic, there were too many bodies to bury; governments in both cases were woefully and criminally unprepared.

The form of the novel is heterogeneous and episodic, stringing together characters, vignettes, official documents, and tables. One of the longest episodes is the story of two brothers and their kinsman. HF mentions the story early in the book, but narrates it completely only much later. He reintroduces it with this injunction, "I come back to my three men. Their Story has a Moral in every Part of it, and their whole Conduct, and that of some who join'd with, is a Pattern for all poor men to follow, or Women either, if ever such a Time comes again" (*Journal*, 100). The import is clear. This is a story with a lesson on how to manage during pandemic times. The three men are a sailmaker, a carpenter, and a baker who leave London to avoid infection but also because they cannot find work. As they wander the countryside, they are denied access to various towns and certain roads under the fear that they are carriers of the plague. They join with a small company of other travelers they meet along the way and build an alternative countryside community that supports and sustains them for a limited time. They practice their individual skills and pool resources and numbers to create temporary stability. One student in class contrasted this "unplanned" community with the planned communities in England and the United States in the nineteenth and twentieth centuries, finding something more meaningful in the modest goals. It is not a perfect community and it is only provisional, but they live in a kind of harmony with each other, with people in the neighboring towns, and with the natural world. Their lives are modest and hard, but they avoid illness, have enough to eat, and are able to build themselves shelters for protection. This makeshift outdoor community depends on the charity and compassion of villagers in local towns. As Rebecca Solnit writes, "If paradise now arises in hell, it's because in the suspension of the usual order and the failure of most systems, we are free to live and act another way" (Solnit, 10). HF's lesson in this parable seems to be the importance of charity, compassion, and collectivity in the face of calamity. This is the opposite to the lesson learned by Crusoe, who prizes autonomy and individuality.

* * *

Many of the sociopolitical failures of the Covid response can be attributed to the persistent myths of individual autonomy and self-sufficiency. Rather than developing compassionate coordinated international surveillance and testing programs, individual nations closed their borders, hoarded precious treatments, and reinforced patent protections. American hospitals competed with each other for scarce resources like ventilators and N95 masks. The collective responsibility needed to care for each other was too often superseded by the selfish individualism of anti-maskers initially and anti-vaxxers later. The rich fled cities to their own island oases, and the burden of disease fell disproportionately on frontline and essential workers who are often the marginalized poor and disproportionately people of color. As one student pointedly remarked, "The pandemic will not end all at once. It will end at different times for different people. And for some it may never end." But the students were also quick to point out how the post-catastrophe situation might point to the emergence of utopia. The years immediately after the pandemic saw a rise in protest culture from Black Lives Matters to Defund the Police as well as gender-based and abolition movements. The Green New Deal and other environmental collectives experienced a refreshed engagement and longing. In our classroom we explored the ideas and ideals that frame our sense of citizenship and responsibility.

Reading *Robinson Crusoe* and *A Journal of the Plague Year* in the context of contemporaneous and contemporary political theory presented us with two competing visions of responding to catastrophe. These are among the first novels written in the English language. Many of the trends or preoccupations that have established our current world order emerged or developed during this period: the transatlantic slave trade, scientific instrumentalism, industrial capitalism, and economic liberalism. Crusoe is the embodiment of this worldview. While the novel is famous for its circumstantial realism, the plot is anything but realistic. The fantasy of Crusoe's survival and success on the island, dependent as it is on the slave trade, an instrumental approach to nature and other humans, a ship full of eighteenth-century material goods, and an imagined sense of complete autonomy, supported the kind of individualistic thinking that led to some of the failures of the pandemic response. But published less than three years later, *A Journal of the Plague Year* promotes a sociopolitical vision of catastrophe in which collective welfare is possible and presents a sensitive sympathy to suffering, especially the suffering of marginalized poor. Sharing bread, we learn, is more important than making bread.

Works Cited

Defoe, Daniel. *A Journal of the Plague Year*. Edited by Paula R. Backscheider. Norton Critical Editions. New York: Norton, 1992.

———. *Robinson Crusoe*. Edited by Angus Ross. Penguin Classics. New York: Penguin, 1985.

Foucault, Michel. *Discipline and Punish: The Birth of the Prison*. Translated by Alan Sheridan. New York: Vintage, 1995.

Jameson, Fredric. "Then You Are Them." *London Review of Books* 31, no. 17 (2009): 7–8.

Locke, John. *Second Treatise of Government*. Edited by C. B. Macpherson. Indianapolis: Hackett, 1980.

Said, Edward W. *Culture and Imperialism*. New York: Vintage, 1994.

Solnit, Rebecca. *A Paradise Built in Hell: The Extraordinary Communities That Arise in Disaster*. New York: Penguin Books, 2009.

Foundations for Nauru Prison Theory
Australian Border Violence, Art, and Knowledge Production
Elahe Zivardar and Omid Tofighian

Australia's border regime is one of the most brutal in the world, involving the construction and management of offshore immigration detention centers on islands in the Pacific and Indian oceans, and onshore facilities across the mainland. At the beginning of 2025 the offshore detention center in the Republic of Nauru (Pacific Ocean) remains in operation; facilities in Manus Island (Papua New Guinea, also in the Pacific) and Christmas Island (an Australian territory in the Indian Ocean) have closed. Several onshore detention centers and APODs (Alternative Places of Detention) remain in operation on the mainland. Australia's policies, political culture, and anti-refugee mainstream media campaigns have inspired other nations to exile people seeking asylum to extraterritorial detention camps where the conditions are inhumane; the access to resources is limited or nonexistent; the potential for abuse is extremely high, with little or no accountability; and no practical pathways to a free and safe life exist. Australia's practices are illegal under international law. In the attempt to justify exiling and imprisoning people, it offers weak and misleading arguments: claiming that it is stopping people who arrive "illegally"; or trying to break the people smugglers' business model; or saving lives at sea; and using other racist and nationalist rhetoric about national security, national identity, and national interest. Asylum seekers reaching Australia by boat are deemed undesirable and expendable. By banishing them to poorer neighboring countries and warehousing them there, Australia reactivates and invigorates dimensions of its own cruel colonial legacy.

Over the last two and a half decades, Australia has built and managed these prisons on islands in the Pacific, thousands of kilometers away from the nation's international borders. Manus Island, part of Manus Province in northern

Papua New Guinea (PNG), and the Republic of Nauru, an independent island nation in Micronesia, have been used by Australia as carceral sites to contain and control people seeking asylum. The facilities in Manus and in the PNG capital, Port Moresby, were designated for men traveling alone, and those in Nauru for women, families, and unaccompanied minors. When the Australian government began exiling and incarcerating people in offshore prisons between 2001 and 2008, this border regime was referred to as the "Pacific Solution." The second iteration of the Pacific Solution began in 2012 with over four thousand people imprisoned in the Pacific islands. The detention centers on Manus were eventually closed and many of the detainees left in limbo in Port Moresby or sent to Australia for medical treatment. Dozens of men are still being held in Port Moresby, having spent over six years locked up in Manus and five years held in Port Moresby. Months after the last refugees were released from Nauru in 2023, new groups were banished to the island, and as of January 2025 over one hundred remain incarcerated there. Many of the people who remain in PNG and Nauru, and those sent to Australia for medical treatment, have no clear pathway to restarting their lives in a third country.

In this context, the Australian border becomes a fluid concept and entity. It extends into Pacific nations with unsettling, debilitating, and irreparable consequences. The agreements between Australia and its neighbors to construct refugee prisons are exploitative. Australia imposes on the sovereignty of poorer nations and disrupts and damages their sociocultural, economic, and moral fabric. Approximately 250 years ago the British Empire established Australia as a penal colony, and this colonial dynamic continues today as Australia transforms other islands into prisons.

Historically, PNG was a colony of Australia and Nauru a former protectorate (PNG gained independence in 1975 and Nauru in 1968). In 2001, when Australia began using these islands as part of its offshore detention regime, people traveling to Australia by boat to ask for protection were warehoused on the islands indefinitely. Significantly, the ecosystems of these islands have been damaged by the construction and maintenance of these carceral sites. Also, multinational companies negotiated the construction, management, security, and maintenance contracts for the prison camps in extremely lucrative agreements that sometimes involved questionable tender processes. Since 2012, Australia has spent at least twelve billion dollars to maintain the offshore detention industry. The economic dimensions of Australia's border regime have enabled many companies to profit significantly from the misery of human beings. Over time, politicians and companies have worked together to create and implement even more complex and brutal technologies for the purposes of border violence. The two major political parties in Australia are complicit in these arrangements, in addition to other political actors, the mainstream media, and a multitude of companies and organizations. Together, they have helped enhance the border-industrial complex. Australia has demonized refugees and ruined countless lives by securitizing and militarizing the border in this way. People seeking asylum by boat are not committing a crime; in fact, they are exercising their right to seek asylum under international law, and thus Australia's immigration detention system has been incarcerating innocent people without trial.

Like the situation in most nation-states, border politics in Australia is a ruthless political and economic enterprise; it is central to many political and sociocultural debates. It is interconnected with issues such as elections, national security, national interest, and national identity. Since 1992 mandatory and arbitrary detention of people seeking asylum by boat has grown to become one of the most significant parts of Australia's political and sociocultural landscape. In 2001, John Howard's Liberal government first introduced the Pacific Solution, constructing offshore immigration detention centers on Manus Island and Nauru, with stage two of the Pacific Solution emerging when Julia Gillard's Labor government came to power in 2012. In 2013, after Kevin Rudd took over leadership from Gillard, a new policy was introduced, according to which anyone arriving by boat after July 19, 2013, would never be allowed to make a home in Australia.

The Liberal-National Coalition led by Liberal leader Tony Abbott defeated the Labor Party on September 7, 2013, and immediately set out to further militarize Australia's borders through draconian policy initiatives spearheaded by the new immigration minister, Scott Morrison. Under this new conservative government, the border-industrial complex became more violent and brutal. Operation Sovereign Borders was implemented, and in 2014 Peter Dutton took over from Morrison as immigration minister. There have been fourteen deaths resulting from detention in Manus and Nauru since 2013 (not including those who lost their lives after deportation).

In 2018, Morrison became Australia's prime minister. He remained in power until 2022, when the Liberal-National Coalition was defeated by Labor. Following the defeat, Dutton became the Liberal Party leader. Prior to that he also became the minister for home affairs—the Department of Home Affairs is a newly created "super-department" (with former secretary Michael Pezzullo [2017–23] replaced by Stephanie Foster). The Labor Party have continued the same policies after their win in the 2022 federal election led by current prime minister Anthony Albanese. Operation Sovereign Borders remains in place.

* * *

Elahe Zivardar fled Iran on that ominous day, July 19, 2013, after experiencing unbearable gender discrimination and increasing suppression of her artistic, cultural, and political activism. She was forced to flee her homeland and leave behind her family, friends, and community, as well as her professional link to her cultural scene, in order to avoid persecution. Women face systemic discrimination at all levels of Iranian society, in particular women who actively resist the prejudice and limitations enforced by the fundamentalist religious government that reinforces misogynist systems and social practices. The 2022 nationwide uprisings in Iran are testament to the deprivation and humiliation felt by women like Zivardar.

After fleeing Iran, Zivardar first traveled to Indonesia, and from there she attempted to reach Australia by boat and ask for protection, only to find herself trapped in Australia's border-industrial complex, like thousands of others fleeing dictatorship, discrimination, and war. She was detained in Nauru from 2013 to 2019 before being resettled in the US as part of the controversial Australia–United States Resettlement Agreement.

From the beginning of her imprisonment until now her creative resistance has been dedicated to exposing this tragedy. She has actively, both inside the prison and after her release, engaged in journalism, media appearances, social media activism, photography, film, writing and research, and painting.[1]

Zivardar has joined scholar, activist, and translator Omid Tofighian to develop what they refer to as Nauru Prison Theory. This project uses an intersectional and multidimensional theoretical and creative framework for critically analyzing Australia's incarceration of refugees; it interprets immigration detention in connection with colonialism, imperialism, and racial capitalism. They argue that the oppression, domination, and subjugation of refugees over the past decades must be understood in relation to colonization and the dispossession and genocide of First Nations peoples. Nauru Prison Theory presents us with theoretical perspectives and artistic production—such as film, painting, and literature—that, among other things, address Australia's colonial imaginary; the appropriation of the land to use as a penal colony for the British Empire; the racial capitalism at the root of the detention industry; the racialized nature of border violence; and the ongoing obsession with incarceration.

Nauru Prison Theory is thus an emerging body of knowledge, a range of artistic works, and diverse activist initiatives. It is based on the experiences, ideas, and visions of the people held in Nauru and the conditions they encountered there. As such, important dimensions of Nauru Prison Theory are the architecture of torture particular to the Nauru facilities and the intersectional discrimination and violence imbedded in the systems and conditions. The Nauru detention regime specifically targeted women, unaccompanied minors, and families. As a philosophical and artistic ecosystem, Nauru Prison Theory combines political action, community advocacy, and transnational collaborations to unpack the logic and machinations at the root of that violence. It has emerged out of years of collaboration between Zivardar and Tofighian in consultation and partnership with other people oppressed by the border-industrial complex. Not only is it a collective project, but it is also a self-generating one that continually incorporates new collaborators. In his own writings Tofighian has referred to this kind of endeavor as a "shared philosophical activity":

> This form of shared intentionality is fluid; it involves a range of diverse agents who occupy different roles but who all work towards the same creative and philosophical objective. The collaborations have the ability to continue and expand the new discourse; to maintain the resistance; and to foster more dynamic critical approaches and invite others.[2]

As such, this form of collaboration contributes to philosophical areas of research in social epistemology: joint commitments, collective intentionality, shared agency, collective purpose, and joint beliefs. A shared philosophical activity emphasizes the value of collaborative knowledge production and promotes the radically important philosophical, political, and ethical outcomes—especially considering the fact that it addresses collaboration with oppressed and stigmatized peoples. It also contributes to discourses pertaining to pedagogy and how this collective way of knowing can help introduce new methodologies for teaching and learning, lead to philosophical discovery, and present rich possibilities for research. Certainly, what is valuable to foreground here is the mode of production, the joint philosophical vision, and the methodology associated with the shared philosophical activity, all of which have deeper scholarly and educational implications.

In Nauru Prison Theory the border-industrial complex is also identified as a dimension of Australia's dominant social imaginary; therefore, it is vital to critique the symmetrical relationship between the Australian border and Australia's sociopolitical structures and institutions. This involves radically transforming the mainstream image of refugees. Australia's social imaginary is intertwined with its colonial imaginary. Its colonial legacy is represented in domestic and international relationships and interactions, and dominates visions of itself in contrast to the rest of the world. Therefore, many perceptions pertaining to displaced and exiled peoples are often determined by a colonial mentality. The conditions out of which the social imaginary is formed include material, symbolic, and epistemic dimensions—all of which function to render displaced and exiled peoples as weak and without agency.

There are many commonplace assumptions about refugees that involve patronizing and debilitating tropes and stereotypes. These elements exist across the political spectrum (including among refugee advocates) and are determining factors when critically analyzing the inhumane punishment and abject conditions of people caught up in Australia's detention industry. Other forms of bordering in Australian society and culture are fundamental components of the social imaginary, and by extension the border violence nexus. Therefore, Nauru Prison Theory proposes new acts of debordering which require a multidimensional approach and radical forms of collaboration that combine translation, coauthorship, collaborative scholarship, joint artistic initiatives, educational initiatives, and shared philosophical activity, all of which cultivate new kinds of pedagogical practices aimed at cultivating decolonial interventions and ways of knowing, freedom of movement, and empowerment of displaced and exiled peoples.

This conversation between Zivardar and Tofighian introduces some of the fundamental elements of Nauru Prison Theory, which relate to core questions about pedagogical purpose and method outside the mainstream university. Nauru Prison Theory focuses on collaborative work and centralizes the significance of teaching and learning when developing a philosophy of resistance. Its core elements are education, writing, creativity, translation, publishing, and healing as acts of resistance.

Omid:

I was educated and trained as a philosopher, but my interests and areas of expertise are interdisciplinary. My research and teaching reflect this diversity, and I have always tried to find new fields and topics for philosophical exploration and inspiration. My activism and community advocacy have played a significant role in my scholarly work, activities I have been engaged in throughout my life—especially during my education, and while researching and teaching.

My own experience of displacement and exile has been paramount. My family and I left Iran around the time of the Iranian Revolution and the establishment of the Islamic Republic. In fact, we were in the United States first for approximately five years before moving to Australia.

My personal experience together with my scholarly interests in borders, race, incarceration, and settler colonialism characterized a lot of the work that I was doing in the community, initially in Australia and then internationally as I traveled and lived in different countries. But for many years there was a separation between my research and scholarship and my activism. I had never really brought the two together. I was trying to move beyond many of the traditional themes and topics in philosophy and my rather traditional training, and I kept searching for themes and topics outside mainstream philosophical questions and traditions.

After studying in Europe, I returned to Australia just after the uprisings and revolutions in the Middle East and North Africa. And at that point, I started to see interconnections between the work that I was doing in the community and in activist spaces, and my own scholarly work. I started to think more about the relationship between themes and topics related to borders, race, settler colonialism, incarceration, oppression, domination, and submission/subjugation. I started to think about all of these in the context of debates within the philosophy of mind, epistemology, ethics, and social and political philosophy. What really interested me was how art and culture factored into many issues; how drawing on theories and methods from aesthetics could enhance a critical analysis of political issues. I grew more interested in the role of art in resistance movements and in activist spaces, and started realizing how important this was from a scholarly perspective, and for teaching and learning.

I started to look into the past in order to see how art had been used in various resistance movements. I saw how importantly narrative and cultural symbolism manifested in revolutionary literature, art, and music in places such as Tunisia, Iran, South Africa, and the US. I was particularly influenced by the role of folklore, street art, and hip hop.

I have been working with people in detention centers in Australia, people who have experienced Australia's border violence, for approximately twenty-five years and in different roles such as translator/interpreter, facilitator for art and intellectual projects, and supporter in terms of legal, social, educational, and community needs and activities.

When I returned to Australia at the end of 2010, I started working again with people held in detention. Unfortunately, a couple of years after that Australia restarted its offshore detention regime. I do not call the prison camps processing centers since they were not designed to process people. It is the offshore incarceration of people seeking asylum. Soon after that I started to work with Behrouz Boochani and other writers and artists, and it just had a roll-on effect. Now I am building on those experiences and successes in my work with Elahe Zivardar.

Elahe:

I was educated and trained in art, architecture, and journalism. I was also heavily involved in the theater community in Iran—an aspect of my life

Figure 1. Render from 3D model of Nauru Prison depicting rooms inside tents (2021). Created by Elahe Zivardar.

I have not discussed before. I performed in theater since the age of ten years old; I actually grew up in the theater community. I was not a full-time professional theater actor or director, but participating in that community has had the biggest influence on my artwork and the way that I think and create art in any field, whether it is painting, documentary making, or even in my architectural work.

When I started working on the documentary titled *Architect* (in progress), which is related to my experiences incarcerated in Nauru, my main aim was to raise awareness by showing the world what happened there. The film also features the 3D model of the prison which I made, and specifically developed in consultation with people who were detained with me. The Nauru detention center was so isolated and hidden from people in Australia and the rest of the world. But as time went by, I realized that talking to people and critically engaging with the central issues related to border violence would enable me to contribute to this conversation. Interacting with people who ask the right questions allows us all to dig deeper into the topic.

It has only been six years since I left the island. But I am still working out how to move on from the aftermath of years of potentially indefinite detention. I have been using my artwork and the artistic skills I developed from when I was in Iran to empower myself.

The film *Architect* is inspired by my final university project in Iran. It showcases my never-before-seen archive from Nauru, and draws on the network of people from my time in the detention center. I expose the architecture of detention though interviews, photography and video, paintings, and my 3D model of the Nauru detention center which, as I mentioned before, I'd made by consulting other refugees who were held there. In my initial university project I had been thinking about ways to help people in need through art. The architectural initiative was dedicated to art and therapy and was called "Abode for Serenity" (*ārāmsāyesh gāh* in Farsi). I considered my university project an important initiative for community outreach, for which I interviewed almost five hundred people between eighteen and sixty years old. After Nauru, the documentary developed into something new.

Thinking of my art as a trajectory of my training and experiences is important to me. It's important to stress that being empowered through art and through strong ideas didn't just begin with my detention experience. It wasn't just an aftermath of prison. Artistic empowerment has been an ongoing journey since childhood. I think this point gets lost in a lot of conversations about refugees and their work: that people had multidimensional and full lives prior to this really traumatizing period of incarceration.

Omid:

This is why challenging and dismantling border regimes must focus on the *epistemic* conditions that characterize and help shape the material conditions. It is necessary to transform the symbolic aesthetic underlying the social imaginary, particularly in relation to beliefs, attitudes, and stereotypes about displaced and exiled peoples. Of course, these elements are reflected in policies and different forms of anti-refugee behavior and systems. And this social imaginary is represented in many examples of racist sentiment. But this social imaginary is so pervasive that it also exists within activist communities and in pro-refugee behavior and systems.

Problems associated with knowledge production, narratives, images, and symbols exist among all of us, including people who want to make change and transform the system. Addressing these problems is key for revising practical political strategies. Changing the social imaginary is critical when developing and choosing the right tactics and engaging with and advocating for displaced and exiled peoples. A combination of methods linking material, epistemic, and aesthetic factors is fundamental when thinking through exactly what needs to happen in order to make positive and sustainable transformation. If the political economy of the detention industry and the political and legal machine that governs it is to be disrupted and radically transformed, this must be done in combination with challenging and changing the disempowering and damaging tropes, images, and narratives constructed to represent refugees among people with citizen privilege.

Abolishing Australia's border regime requires structural changes in multiple spheres. Of course, this involves a serious consideration of racial capitalism and the role of colonialism. Multinational companies are making massive profits out of this particular border regime. And many of them work internationally as part of the military-industrial complex; they work in prisons as part of the prison-industrial complex; and, of course, the companies have close ties with governments and politicians. But they also operate in hospitals, schools, universities, and places where you would never even imagine. Essentially, the issue is really about power and profit. The reason why these companies are running these centers and complicit in the atrocities that occur in these places is because they are making money. Imprisoning and torturing people seeking asylum is profitable.

I feel that in terms of activism, not enough has been done to cut off that cash flow. And I think once corporations stop making money, then we will be one step closer to changing things. The other issue is political profit. Why are politicians wasting so much money? We are talking about well over $12 billion spent in the last twelve years on the immigrant detention industry in Australia. Why are so many voters fine with the fact that their tax money is being spent on torturing people?

I think one way to answer that question is that, unfortunately, what we see on the border is a reflection of a particular colonial mentality and political strategy that pervades Australian society. This kind of treatment of people seeking asylum is interconnected with the way marginalized and stigmatized peoples are being oppressed today and the historical injustices that this oppression is rooted in. Violence against noncitizens must also be interpreted in connection with abuse of citizen rights. One aspect of this violence is the reduction of people's capacity for compassion so that atrocities committed on the border do not illicit moral indignation and community outrage. To achieve this, strategies need to be implemented involving anti-refugee narratives, images, and symbols in cooperation with the media, cultural institutions, and throughout all levels of education and research. As a consequence of these different programs, violence against refugees is taught to citizens and internalized, violence at the border is turned around and used against citizens and normalized—it is inevitable that citizens eventually reproduce this violence against each other.

For us to talk about all of this, we need to look at history and we need to look at the education system. It is really important for schools and universities to work in ways that bring activism into the classroom. Education needs to include more critical analysis of the complexities of border violence and its connection to colonialism, and critical discourses and approaches need to be central in research spaces and pedagogical spaces. In order for this to be successful, it is necessary to make significant epistemological shifts, as I mentioned earlier. One way is for educational institutions and funding bodies to look into investing in collaborative work in these spaces, partnerships that bring together educators with people who have lived experience of displacement and exile, also with activists and community advocates.

The boundaries separating different groups need to be removed; it is important for researchers and educators to collaborate with activists and communities in meaningful and dignified ways. Institutions and funding bodies have a lot of responsibility to help make collectives; consultation and collaboration are essential here.

Activism directed at changing legislation and transforming the political establishment, for instance, is important. But that work must be coupled with intellectual and creative forms of activism; it is necessary to include and foster new images, new imaginaries, new ways of understanding identity, new forms of knowledge production, and new epistemic criteria. It is important to rethink support mechanisms and infrastructure so that different contributors and voices can interact and build. These aims and objectives are at the core of Nauru Prison Theory, they drive the artistic and creative work we engage in, they inspire us to continue disseminating these perspectives and plans in different forms, they guide us in bringing in others and expanding the shared philosophical activity.

Elahe:

I agree: our work should communicate to create epistemological shifts. Just "spreading awareness" as some activists describe it is not enough. After my experiences incarcerated in the border-industrial complex, I am more critical of support networks—we also have to address gender discrimination in activist spaces. I think one of the reasons that I was being denied a lot of support and exposure when I was incarcerated in Nauru was because I did not play the familiar role of a victim. I do not know why, but a lot of activists are more interested when we talk about displaced and exiled peoples as being in poverty or in different positions of weakness and need. They seem to respond better to narratives and depictions of people who need food or clothing, or similar kinds of things. Of course, those things are important, but some pro-refugee entities do not seem to be open to the image of the refugee that empowers and humanizes refugees.

I have encountered a lot of supportive people, but I have also often encountered activists who have discriminated against me based on gender and race. In

Figure 2. Refugees protesting from inside the Nauru immigration detention center or Nauru Prison in 2016. Signs refer to then Australian immigration minister Peter Dutton, Australian Border Force (ABF), and contracted private companies: Wilson, Serco, Connect, and International Health and Medical Services (IHMS). Photo credit: Elahe Zivardar.

the US, where I now live, there have been times when people have tried to censor me by creating obstacles when our perspectives do not align, or they somehow request that I redirect/modify/temper my message. This also happens when I work with mainstream media in Europe or in Australia: people are not interested in many things I have to say because I want to dig deeper into the issue, go beyond the victim discourse. Yes, racism and capitalism are at the root. This is all about money and exploitation of marginalized peoples, this is all about corruption and power. And this is something that, unfortunately, the mainstream media do not like to discuss because it threatens big donors, big corporations. People with power and money do not approve of this discourse. So even in our advocacy a lot of discrimination occurs; other people make decisions for us, they decide which part should be heard, which part is better off censored.

I believe my experiences as a researcher, journalist and educator in Iran—before my incarceration—fed into my time in Nauru. I had always used art and design in liberating ways from when I was challenging gender discrimination in Iran. In Naura I developed this further: I worked with other refugees in the prison camp to expose the unjust incarceration and attract international attention. And my work kept developing when I moved to the US and found new obstacles here.

Eventually healing became part of my activist vision. Whether we face social and political struggles, or just have nightmares about them, we can find ways to heal through the radical use of art and creativity. I mention nightmares because I personally had to overcome those that involved my father whom I was very close to—I was in Nauru when he passed. I incorporated mindfulness techniques such as meditation into my work, which though sometimes triggering, were also helpful. (Of course, for many, personal pain and trauma or other difficulties require other methods.)

In my workshops I consider healing to be one of the basics of teaching design or the foundations of visual arts. Treatment, in its various forms, should be part of educational practices. And the word "workshop" is intentional. What I learned—about art, ideas, architecture, and culture—needs to be shared collectively in the format of a workshop: it is not something that I can describe or instruct or teach without close practical interaction.

The workshop stresses the shared collectivity of the teaching experience. Not only is a single approach insufficient to help people with different learning needs, identities, or capacities, but even I learn new things during the pedagogical process. Often, it's better if the participant does not even have a basic understanding of design. The educator then stops expecting that the learner have specific or specialized knowledge or artistic skill. When the learners' feelings toward the project are pure and they have not been preconditioned in any way, excellent results can be achieved. The aim is that education should be therapeutic and empowering.

This isn't to say that I *don't* use my specialized training in art, architecture, and culture whenever I engage in any kind of teaching. Of course, I use universally recognized essentials such as points, lines, shapes, or volume as starting points for any art project. Only I connect these to other, personal emotions, experiences, and concepts. Every learner is expected to create something different, whether it is an artwork or other forms of expression such as writing, based on their background and interpretation. Responses are diverse and meaningful. I practiced this approach when teaching art in the detention center even though we had very limited resources and were always under surveillance and pressure. But I managed to conduct activities with friends, and I noticed that more and more people, regardless of skill level, would join after witnessing my workshops.

These design-based teaching experiences helped my own art projects. I spent one year on my painting titled "Concealed Borders" (part of my *Border-Industrial Complex* series). Like a lot of my art, the work changed significantly during the process. In the beginning I used realism (I painted the face of Peter Dutton) and then changed it to something abstract. But there is a reason for every stage and change. I spent weeks sometimes repainting or changing something. For me this process represented the removal of some trauma or pain and the ultimate production of a beautiful work of art.

When I remember my nightmares during my time in Nauru I think about the surreal atmosphere that was being created for me there. It has been helpful to draw on Freud and research on dream analysis to interpret my experience. When I see a nightmare every night, over and over again, I need to work it out. There is no way to get the help you need in detention. Art helped me to move on from that state, even when the nightmares got more complex. In the prison I often experienced multiple levels of nightmares. At a certain point I learned how to wake myself up when I was in the middle of a nightmare. After a while I realized, oh, this is a nightmare, this is not real. My art helped me arrive at this point. I was expressing in art what I was seeing every night, and then I could control it.

I am still finding ways to move on from that experience in detention. I even remember four levels of nightmares. I wake myself up and it is another nightmare again. My artwork, my paintings, represent the atmosphere of those nightmares. I can make them calmer and softer with the help of colors, for instance, but later at the end of the day, I find the bright colors in my paintings kind of ugly. It is that absurdity that helps depict the surreal environment of indefinite detention. Some things just don't match. It feels like beautiful colors have been injected into a bitter painting. Still, even if it is scary to express all this in art, that is how I can transcend the experience and teach others.

Omid:

Of course, one of the key aspects of surrealism is dream visions and the kind of uninhibited, unrestricted expression associated with dream experiences. Dream visions and dream logics pervade a lot of art and writing by people in detention, and that is prominent in your paintings. So it brings in all the contradictions, the conflicts, the absurdities and puts them alongside each other.

Elahe:

And that's the main inspiration for my painting. Overcoming the horror of those surreal experiences through art, design, and storytelling is one of the aims of my teaching and treatment.

Omid:

Thinking about using art to heal, and helping others to heal, and how all this affects the communities in which we live, raises questions about the causes of abuse in places like detention centers and the purpose of carceral sites in gen-

FOUNDATIONS FOR NAURU PRISON THEORY

Figure 3. Elahe Zivardar, *Nameless*: part of the *Border-Industrial Complex* series of paintings, acrylic on canvas, 2017.

eral. Why would any state, or anyone, want to imprison people who are just exercising their human right under international law? Exercising their right to seek asylum. There is no need, at all—in any way, shape, or form—to detain people who are fleeing violence: men, women, children, families. And it is important to think about this in a broader sense; once we allow states to

Figure 4. Elahe Zivardar, *Purple Pain*: part of the *Border-Industrial Complex* series of paintings, acrylic on canvas, 2019.

conduct these sorts of practices on vulnerable people it then imbeds that behavior and those practices deeper into the culture and social fabric. It is replicated in more government policies. How are we as citizens made vulnerable by allowing it to happen to others? How does that reduce our capacity for compassion? How does that transform our way of engaging with our neighbors, our family members? How does this violence multiply within us?

Elahe:

Exactly. We need virtuous experiments, virtuous designs. Places and programs that heal and empower rather than torture. That is what I have been thinking about in my work. To build relationships with architects and designers, for instance, and talk to them about the moral consequences of their creations. It is their duty to convince people in power that we do not need prisons or detention centers. They need to collaborate with the appropriate researchers, educators, activists, and advocates to make change through art and design. Especially after Covid-19 so many people have been traumatized by some form of confinement or isolation. The right policies, the right environment, the right workshops can be helpful.

Omid:

Australia was founded as an offshore prison nearly 250 years ago and it seems like it has not been able to move beyond that identity, that colonial character. Prisons have been multiplying, morphing, replicating all over the place. Incarceration seems to be Australia's answer for so many things. We need to develop a more radical ethics, create more radical ways for how to deal with issues rather than just creating a prison and locking people up.

Elahe:

Yes. The scale of the prison/detention industry that we have right now, we really do not need that. And this could be interpreted as partly a failure of architecture, that we still design and build these kinds of places in our world. But creative people like architects can—should—contribute much more than this.

During my time in Nauru, especially after the death of Omid Masoumali, I was reaching out to people to help me raise awareness, to help me make connections with journalists. It was hard to get journalists to see my work. The interviews that I used to do with people needed to get out to the public, but publishing this work was difficult. There were obstacles to publishing my work under my own name in the Australian and international media. And then there were those who were simply not willing to help, or had no idea how to help. Sometimes people could not think beyond basic forms of support, they thought I just needed money, or a second hand phone, or something like that, they had no idea how they could help otherwise.

For some advocates it seems that the end goal is to attract views on Facebook and other social media. The stakes are different for them. For some people, it is

Figure 5. Nauru immigration detention center or Nauru Prison in 2016. Toxic mold covers the inside of the tents and contaminated condensation drips onto bedding. Photo credit: Elahe Zivardar.

about followers. Who does it help to post something about a refugee who has been in prison, and what is the benefit for those agents to "spread awareness" about others? What does this kind of exposure do? For me, working with people on the inside, recording interviews, taking photos, my stakes are higher. Yet on many occasions people even published what I collected and took the credit for themselves—which is, of course, abuse.

Omid:

A particular narrative about refugees is created by some supporters, one that is limited to their being poor, needy, vulnerable, broken people. This is represented too many times on social media and attracts a lot of attention from certain groups of people. There are damaging tropes that are repeated over and over again in the media and in activist spaces.

In our collaborations we critique how particular stereotypes, particular images of refugees are constantly reproduced in government spaces and among anti-refugee sites. And sometimes these stereotypes and images are similar to those circulated among the people who want to help. There's the image of the "caged person" who is oppressed in the Global South but escapes to the West for freedom. With this trope there is a problematic dichotomy between the Global South and Global North: one location is reduced to a place of oppression, and the other one is reduced to a place of opportunity and freedom.

Another trope pertains to the refugee as simply desperate. A supplicant, someone in constant need. Another one that I think is disturbing is the "struggling overcomer" or the "battler," the person whose identity is determined by constantly fighting to overcome odds. Also, a common trope involves reducing people to the tragic or miserable victim. And there is a stereotype that I often come across and think is really problematic: the mystic sage. This involves depicting a quirky and mysterious person, a trickster or kind of exotic refugee.

You can deny someone dignity and respect by distorting their identity or reducing them to one element of their experience. We all deserve to be acknowledged and respected for the multidimensional elements of our personalities, experiences, talents, and desires.

One of the most important aspects of our collaboration, this shared philosophical activity then, is that it defies these reductive tropes. In our work we represent the refugee as a knowledge producer, as a creative, as someone with insight and the ability to teach and lead.

Notes

1. Zivardar's work is listed on her website: shakibaproductions.com.
2. Omid Tofighian, "Introducing Manus Prison Theory: Knowing Border Violence," in "Law, Love and Decolonization," special issue, *Globalizations* 17, no. 7 (2020): 1149.

Politics Was in the Very Air We Breathed
Conversations with Khaled Fahmy and Ahdaf Soueif

Khaled Fahmy and Ahdaf Soueif are two of the most prominent international voices from Egypt. The first rose to fame with his scholarship, the second with her fiction. Over decades, both have also consistently produced essays, journalism, and translations. What does it mean to be an Arab public intellectual writing on an international level? We thought it best to let them speak for themselves.

When did you first realize you were "political"? Was there a particular moment?

Ahdaf:

I am trying to find my way into this question; leaving it and coming back to it. Because, on the one hand, in my upbringing—my childhood, my teenage years—I would say politics was in the very air we breathed and, on the other, one didn't—*I* didn't—see political action as a possibility . . .

1954

My mother leaves for the UK to start her PhD. My father and I move in with my mother's family. I am four. I love being at my grandparents'—but I understand that "the government" is preventing us being with my mother. When my father's travel permit finally comes through, my mother's uncle, a judge, accompanies us till we board. He doesn't leave us until the *Stratheden* is about to leave the dock. I understand that "the judge" gives us protection against "the government."

1956, Autumn

We are in London when Britain, France, and Israel attack Egypt. When we march against the war my parents' British friends march with us. I understand that there's a difference between "the country" and "the government"—and that it is somehow noble to stand against what your government is doing to people in other countries.

1956, Later

My parents' tiny student flat in Stockwell is the scene of arguing and mourning. The USSR has invaded Hungary. It seems very natural that there is an idea, a feeling, that spans the whole world and makes people in one part of the world grieve and "take a position" about what's happening in another part.

1958

Back in Cairo, enrolled in Amoun Private School, Zamalek, we salute the flag of the new United Arab Republic every morning. Every year on July 23 in the evening we, us children and the nanny, look down into the garden of the Officers' Club one block away from our balcony: the cars arriving, the many, many formally dressed people going in, and then the open-air concert in honor of the anniversary of the (1952) revolution. The concert we're watching from six floors up is also being shown on state television in the living room behind us. But the television is off; my parents aren't watching.

My parents keep their distance from the government. They somehow avoid becoming members of the Party: al-Ittihad al-Watani, later al-Ittihad al-Ishtiraki. But there is *never* an occasion where adults are together—whether just sitting at the lunch table at home, or in larger family gatherings, or when my parents' friends come to our house—there is never an occasion where most of the talk isn't about politics. But no one that I can see *does* anything with politics—I didn't imagine one *could* do anything about politics.

I am a child of the 1952 revolution. I love Nasser. He's big and handsome and I love his ready smile and his ease with the crowds that mob him. I agree with the redistribution of land ("They're five acres/acres five/I'll plant them pepper and chili/to fling at the guy with the hat silly"), the industrialization ("from the needle to the rocket"), the building of the High Dam ("With our money/Our workers' arms"), with the Pan-Arab vision ("We're a nation that defends, not threatens/We're a nation that conserves, not destroys") and most of all with Egypt's support of anti-imperialism in the Global South and the ideals and

"Positive Non-alignment" of Bandung. Like most children I know nothing about the executions, the purges, and the prisons. For me, prison is where my father and my uncle spent a year each when they were Leftist students in the time of the Unjust King. My uncle was tortured. I question my mother: What is torture? She tells me they made him put his feet in a tub of warm water then a tub of cold water. It doesn't sound pleasant but it doesn't sound too bad either. I feel special that when I was born, the first time I went out was to be held up in the street outside Qara Midan Prison for my uncle to look out through bars high up in the walls and behold the baby; the first of the new generation.

(One generation later I will take my sister and four-year-old Alaa to show baby Mona to Ahmad Seif, their father, in Tora Prison. Another generation later, baby Khaled will be taken to be shown to Alaa, his father, in Tora Prison.)

June 1967

School, exams, life—all are suspended because of the war. Windows and the glass panes above the doors are pre-splinted with tape and blinded with dark blue paper. In the windowless hall of our apartment I fight with my mother over joining the Civil Defense. I'm on shaky ground because I don't know how to join the Civil Defense—where would I actually head to if she let me out of the flat? Our quarrel is resolved by the war ending so quickly.

But I've fallen in love with Palestine and the Palestinian cause. "The children of '48 are the commandoes of '68." Palestinian posters adorn the walls of my half of the room I share with my sister, along with Che and "Facciamo l'amore non la guerra!" Yet it is my sister who springs into political action in her teens and has never stopped.

1973 onward

Studying, living, alone, in England I am awakened to the politics of race, identity, representation and misrepresentation. I arrive at Lancaster University on October 4, 1973. Within forty-eight hours, war breaks out, and in front of the TV in the Common Room I realize that my colleagues are cheering Israel.

It takes time to comprehend that the Zionist position *is* in fact the position of British politicians, intellectuals, media. Everything falls into place the moment I figure how that's linked to issues of race and empire.

Then, in a decade, Islam goes from being exotic and sexy to being backward and threatening. And I go from being a representative of something exotic and different to someone who can only be made sense of as "against" her own culture.

But by then I'd come to accept that people I met in the North would always make assumptions about me—and they would always be wrong.

1980s

I start writing stories, essays, reviews. After a few stumbles I see the "exotic" ghetto I'm being admiringly nudged toward and I change tack.

2000

The Big Break. With *The Map of Love* shortlisted for the Booker I'm invited by *The Guardian* to write on Palestine. They'll pay for me to go, and to stay for a week. I'm to produce three thousand words. Sitting up nights in the American Colony Hotel in Jerusalem, writing the pain, the grace, the brutality, the humor—I find myself. I find what I am *for*. I deliver ten thousand words and *The Guardian* publishes them and readers insult me and bad-mouth me and praise me and I've entered the arena—to stay.

So I guess that was the moment. After that no action was free of politics. Not one.

Khaled:

I don't think I was ever drawn to politics, narrowly defined, e.g., running for office, joining a political party, etc., mostly because politics so defined is either blocked or corrupt (or corrupting) in our societies. But I have always believed in a wider definition of politics, i.e., the duty to "give back" to society, to serve a community wider than one's immediate family.

I grew up in what can be described as a typical bourgeois environment: study hard; have good manners; get good grades; search for a good, stable job; get married and have a family; pass on these values to your children. It is not that I didn't believe in these values; rather, I thought they were limited and precluded the possibility—or responsibility—of giving back to society, and limited one's energy to one's immediate well-being and happiness.

But it was mostly in my university years that my doubts about this bourgeois upbringing deepened, and it is then that I realized that there is more to education than having good grades, and that one's aims upon graduation should not be limited to landing a good job. I was fortunate to have gone to the American University in Cairo where there were many opportunities to "give back." In my first week, I joined the AUC Library as an employee in the Reference Department, where I worked for seven years (my BA and MA years). I also learnt that there was a large number of student clubs that catered to many tastes. In my first year, I joined a club called the Community Service Society, and soon became its president. But then I discovered Nadi Asdiqa' al-Quds, Jerusalem Friends Club. This was in 1982 during Israel's invasion of Lebanon. I remember participating in a poster exhibition depicting Israel's siege of Beirut and the Sabra and Shatila massacre. This was the beginning not only of a commitment to the Palestinian cause but also of knowing what it means to be involved in collective work: attending meetings, coordinating efforts, assigning duties, etc. Modest beginnings, it is true, but they proved to have long-lasting effects.

As Ahdaf says, politics is in the air we breathe. There are obvious instances of political work, but more often politics are inadvertent to one's professional life, right?

Ahdaf:

Well, in my case, the inadvertent was of such importance that it very quickly took up the main space.

The turning point, really, was *Map of Love*. What started out as a kind of Mills and Boone-ish romance of the desert transformed itself in the writing into a romance with politics at its core. The reviews were a complete departure from reviews of my earlier work. Reviewers were prickly and demanded the novel make up its mind whether it was about love or about politics! The *TLS* actually published a spoiler *before* publication date in which Robert Irwin announced he was fed up with being made to feel guilty about Britain's colonial past. There were two serious (and favorable) reviews: one in the *LRB* and one (my favorite: "The Real Thing") in the *Big Issue* (the magazine of the homeless). Then the Booker nomination came and the book took off.

And your work with PalFest or the British Museum, for instance?

On the back of the nomination, as I've described above, came the Palestinian involvement, and from that the Palestine Festival of Literature—"PalFest"—was born. So I guess that when the "inadvertent" happens, one has a choice to use it to create a willed action.

The British Museum Trusteeship was also like that. It was not a political act to accept the position—it was a big honor and I knew it. It was not the best moment for me; I'd rushed to Egypt when the Revolution broke out and we were (in June 2011) at the height of our engagement, but my mother had loved the British Museum and I reasoned it was a good way to somehow "serve" in my second country. And I suppose I thought of lingering racial and colonial residues and how one could help scrub them away. It was over time that I came to recognize how set in its ways the institution was, and over more time how impossible it would be—for me—to change anything from within the board. Then came the realization that the only way I could create waves which might be useful to the two immediate issues I was very troubled by (Big Oil sponsorship and workers' rights) would be to resign. I'm only grateful I realized that when there was still time to resign!

Khaled:

Teaching has always been deeply political in my case. I have been teaching modern Middle Eastern history in Western universities for nearly thirty years, and, naturally, the subjects I touch upon in my courses are political in an immediate sense of the word. I teach the history of European colonialism in the Middle East, the history of the Arab-Israeli conflict and the politics and economics of oil in the region, among many other subjects. So the subject matter of what I teach is deeply political.

But apart from the subjects, the very context of what I teach—institutional, academic, and geographic—makes it doubly political. In all the Western universities where I have taught, I was employed not in history departments, but in Middle Eastern studies ones. There, the question of Orientalism has always been present. And even though most undergraduate students nowadays start their university education having already read Said's critique of Orientalism, I still find it important to point out to my students their positionality, and to urge them to think of the history, the politics, and the academic department (and discipline) that they had just joined. Long before decolonization became a buzzword on campus, the field of Middle Eastern studies has been undergoing a deep process of decolonization. The awareness of the connection our field has with colonialism; the connection some leading Middle Eastern studies departments have with policy circles, intelligence agencies, and conservative think tanks; and the structural inequalities that characterize our field—these are issues I repeatedly point out to my students. To drive the last point home, I often urge them to wonder if their counterparts in the countries they study, i.e., university students in Baghdad, Beirut, Tunis, or Cairo, have the resources—the libraries, travel grants, language teaching facilities, etc.—to study a culture other than their own, e.g., medieval English history, Basque language, or the power dynamics of a small Austrian town. These structural inequalities cannot be more political.

Even during the short period in which I taught modern Middle Eastern history in the Middle East, the political was central rather than inadvertent. This was from 2010 to 2013 when I chaired the Department of History at the American University in Cairo. Most AUC undergraduates (as well as their parents and the majority of the staff) have a very limited understanding of history and equate it with the study of a past that is unconnected to the present. Maybe it was the peculiar moment in which I landed this job, coinciding as it did with the January Revolution, but I found my students very eager to approach history in a different manner. And this different approach to history, of course, is at the core of my research: the history of the present. Whether it is Mehmed Ali's army, the history of biopower (vaccination, census taking, forensic medicine, etc.), or the 1967 defeat—all my research subjects have given me opportunities to understand the nature of our present predicament. And it was a pleasure to share with my students insights from my research. I felt they, too, were struggling to understand the present by probing the past.

Ahdaf, might pedagogy itself be inadvertent in your case? For many of your readers in the Arab-speaking world, and in Egypt, you are an inspiring founding and major voice of Anglo-Arab fiction, a voice of intellectual activism, and a gracious public speaker. There is an inseparable pedagogical expectation from intellectual work in Arab societies. Would you consider such roles as pedagogical in any way? For instance, as a role model? A leader?

Ahdaf:

No. I don't think like that. I mean, what sort of person thinks of themselves as a role model? I'm just really grateful when people like what I do, and I'm touched when they like *me*. If something I've done or written has a good effect on someone's life then that's great. But that's as much the person's doing as mine. They read some words, interpreted them, took them to heart, and acted. My words would have sat on the page, un-alive, were it not for that reader's initiative and energy. So, really, I just do my best and my most honest for the task in hand, then I put my trust—as we say in Egypt—"first in God, then in the reader."

If I ask you off the cuff to write a short list of political categories, catchphrases, or assumptions that you would like to see dismantled in the discussions on Middle East politics, what would you come up with?

Ahdaf:

- The Arab Israeli conflict is an ancient conflict
- Ancient hatreds (as in "between Jews and Arabs" *sic*)
- Islam oppresses women
- "Shari'a Law" as understood in the North
- "Conflict," "peace," "terror"

Khaled:

- The Arab-Israeli conflict is a religious conflict.
- Israel is the only democracy in the region.
- A corollary: Arabs are genetically unfit for democracy.
- Palestinians sold their own land and therefore they deserve whatever calamities they are currently suffering from.
- Terrorism can be defeated by waging a war on terror.
- Austerity measures are the only means to put the region's economies on a sound footing.
- Strong men are the only guarantees of stability in an inherently volatile region.

Earlier, Khaled mentioned probing the past as well as the present. History seems to figure importantly in the work you both do. Egypt's streets and landscapes, neighborhoods, its buildings, the small professions of its many pedestrians carry their own history. Yet a lot of this history is not written down, not known to the public, or not really a general concern. This makes change a sad event. When the infrastructure of a city is changed, the history or the memory of its communities is lost. It clearly doesn't help that the biggest cultural machine for knowledge production and media dissemination is the state, which has a specific agenda to impart. Does this precariousness of historical tangibility affect social movements, or everyday collective resistance?

Ahdaf:

I guess I would say that the changes are sad whether or not they're recorded—being recorded doesn't make them less sad. Also, the written archive isn't really a resource that's available or in the mental landscape of the ordinary citizen. Old ways are preserved and remembered in stories, in song, and in film. But, yes, most of the ordinary lived communities' histories is ephemeral.

Was that true of the case with the Zamalek houseboats?

The Zamalek houseboats are one instance of the regime's complete blindness to what makes a city a city, urban fabric and what it means, the value of history and of community. The houseboats of Cairo were well documented, they had occupied half a kilometer of Cairo riverbank for almost a century, were connected to the city's services, and had an outsize place in the city's sense of itself because they'd featured in iconic novels and films.

The government took a decision to remove them and we were served with fourteen-day evacuation orders. They also imposed heavy "fines" for being there after they had passed a law delegitimizing living on the river. But we had not known about that law because they had kept it secret. The fines were payable alongside the removal.

What was surprising and heartening was the groundswell of public opinion that the event instigated. It seemed that everybody had a soft spot for the houseboats—except the government, which fielded senior spokespersons onto talk shows to smear the boats and the residents. So even vociferous public opinion and an international outcry were not enough to persuade an obtuse dictatorship to leave the tiny stretch of some thirty historic boats alone.

In scenes reminiscent of Palestine, people were weeping as they broke up their boats to sell for scrap. What used to be our gardens have become derelict garbage dumps in the six weeks since we were unmoored. Gardeners, boatmen, guards have lost their livelihoods. The local market and workshops have all lost good custom—but they too are going to be evacuated soon anyway.

Nine boats are sticking it out. We're still parked where the authorities put us when they dragged us out of our docks. We're demanding that they provide us with new moorings and—since their motivation seems to be that every inch of the country and every soul of its inhabitants produce money—with commercial licenses. They won't allow us to live on the Nile, so we will comply and we will work on the Nile. And we will once again create community and meaning.

Khaled:

Yes, when you have no historical memory, you lack a narrative, which means you have no trajectory that you can situate yourself in. It means that the process of imagining a future is much harder. I sensed this deeply during the January Revolution when I came across hundreds of your men and women who are full of energy and enthusiasm and who were moved by high hopes for the country and deep belief in a brighter future, but who could not think of themselves historically. They had no understanding of the history of labor struggle, of the youth movement, of student protests. Of course, this amnesia was partly responsible for their boldness and courage. But I believe it proved fatal in the end. With no awareness of the history of their own struggle, it proved impossible for them to imagine a future.

So how would you define an "archive"?

Khaled:

The word "archive" has been used so loosely lately that I think it has lost much of its descriptive potential. I have a very old-fashioned understanding of the archive based on my formative experience in Dar al-Watha'iq al-Qawmiyya, the Egyptian National Archives. Accordingly, by "archive" I mean an institution housed in a building where historical documents are preserved, catalogued, and made available to the public.

My struggle with this archive is not semantic, however. My struggle with the ENA is that it is a state archive. It is not the people's archive. With the exception of the voluminous collection of the shari'a court records which date from the beginning of the sixteenth century, and which record inheritance, sales, manumissions, and many other social transactions, the bulk of the ENA is composed of government correspondence with little or no reference to the actual citizens. My struggle, therefore, was to read this archive against the grain, so to speak, to locate the voice of the citizen in the middle of the deafening chatter of state officials.

As mentioned above, there are numerous institutions, e.g., charities, sports clubs, firms, and even families, which have historical documents but which have little or no recognition of their historical value. My hope is that other institutions, the institutions of civil society, will start creating their own archives. Some institutions have already done so, thankfully, but there is much more to be done.

I have become deeply disenchanted with cultural institutions in Britain, not only because of the heavy colonial legacy that I believe is in their DNA, but also because of the elitist orientation of many of their directors and curators. Still, I am always amazed by the eagerness of the public to make use of these institutions, to visit these museums for amusement, edification, or both. I am also reminded that people have a way to turn these institutions around and own them, make them their own. In my visits to the National Archives in Kew, for example, I often come across visitors looking for historical evidence that can help them figure out their own family's history, or write the history of their little village. Back in Egypt, I struggled for many years to make the ENA accessible to the wider Egyptian public, a struggle in which I have failed miserably as I came up against multiple security agencies which want to tighten their grip on the ENA and which are keen to deprive Egyptians of their right to consult their own history. Still, I hope that the ENA will one day be the people's archive, not the state's archive.

What about history that goes beyond local communities? The year 1967, for instance, appears as a turning point in your scholarship/fiction writing. Why?

Khaled:

It is true that 1967 can be seen as a turning point. After all, it is following that catastrophic defeat that Egypt lost its bid for hegemony over the Arab World, with Saudi Arabia now taking over the baton. The Nasserist dream of establishing an Arab regional order impervious to outside diktat was defeated in the most humiliating manner. Arab socialism (whatever that meant) was also defeated and a noticeable turn to religion as a means of personal salvation could also be traced back to the year.

But I also think that it may be more fruitful to ask whether 1967 can be understood not as a turning point but as a revealing moment. For the past five years, I have been studying 1967 to see what it tells us about the Arab state system, the nature of the Egyptian state, and the dynamics of civil-military relations. Accordingly, I have come to think that looking at 1967 as a turning point might be blinding us from recognizing how little things have changed. The so-called Arab cold war which was a feature of pre-1967 regional politics and which contributed significantly to the defeat continues to be a defining feature till today. The manner in which the Egyptian state deals with its citizens—haughty, condescending, impervious to criticism, resisting all forms of transparency and accountability—has not witnessed any qualitative change since 1967. And after a forty-year hiatus in which the military slightly lost its center stage, it has now returned to its privileged position on the Egyptian political landscape, recapturing territory it lost in June 1967. *Plus ça change, plus c'est la même chose.*

Ahdaf:

It's only a turning point for me in so far as it was a turning point for the country and the region. And I think that's reflected in how it's dealt with in *In the Eye of the Sun*.

Is this why Palestine has been one of your committed causes?

Ahdaf:

Palestine is a global issue. It doesn't just concern Arabs. In fact I would argue that in the first decade I was writing about it—from 2000—it was more important to write for the Western public; to bring the information/the Arab voice to the West, to rally public opinion in the West, to change or at least affect the discourse in the West. And since I lived in London, worked in English, and had a public and a platform, it was my clear duty to take this on.

Also, really, the more you see of the Palestinian story the more you realize it's the stuff of myth and legend. Generations born into a fight for their literal survival against a brutally powerful enemy who has the backing of the bad boys of the world. The Palestinians, as well as fighting for their survival, are fighting to maintain grace, dignity, meaning, history, and culture. For me, whether you understand and support the Palestinians is the litmus test for whether I can be friendly with someone or not.

Finally, Israel is really the primary author/reason/excuse for a great many of the issues in the region. So from a position of pure self-interest as an Egyptian I need to see a just resolution of the Palestinian situation.

Khaled:

More than the subalterns whose lives I was reading about in the ENA, Palestinians in their present, ongoing tragedy have my full respect. There is no other people whose struggle is as honorable, tragic, and inspiring—all in equal measure—as that of the Palestinian people. Fighting against one of the most ferocious examples of settler colonialism in modern history, that of Zionism; confronting one of the most imperious of superpowers, the US; betrayed repeatedly by corrupt Arab leaders and by large segments of Arab masses who love Palestine but hate Palestinians; and being cursed by a bankrupt, complicit leadership, Palestinians, generation after generation, have stood fast against all these odds and have done so with dignity, bravery, and honor.

This last summer (in 2021), during the onslaught on Gaza and the incredible solidarity shown by Palestinians in the West Bank and those of 1948, I had an opportunity to participate in a podcast on the history of Palestine, and to watch and listen to many public forums in which Palestinians were chatting among each other. These were profound experiences for me. It is as if I were listening to the story of the Palestinian tragedy for the first time, this despite having been teaching this story for many, many years. At a certain moment during the podcast I was participating in, I had to stop to reflect deeply about the words of my Palestinian friend who was sharing the platform with me. The clarity of vision that makes them appreciate the difficulty of their predicament; the righteousness of their cause that allows them not to lose their moral compass; their deep conviction that despite the dark moment of the present, the future is theirs—these are the hallmarks of Palestinians and how they carry on their struggle. It is truly inspiring.

Is it dual local/global outreach that motivates you to use both Arabic and English? Your public writing is of course iconic in that it uses both languages, even as you deal with issues at the forefront of contemporary Egypt like the 2011 revolution or the imprisonment of journalists and cultural workers.

Khaled:

I think I actually use three languages, not two, for in addition to English and *fusha*, I occasionally write in *'amiyya*!

Seriously, though, writing in Arabic and English obviously addresses two different audiences. I have already explained whom I have in mind when I write in Arabic. In English, I have a slightly different audience. In this case, and even when I write about Egypt, I mostly address people who lack Arabic, and therefore, mostly non-Egyptians and non-Arabs, who, I believe, are eager to know something about the region. Whether it is the occasional op-ed or the more numerous tweets and Facebook posts, the audience I have in mind are not politicians or policy makers, given that a long time ago I have given up the idea that Western governments are interested in promoting democracy in our region. And since most of my writing is about the human rights grievances, the ongoing suspension of our most basic democratic rights, and the flagrant abuses of power by our rulers, I am not keen on reaching out to Western governments who are too supportive of our regimes to be embarrassed out of their complicity by an op-ed. Rather, I have in mind citizens in the West who are equally dismayed by their own political systems and who, like us in the Arab World, believe that a complete overhaul of our political system is long overdue. The challenge then is to explain that what our region suffers from is not due to some intrinsic fault (e.g., Islamic fundamentalism, some oriental proclivity to violence, etc.) but structural problems not that different from what Western democracies are suffering from: lack of accountability, corruption, a widening gap between the haves and the have nots, and reckless policies when it comes to the environment. The aim is to say, basically, that we, the people, are in the same boat, and that our leaders, who are only too eager to do business with each other, need to be held accountable.

Ahdaf:

Pre-2011 I wrote completely in English, and most—maybe all—of my non-fiction was about the Arab world. I think we need to note a couple of things here:

1. In fiction you don't write for a specific audience. Your first readers are the ones who read the language you write in. They can be of any nationality or background. Then there are the translations.
2. From 2011 to 2015 I wrote a weekly column in Arabic in the Egyptian national daily, *Shorouk*. That was a unique experience in the feeling of connection it gave me, the back and forth between events, the column, readers. It was a unique time—and I still feel its reverberations—sadly mostly in messages I get from people in prison.
3. I have actually stopped writing (nonfiction) about the Arab world in the West (except in the context of specific campaigns). I think the location of the necessary struggle is now broader and the changes that need to happen in the world are systemic and cross all borders.

Ahdaf: Is this development toward wanting systemic change related to the move from fiction writing to more physical instances of activism?

I think it's related to what's actually happening in the world—like climate change, surveillance, the erosion of democracy—and what needs to happen counter to it.

If you live for long periods outside a country, how do you relate to a "public" outside of a national context? What kind of public can be imagined?

Khaled:

Despite long years living outside Egypt, I have always been working on Egypt. All my academic research and publications and a big part of my teaching is about Egypt. And while my scholarship is conducted in English, I always have an Egyptian public in mind, and this is why I am keen to translate all my work into Arabic, and also to write increasingly in Arabic. Five years ago, I also launched a blog to collect all my writings in it. I haven't made any exact calculation, but I guess that 80 percent of the blog is in Arabic and the remaining 20 percent is in English.

In my writing, whether academic or journalistic, I always have an Egyptian (and to some degree a wider Arab) public in mind. It took me a while to know this public. By "know" I don't mean to canvass this public or to have a direct contact with it, but to define it, and to try my best to find out how best I can be of value to it.

As academics, we are not trained to think of this question, the question of who our public is. By default, we are trained to write for, and to address, our peers. Hence the importance of academic presses and peer-reviewed journals. We are not trained to address a wider audience, be it policy makers, the press, or the nonacademic reading public.

I have always felt that this is not healthy. Apart from the "ivory tower" problem, apart, that is, from limiting our impact to a handful of like-minded scholars who may end up reading our journal articles, problems that academics in all fields of the humanities and social sciences suffer from, this problem is compounded within the field of Middle Eastern studies by the fact that our discipline, as defined and practiced in Western universities, is designed in such a way as to ignore the people we are writing about. Not only do we have very limited interaction between Western academics working on the Middle East and their counterparts in the Middle East, but we never address our scholarship to the wider reading public in the societies we study.

When I look at my colleagues in the History Department here at Cambridge who work, say, on German history, I see many of them publish in German. I see them attending conferences in Germany. And, most significantly, I see them thinking of a wider, nonacademic audience in Germany being interested in their own scholarship.

I think this engagement with a wider public can only enrich our scholarship academically. And this is why I am eager to publish academically (i.e., in academic presses, and in peer-reviewed journals), *and* also to translate my work into Arabic, knowing very well that once translated, my scholarship will then be accessible not only to my fellow historians but also to a wider Arabic-speaking public.

And this brings me back to your question: What kind of "public" can be imagined in this process? I have been struggling with this question for a long time. And in trying to come up with an answer, I was helped by members of this public themselves. In numerous emails, in DMs I receive on X (formerly Twitter) and Facebook, I receive messages from "the public" expressing appreciation for something I had written based on my academic scholarship. I remember the most moving of these messages was one that I received two years ago from a conscript who had come across my book on Mehmed Ali's army (*All the Pasha's Men*) while doing his national service. He wrote to me to say how his experience in the army suddenly made sense to him, that he suddenly understood what until then appeared to him as a violent, humiliating, nonsensical experience. He added that he would look forward to the leaves every few weeks so as to go home and read a chapter from my book. (Books are not allowed in military camps, least of all my book, he added.)

A message like this means much more to me than the most positive academic review of any of my books. It gives me purpose for writing. And it helps me clarify whom I am writing for. Through time, I came to realize that the most treasured audience I have in mind are young, educated people, men and women in their twenties and thirties, say, who are eager to figure out the roots of our common predicament. My responsibility toward them, I believe, is to figure out what historical questions they may have in mind, and then to see if I can be of any help in providing some answers. I would like to think that having this public in mind has considerably enriched my academic scholarship.

Khaled: You are an eminent academic, but do you ever find your authority as historian questioned because of your interest in the contemporary? And on the other side of that, for those who work on areas like the Middle East outside the Middle East, how do you stop your work from being too foreign and distant, or even worse, something of the exotic?

Khaled:

Of course, there will always be those who think that history is concerned only with past events, and that being a historian does not entitle one to comment on current affairs. But as I said above, there is a large, eager public who understands the connection between the present and the past. You don't have to be an academic to understand what historicism is, and I have been approached by many, many young people who want to study the past to figure out the present.

What I deeply bemoan is that this sensitivity to the importance of the past is not as commonplace with older generations. I am thinking specifically of members of our different professions, e.g., doctors, engineers, lawyers, artists, athletes, etc., who the lack the most rudimentary knowledge of their own profession's history. I often wonder how beneficial such knowledge can be in addressing current problems. For example, I'd like to believe that my last book (*In Quest of Justice: Islamic Law and Forensic Medicine in Modern Egypt*) is helpful to understand the origins of the Egyptian public health system (the book has a large section on quarantines, census taking, and smallpox vaccination), and in fact I wrote large segments of the book with my doctor friends in mind to help them understand the historical roots of the problems that our current public health system suffers from.

Few Egyptian doctors have adequate knowledge of the history of their profession. Engineers do not know how their profession has evolved. There is not a single sports club that has a proper archive to document its own history despite the fact that some of these clubs are nearly a century old. Even academic historians lack the knowledge of how their profession has evolved.

The only institutions which have a keen interest in their own past and which are eager to produce cohesive narratives of their own evolution (no matter how distorted or misconceived this narrative may be) are the army and the Muslim Brotherhood (and to a lesser extent Al-Azhar and the Coptic Church). And I think this speaks volumes to the ability of these institutions to act with the boldness and self-confidence with which they have been acting. By contrast, our civil society institutions—our professional syndicates, universities, sporting clubs, newspapers, etc.—have been living only in the present with no awareness of their own historical roots or their historical trajectory, which is one crucial reason for their lack of a vision of their own future.

By reducing history to antiquarianism, we miss the opportunity of having our own narrative of where we have come from and where we are heading. We end up being beholden to learning only from foreign countries rather than from our own past.

Ahdaf: Your fiction writing has often been set in Egypt and England. Were you ever tempted to explore different terrains that took you out of these specific regions? What's at stake if your imagination goes elsewhere? Would that even be possible?

Ahdaf:

Location isn't really the point, is it? I mean, in *In the Eye of the Sun* there are sections set in Italy and in New York. The novel revolves around characters—characters whom I can understand and whom I find interesting.

But characters also engage with space and time, call it geography and history, or setting and plot, right? One thing that your fiction and Khaled's writing have in common, for instance, seems to be the concern with power. Is that at all germane to your work?

Yes, of course. Well put.

OK, so how do you avoid giving the inevitable "history lesson" when writing a novel like In the Eye of the Sun, *or the threat of inevitable pontification when writing about politics, or, as in* Aisha *when talking about women, the threat of exoticization?*

I'm not sure you can avoid the history lesson completely, or the opinion-piece feel when writing about politics. Even Tolstoy couldn't avoid them. But you can lighten and mitigate them. You can certainly avoid exoticization—of both women and men. I guess you do that by writing well, and by being mainly interested in character and motivated by it rather than by pedagogy.

Khaled: Your writing has been on one of the most interesting periods of time in Egypt, namely the late eighteenth through to the twentieth century, when the modern state was being "set up," so to speak. Across the different institutions which you have looked into (legal, military, or popular), the primary thematic concern seems to be power: the power of the institution, the power of the individual, the power of the public, and the interrelations and dissonances between the ways each of these entities perceives, is cognizant of, and uses this power. Why is this important to you?

Khaled:

You are right, I am mostly concerned with the rise of a modern state in Egypt, and with the power that state had on all of us. I wanted to understand how this state was formed, how it was resisted, accommodated, or embraced. By looking at such institutions as the army, the police, and the judiciary; and by cataloguing the myriad ways this state had made itself felt by its citizens (e.g., conscription, vaccination, census taking, urban planning), my aim is to understand the state historically.

By this I mean that there is nothing that this state does that is inevitable or preordained or natural. And I think this is politically important because our politicians speak about the state as if it is some primordial entity, outside time, outside space, that somehow it precedes society, that is, precedes us, the people, and claims precedence over us. By analyzing how the modern Egyptian state came to be formed historically, and how it lay its hegemony on the people who came to identify themselves as Egyptians, I aim to empower us, the people, to better understand how it works. The hope is that one day we can make this state serve us, rather than we it.

So beyond pedagogy, intellectual activity, diasporic solidarity: what does it entail to be political in the immediate sense in the Arab world?

Ahdaf:

At the moment I think the options are:

> To be murdered (in a variety of available ways)
> To be in prison
> To be engaged with the Arab world but physically outside it
> To be trying to maintain some kind of not-too-compromising politico-washing relationship with the regime—and watch any value or credibility you had slip away as you do that
> To be in with the regime and trying to maintain a space within it at any price as it constantly shifts and maneuvers

Of course, the option you take depends on both your character and your circumstances . . .

Khaled:

I have little doubt that we Arabs are living one of the bleakest moments in our long history. Being political in my view means to be critically aware of the bleakness of this moment and avoiding being ensnared by the phony comfort that our political and economic elites offer us. In the wake of the Arab uprisings of 2011–13, and with the triumph of the counterrevolutionary regimes in the Gulf, Egypt and Syria, the very existence of the political arena, an arena of peaceful disputation, critical engagement, of negotiation and compromise, is in jeopardy. What our political, economic, and cultural elites offer us is nothing less than the total abdication of our political rights. Being political means insisting not only to hold these rights but also to practice them as duties. It is our duty to be critically engaged, to question what our leaders do, and to hold them accountable.

It sounds flippant maybe ending with this: What do we do with fear?

Ahdaf:

As the Counterrevolution sludged into action, my apartment in Cairo was raided twice. Both times I was abroad. Both times nothing was taken. It was a warning. The apartment is on the sixth floor, and every time I hung laundry out the window to dry I would get a strong sense of someone coming up behind me. There was no one, of course. But I had a totally vivid sense of two men coming up behind me and quickly tipping me over the windowsill. I continued to hang out the laundry, but every time I had the sense in my chest and stomach that someone was coming up behind me. By the time the washing was hung I would be breathless. When I moved into the houseboat, one of my first thoughts was "Well, this time I'll hit water."

Fear is different for each of us. For me, when I do feel fear, it is almost always fear of something imagined.

As for fear of real things, political fear, perhaps our only antidote against it is solidarity; the certainty that there are people who will not let go of you whatever happens. Community breeds courage.

Khaled:

Fear can be a very healthy sensation. It alerts one of danger. Instinctively, one immediately seeks cover or flight. But then comes the sober reflection of the source of danger and how best to deal with it.

We live under a regime that is constantly terrifying us. It seeks our cover, i.e., our silence, or our flight, i.e., repudiation of our principles. The challenge has always been not to give in to these instinctive reactions; to look this regime in the eye; and to stick to one's principles.

I have always found that work—research, teaching, and writing—to be the best antidote against this policy of state terrorism.

My research has been primarily informed by a desire to study the institutions of the state, the very state that is constantly terrorizing us. I have been studying the history of the army, the police, and the courts, foundational pillars of the modern state apparatus. It is my way of dealing with the fear that we, Egyptians, all feel when we approach the state. Studying these institutions of terror has been my way of dealing with this fear.

Studying—rather than teaching, writing, or leading? Is this traditionally the role of the public intellectual in the Arabic context?

Khaled:

Intellectuals like to pontificate. And I don't mean this facetiously. Intellectuals *should* pontificate. They should think, read, engage with one another and, if they are "engaged intellectuals," pass on the fruits of their intellectual labor to a wider public. In Egypt in particular, there is an expectation that intellectuals should "enlighten" the masses and should dislodge them from their ignorance, their apathy, and their illness. But I believe that intellectuals should also listen to this "wider public," to the masses, to the subalterns. This is often difficult for intellectuals to do as their training, as well as the public expectation, ill prepare them to listen. It is also difficult for them to do so given that the modern Arab political system, from the Ocean to the Gulf as the saying goes, is purposefully built to silence the masses and to render them powerless. We lack institutions in which the masses can speak and in which their voices can be heard. We have no forums that allow members of the public to exchange ideas with each other peacefully and respectfully. We also lack expertise in how to disagree, how to negotiate, and how to reach compromises. But above all, we lack expertise in how to listen.

So I believe that one of the prime duties of intellectuals is to listen to the "masses" and to engage with them, not in a condescending manner telling them how to lead their lives, but on the contrary, by being ready to be taught by them. I am a historian, and I learnt the tricks of my trade in the Egyptian National Archives (ENA). For over ten years, I conducted research in the ENA consulting police and court records from the nineteenth century. I believe this was the most humbling experience of my life. By this I don't mean the difficulty of deciphering the script or understanding the logic of the documents. These tasks were humbling enough, for sure. What I mean, rather, is recognizing the tragic lives the people I was reading about lived, and standing in awe in front of the dignity with which they handled truly tragic situations. A little more listening can do us all a lot of good.

Contributors

Dimitris Christopoulos is a Greek scholar, writer, and public intellectual. He is Professor of State and Legal Theory at the Panteion University of Athens, Dean of the Political Science Faculty, and former President of the International Federation for Human Rights (FIDH 2016–19). His writings on human rights, the far right, minorities, migrants, and citizenship have appeared in Greek, English, French, Portuguese, Hebrew, Albanian, and Serbo-Croatian. His many books include *Droit, Europe et minorités—Critique de la connaissance juridique* (Sakkoulas, 2000), *Η ετερότητα ως σχέση εξουσίας* [Otherness as a power relation] (Kritiki, 2002), *Ποιος είναι έλληνας πολίτης; Το καθεστώς της ελληνικής ιθαγένειας από την ίδρυση του ελληνικού κράτος στις αρχές του 21ου αιώνα* [Who is a Greek citizen? The status of Greek nationality from the creation of the Greek state to the dawn of the 21st century] (Viviliorama, 2012), *Στο ρίσκο της κρίσης—Στρατηγικές της αριστεράς των δικαιωμάτων* [At risk in the crisis—Left human rights strategies] (Alexandreia, 2013), and *Η κρίση των δικαιωμάτων* [The crisis of rights] (Xbooks, 2015). He is coauthor of *Προσφυγικό: "θα τα καταφέρουμε"· Ένας απολογισμός διαχείρισης και προτάσεις διεξέδου* [Refugees: "Will we make it?": A management account and recommendations for a way out] (Papazisis, 2016), and *10 +1 Ερωτήσεις & Απαντήσεις για το Μακεδονικό* [10 + 1 Questions & answers on the Macedonian Question] (Polis, 2018). Christopoulos is also cofounder of the Minority Groups Research Centre (KEMO), the first Greek independent think tank on minority issues, and a regular contributor to international and Greek media and the press.

Dimitri Dimoulis is an academic and writer. Born in Athens (November 1965), Juris Doctor (University of Saarland, 1994). Professor at the São Paulo Law School of the Fundação Getulio Vargas since 2007. Director of the Brazilian Institute of Constitutional Studies (Instituto brasileiro de estudos constitucionais). In addition to specialized legal studies, including on freedom of expression and censorship, he has published the books *Nations, classes, politics: The dialectics of war* (in Greek, coauthor, Kritiki, 1995); *Justiça de* *transição no Brasil: Direito, responsabilização e verdade* (coauthor, Saraiva, 2010); *Estado de direito e desenvolvimento* (editor, Saraiva, 2011); *States against workers: The Greek crisis* (in Greek, coauthor, Taxideutis, 2016); *Karl Marx and the Classics: An Essay on Value, Crises and the Capitalist Mode of Production* (coauthor, Ashgate, 2017); *Direito de igualdade: Antidiscriminação, minorias sociais, remédios constitucionais* (Almedina, 2023).

Khaled Fahmy is Edward Keller Professor of North Africa and the Middle East at Tufts University. He is a historian of the modern Middle East and an active contributor to the press in Arabic and English. His books and articles deal with the history of the Egyptian army in the first half of the nineteenth century, and the history of medicine, law, and urban planning in nineteenth- and twentieth-century Egypt. He charts the specific ways in which a modern state was established in Egypt and the manner in which Egyptians accommodated, subverted, or resisted the institutions of this modern state. He is also a prolific writer for the press in Arabic and English, on social media, and on his blog (www.khaledfahmy.org). He has taught at Princeton, NYU, Columbia, and Cambridge, and is a fellow of the British Academy. His books include *In Quest of Justice: Islamic Law and Forensic Medicine in Modern Egypt* (University of California Press, 2018), *Mehmed Ali: From Ottoman Governor to Ruler of Egypt* (Oneworld, 2012), and *All the Pasha's Men: Mehmed Ali, His Army and the Making of Modern Egypt* (Cambridge University Press, 1997).

Rishi Goyal, MD, PhD, is Director of the Medical Humanities major at the Institute for Comparative Literature and Society at Columbia University and Associate Professor in the Department of Emergency Medicine at Columbia University Irving Medical Center (in Medical Humanities and Ethics and ICLS). His research interests include the health humanities, social medicine, the study of the novel, and medical epistemology. He is a cofounding editor of the online journal *Synapsis: A Health Humanities Journal*, cofounding director of the Health Language Lab, and a recipient of a National Endowment for the Humanities grant. He most recently coedited the volume *Culture and Medicine: Critical Readings in the Health and Medical Humanities* from Bloomsbury Press.

May Hawas is Associate Professor in World Literature at the University of Cambridge, and Valerie Eliot Fellow of English at Newnham College. She is the author of *Politicising World Literature: Egypt between Pedagogy and the Public* (Routledge: awarded the Anna Balakian Prize, 2022) and *The Diaries of Waguih Ghali* (American University in Cairo Press, 2 vols., 2017–18), in addition to a number of articles and essays; editor of *The Routledge Companion to World Literature and World History* (2018); and coeditor, with Theo D'haen, of the special issue of *The Journal of World Literature*, "What Is World Literature—of Arabic?" (2017). She has taught in Egypt, the US, and England, and is a former EUME fellow (FU Berlin).

Bonnie Honig is Nancy Duke Lewis Professor of Modern Culture and Media (MCM) and Political Science at Brown University. In 2017–18, she served as inaugural Carl Cranor Phi Beta Kappa Scholar. An affiliate of the Digital Democracy Institute at Simon Fraser University and the American Bar Foundation, Chicago, her work in democratic and feminist theory studies the cultural politics of immigration (*Democracy and the Foreigner*, Princeton University Press, 2001), emergency (*Emergency Politics: Paradox, Law, Democracy*, Princeton University Press, 2009), mourning (*Antigone, Interrupted*, Cambridge University Press, 2013) and refusal (*A Feminist Theory of Refusal*, Harvard University Press, 2021). Her book *Public Things: Democracy in Disrepair* (Fordham University Press, 2017) came out days after Trump's 2017 inauguration, and her first piece of public writing about that presidency, "The President's House Is Empty," appeared on that inauguration day in the *Boston Review*. A collection of her public writing, *Shell Shocked: Feminist Criticism after Trump*, appeared with Fordham University Press in 2021. In 2023, her first book, *Political Theory and the Displacement of Politics*, was republished as a thirtieth-anniversary edition by Cornell University Press.

Mona Kareem is Assistant Professor of Arabic and Comparative Literature at Washington University in St. Louis. Her research focuses on literary cultures of race and ethnicity in the Global South, with an emphasis on Afro-Asian encounters in the Arabian Peninsula/Persian Gulf region. Her articles have appeared in *Arabian Humanities, Jadaliyya, Arab Studies Journal, The Los Angeles Review of Books,* and *The Common,* among others. Kareem has been a visiting scholar at the Center for Humanities at Tufts University, the Program in Translation and Intercultural Communication at Princeton University, the Arabic program at the University of Maryland College Park, and the Forum Transregionale Studien in Berlin. Kareem is also a poet and translator. She has published three poetry collections, and her work has appeared in *POETRY, Poetry Northwest, Michigan Quarterly, Poetry London,* and *Modern Poetry in Translation,* among others.

Benjamin Mangrum is Associate Professor of Literature at the Massachusetts Institute of Technology. He is the author of *The Comedy of Computation: Or, How I Learned to Stop Worrying and Love Obsolescence* (Stanford University Press, 2025) and *Land of Tomorrow: Postwar Fiction and the Crisis of American Liberalism* (Oxford University Press, 2019). He has also published articles in *PMLA, Diacritics, New Literary History, Modern Fiction Studies, American Literature, American Literary History, Contemporary Literature,* and elsewhere. He received the 2023 Levitan Prize from MIT and is a past member of the Michigan Society of Fellows.

Nora E. H. Parr is a Research Fellow at the University of Birmingham, where she is a co-Investigator on the Rights for Time research network. She coedits the *Journal of Middle Eastern Literatures*. Her monograph *Novel Palestine: Nation through the Work of Ibrahim Nasrallah* came out in 2023 with the University of California Press's New Directions in Palestine Studies series.

Bruce Robbins is Old Dominion Foundation Professor of the Humanities at Columbia University. He was educated at Harvard University and previously taught at the universities of Geneva and Lausanne and Rutgers University. His most recent book is *Atrocity: A Literary History* (Standford University Press, 2025). A collection of essays entitled *Cosmopolitanisms,* coedited with Paulo Horta (NYU Press), came out in 2017. His other books include *Criticism and Politics: A Polemical Introduction* (Stanford University

Press, 2022), *The Beneficiary* (Duke University Press, 2017), *Perpetual War: Cosmopolitanism from the Viewpoint of Violence* (2012), *Upward Mobility and the Common Good* (2007), *Feeling Global: Internationalism in Distress* (1999), *Secular Vocations: Intellectuals, Professionalism, Culture* (1993), and *The Servant's Hand: English Fiction from Below* (1986). He is the director of a 2012 documentary entitled "Some of My Best Friends Are Zionists," available at bestfriendsfilm.com, and another short film about the Israeli historian Shlomo Sand, "What Kind of Jew Is Shlomo Sand?," which came out in 2020 and is available at mondoweiss.com.

Ahdaf Soueif is a celebrated Egyptian novelist, political commentator, cultural producer, and activist. Her work, which engages with the legacies of British and American intervention in the Middle East, especially Egypt, has made her an important international figure for those concerned with human rights and literature, not least in relation to the Arab world, as well as an iconic figure for Anglo-Arab writers and journalists. Soueif is a Booker Prize nominee, and has received many awards, including the Cavafy Award, the Mahmoud Darwish Award, the Lannan Literary Fellowship, the Bogliasco Foundation Fellowship Award, and most recently, the ECF Princess Margriet Award for Culture. Her work has been translated into a large number of languages. She has contributed regularly to *The Guardian, The Observer, Cosmopolitan, Granta, The London Review of Books, New Society, The Sunday Telegraph, Times Literary Supplement, Washington Post,* and others. She also writes in Arabic, and has contributed to *al-Shorouk, Akhbar al-Adab, al-Arabi, al-Hilal, al-Katibah, Nisf al-Dunya,* and *Sabah al-Kheir*.

Omid Tofighian is an award-winning lecturer, researcher, translator, and community advocate, combining philosophy with interests in citizen media, popular culture, displacement, and discrimination. He is the translator of Behrouz Boochani's multi-award-winning book *No Friend but the Mountains: Writing from Manus Prison* (Picador, 2018); the author of *Creating New Languages of Resistance: Translation, Public Philosophy and Border Violence* (Routledge, 2025) and *Myth and Philosophy in Platonic Dialogues* (Palgrave, 2016); cotranslator/coeditor of *Freedom, Only Freedom: The Prison Writings of Behrouz Boochani* (Bloomsbury, 2023); and coeditor of special issues for the journals *Southerly* (2021), *Alphaville: Journal of Film and Screen Media* (2019), and *Literature and Aesthetics* (2011). He is currently adjunct lecturer at the University of New South Wales.

Elahe Zivardar is an award-winning Iranian American artist, architectural designer, journalist, and documentary filmmaker who currently lives in Arizona, United States. Zivardar fled Iran in 2013 and attempted to seek asylum in Australia, but was instead imprisoned on the remote Pacific island the Republic of Nauru until 2019, when she was granted refugee status by the United States. During her years of imprisonment in Nauru, she returned to her activist roots and began using photos and video to document and expose the horrific treatment and conditions endured by refugees imprisoned offshore. Using diverse mediums including painting, photography, and documentary filmmaking, Zivardar seeks to depict and raise awareness about the powerful stakeholders who benefit from the victimization and detention of refugees. In addition, Zivardar has served as advisor to international refugee rights campaigns and organizations in Australia, the UK, and the US.

Index

9/11, 65, 121

Abdel Raziq, Ali, 110
Abode for Serenity, 159
absolutist, 15, 22–30
Abu Zaid, Nasr Hamid, 111, 118–23
activism, 18, 112, 133, 153–56, 160–61, 176, 183
Adichie, Chimamanda Ngozi, 16, 134
Adonis, 111
advocacy, 11, 48, 133, 155–56, 162
agency, 58, 64, 136; without, 155
Ahab, 21–36
Al Azhar, 111, 186
Al Zaytuna, 111
al-Aqqad, Abbas Mahmoud, 110
al-Azm, Sadiq Jalal, 111
al-Haj Saleh, Yassin, 113–15, 118–19, 122–23, 124
al-Ittihad al-Watani Party, 171
al-Ittihad al-Ishtiraki, 171
al-Nadim, Abdallah, 111
al-Sayyid, Ahmed Lutfi, 110
Alexandria, 115–17
American Civil War, 23
American University in Cairo, 115, 176
American, 4–6, 14–15, 21–22, 27, 38, 40, 45–46, 48–49, 54–70, 74, 93, 108, 110, 117, 130, 132, 149, 173; un-American, 129; United States, 4, 11, 15–16, 22, 32, 41, 44, 58, 60, 62–65, 108, 111, 119, 148, 154; US, 44, 46, 60, 62
Americanah (Adichie), 16, 134, 136

animal body, 26
Ann Arbor, 115
anti-maskers, 149
anti-refugee, 151, 159, 160, 169
anti-vaxxers, 149
antitotalitarian, 16, 126–27, 130
apostasy, 119, 121
Arab World, 1, 3, 12, 18, 82, 112, 121, 180, 182–83, 188; Gulf, 15, 67, 82, 188, 190, 193
Arab-Israeli conflict, 175–77
Arabia, 68, 180
Architect (Zivardar), 158
architects, 167
architecture, 154, 157–69
archive, 86, 179–80, 190; anthropological, 15; Israeli, 73; written, 177–81, 189–90
Arkoun, Mohammed, 120
army, 15, 95, 186; Egyptian, 186, 189; Greek, 89; Japanese Red, 80; Mehmed Ali's, 176, 185; Ottoman, 77
asylum, 151–65
atrocities, 4, 12, 13, 16, 130–38; against non-citizens, 160; against Greeks, 89; Greek history of, 93–94
austerity, 177
Australia–United States Resettlement Agreement, 153
Australia, 12, 17, 99, 151–69
autistic, 72
autonomy, 2–18; of the individual, 143

195

Baconian, 144
Baghdad, 175
Balkan Wars, 89
Bazarov, 137
BDS, 4
Beirut, 68, 79–80, 83, 174, 175
bell hooks, 6, 10, 14, 19, 47, 57
Ben Ezra Synagogue, 115
Bible, 33–34, 132
Bildung, 111
bilingualism, 182–83
Black, 6, 128; educable, 7; educators, 66; hire, 123; scholars, 19; South Africans, 136; students, 60; woman professor, 66
Black Lives Matter, 149
blackness, 47
body politic, 1, 16, 110, 118, 112–13, 121, 123
Boochani, Behrouz, 157
The Booker Prize, 173–74, 194
Border-Industrial Complex series (Zivardar), 163
border, 23, 151–69; detention, 17, 153–69; industrial-complex, 153; police, 84; politics, 163; regime, 152; stop, 82; violence, 152
British Mandate, 42–43, 75, 77
British Museum, 174–75
Brookfield, Stephen D., 42–43
Brown University, 20–21, 29, 33
Bsharat, Ahlam, 74–79
Bulgarian, 13, 89–90, 100

Cairo, 59, 83, 111, 115–17, 119–21, 171, 173, 175–76, 178, 188
Cairo University, 119–22
Cambridge University, 115, 117, 184, 192
Camus, Albert, 137–38
Cavafy, C. P., 133
censor, 10, 12–13, 47, 61, 89, 90–102, 112, 162
Cities of Salt (Munif), 67
citizen privilege, 160
citizenship, 3, 5–6, 18, 39, 51, 101, 112, 149, 191
class, 8, 130, 134, 135; anxiety, 51; class-based, 63; class solidarity, 64; class struggle, 40; classes, 112; classless, 23; middle-class, 65; working-class, 10, 16
close reading, 62
Coetzee, J. M., 72, 83, 86, 136
colonialism, 64, 117, 132, 137, 146, 154, 156–57, 160–61, 175, 181
Columbia University, 40, 45, 132, 141
communism, 38, 40

"Concealed Borders," 163
constitutionalism, 26; constitutional check, 29; constitutional democracy, 12–13; Greek constitution, 99; unconstitutional, 97
Coptic Church, 186
Cossery, Albert, 68
counter-discourse, 94
counter-history, 68
counter-public, 13
counterrevolutionary, 188
Covid-19, 11, 16, 140–49, 167
Crete, 97
criticism, 5, 8, 9, 10, 13, 16, 48, 68, 90, 91, 98, 111, 117, 118, 122–23, 180, 193
Crusades, 132
Cuba, 5
cultural homogeneity, 99
Czech, 126, 129

decolonization, 175
Defoe, Daniel, 140–50
democracy, 2, 4, 6, 13–15, 17, 21, 33, 37–54, 99, 102, 104, 177, 182
demos, 51
depoliticization, 93; depoliticized, 102
detachment, 1, 54
Dewey, John, 44, 47–48
dictionary, 89–91, 95
disability reading, 72–74, 80–83
discomfort, 6, 10, 17, 62, 64, 66, 71, 139
displacement, 12, 51, 75–76, 80–82, 156; displaced feelings, 51; displaced peoples, 155, 161
dissent, 3, 100
dissident, 89, 96
diversity, 15, 48, 75, 123, 156
ecosystem, 17, 124, 152, 155
educable, 7–8
Egypt, 17, 59–60, 64, 68, 77, 107–22, 171–90
Egyptian healthcare system, 185–86
Egyptian Revolution, 171
El Shorbagy, Mohamed, 108–9
Eliot, George, 139
"The Embassy of Cambodia" (Smith), 139
emergency, 141–46
empathy, 4, 15–16, 50, 118
engagement, 9, 30, 51, 65, 93, 138, 146, 149, 174, 184, 188
England, 15, 24, 29, 108–9, 115, 117, 118, 148, 172, 186
English Civil War, 24

INDEX 197

epistemology, 155, 157; epistemological shifts, 159, 161
ethical, 18, 62, 126–27, 129, 132, 155
ethnic cleansing, 89, 98, 132
exile, 80, 113, 114–15, 118–24, 151
exiled peoples, 120, 146, 155, 156, 159, 161

fake news, 96, 100, 101
Fathers and Sons (Turgenev), 137
Ferrante, Elena, 134
First Nations people, 154
folklore, 157
France, 22, 171
freedom, 2–4, 6, 9, 11, 12, 14, 19, 22–24, 30, 32, 60, 75, 90–145, 156, 169
Freud, Sigmund, 164

Gallic War, 132
Gaza, 3, 4, 13, 83, 85, 181
gender, 7, 47, 60–61, 64, 80, 135, 136, 149, 162
general education, 39–42, 46–48, 54
Geniza, 115, 117
genocide, 91–92; of First Nations People, 154; in Gaza, 3; Greek denial of, 97–98
Ghosh, Amitav, 67, 115–17
Gibran, Khalil, 111
Global North, 16, 169
Global South, 67, 169, 171
Great Books, 46–47, 50, 132
Great Conversation, 47
Great Depression, 46
Greece, 12, 13, 88, 89–105
Greek antiquity, 16, 91–93
Green New Deal, 157
The Groves of Academe (McCarthy), 37–41

Harvard University, 39, 54
healing, 156, 162
Hellenic, 97–98; Hellenism, 94; Hellenization, 99–100
hermeneutics, 119
hip hop, 157
Hitler, Adolf, 129
Hobbes, Thomas, 15–16, 20–36, 141
Holocaust, 97, 132
Homo economicus, 142
human rights, 73, 83, 95, 100–1, 105, 131
humanities, 1, 11, 13, 19, 40, 43–45, 58, 61–62, 65, 68, 141, 184
Hungary, 171
Hussein, Taha, 110
hyperpoliticized, 102

Ibrahim, Sonallah, 68, 70
ideological, 14, 62–64, 67, 92–94, 102
If This Is a Man/Survival in Auschwitz (Levi), 131
immigrants, 23
imperialism, 63, 87, 128, 150, 154; anti-imperialism, 171; empire, 32, 62, 77, 91, 92, 129, 152, 172; imperialist, 62–63
In an Antique Land (Ghosh), 115–17
In Quest of Justice (Fahmy), 185
incarceration, 17, 151–69
Indonesia, 17, 154
inequality, 84; inequalities, 72, 175
international law, 151, 165
Intifada, 76–77
Iran, 17, 154, 156–58, 162
Iranian Revolution, 156; society, 152
Iraq-Iran War, 69
Irwin, Rober, 174
Ishmael, 21–36
Islam, 118, 121; anti-Muslim sentiment, 122; Islamic philosophers, 120; Islamic Republic, 156; Islamic thought, 122; Islamic universities, 111; Islamists, 117, 119; Muslim, 92, 101, 119; Muslim Brotherhood, 112
Israel, 12, 72, 78, 7, 122, 133, 138, 139, 171–72, 174–75, 177, 181; bombing of Gaza, 13; Israeli, 8, 72–78, 84–86, 88, 194; invasion of Lebanon, 174
Israeli-Arab War, 180–81

Japan, 80, 120, 132
journalism, 8, 17–18, 110, 154, 157, 170
A Journal of the Plague Year (Defoe), 141–50
Julius Caesar, 132

Kanafani, Ghassan, 74, 79–82, 87
Kant, Immanuel, 7, 11, 127–28, 133
king: two bodies, 25–26, 29, 30; and lord, 144; Unjust King, 172
kitsch, 127
knowledge, 28, 30, 50, 53, 74, 92, 107, 110, 131–32, 135, 185–86; count as "knowledge", 73; criminalization of, 97; democratic, 33; disciplinary, 49; discomforting, 17; emerging body of, 154–63; gentleman's, 40; law of, 122; liberal, 39, 41; mass, 4; politics of, 87; production, 47, 177; specialized, 45
Kundera, Milan, 16, 126–39

LEAN model, 142
lecture, 13, 34, 42, 43, 44–7, 56, 111–12, 120, 128–30
Levi, Primo, 131, 139
Leviathan (Hobbes), 15, 20–36
liberal education, 37–57
Locke, John, 144

Macedonia, 13, 89–91, 99–101, 104–5
Mahfouz, Naguib, 58–59, 61, 63–65, 70, 71
mainstream: cultural phenomenon, 60; image of refugees, 155; media, 13, 153, 162; philosophical traditions, 157; university, 156
Malayalam, 67
The Map of Love (Soueif), 173–74
McCarthy, Mary, 37–42
media, 8, 13, 54, 92, 95–100, 109, 140, 154, 162, 169, 177
Medical Humanities, 141
Mediterranean, 117
Melville, Hermann, 15, 20–36
Men in the Sun (Kanafani), 79–82
mentorship, 16, 106–24
Mexico, 23, 32
Micronesia, 152
Midaq Alley (Mahfouz), 58–59
Middle East, 1, 2, 11, 112, 138, 157, 185; history, 175–76; studies, 65, 184
Middlemarch (Eliot), 139
Midianite, 132–33
military, 58, 72, 76, 84–85, 95, 111, 160, 180, 185, 187; militarizing the border, 153
Mill, John Stuart, 51
Minor Detail (Shibli), 72–73, 83–86
minorities, 7, 13, 93, 116; Bulgarian, 89; Greek-speaking, 91; Turkish minority, 92, 99, 101–2; nonminority, 100, 104; Macedonian minority, 101; minority rights, 105
Moby-Dick (Melville), 15, 20–36
Moll Flanders (Defoe), 112
moral, 148; ground, judgment, 110, 127; impulse, 40; moralistic basis, 60, 117; morality, 26; 110; moralizing, 143; perspective, 146; perversity, 129; policing, 61; progress, 16, 133; of the story, 136; training, 99; turmoil, 131
Moses, 133
Munif, Abdelrahman, 67
Musa, Nabawiyya, 111
My Brilliant Friend (Ferrante), 134–35

Naimy, Michail, 111
Nasser, Gamal Abdel, 64, 171, 180
Nassif, Malak Hifny, 111
nationalism, 75, 94; allegory, 3, 137; national education, 91; national issue, 90–102
Nauru, 17, 151–69
Nazis, 103, 131–32
Nea Dimokratia, 94
Netherlands, 119
New York, 16, 20, 22, 59–60, 186
Nietzsche, Friedrich, 126–28
Nigeria, 134
non-alignment, 172
North Africa, 15, 77, 157

Occupied East Jerusalem, 72
Ōe, Kenzaburō, 132
oil, 28, 30, 35, 67–68; Big Oil, 175
Operation Sovereign Borders, 153
Orientalism, 73, 175; Orientalist, 128
Orthodox Christians, 89; Church, 94; Patriarchate, 90
Ottoman, 75–78, 91–92, 98, 192

Pacific Solution, 152–53
paideia, 111
Palestine, 3, 4, 62, 172–82; Festival of Literature (PalFest), 174–75; teaching of 72–88
Pamuk, Orhan, 136
Panopticism, 146
Papua New Guinea, 152
pedagogy, and autonomy, 2–19; apolitical, 133; in Arab societies, 107–22; Arabic literature, 62; of class discussion, 120; democratic pedagogy, 25, 30; discussion-based, 38–54; and national issues, 91; new kinds of, 156–69; for politics, 22; in schools, 102; and writing, 176
Pequot, 22
"Petrofiction: The Novel and the Oil Encounter" (Ghosh), 67
philosophical investigations, 36, 55; activity, 155; ecosystem, 155; excursions, 130; reasons, 48
plague, 137–38, 141–50
The Plague (Camus), 137
political novel, 136–37
politics, 1–18, 24, 28; bans on, 94; borders, 153; a call to, 80; class, 64; of close reading, 71; communist, 68; element of,

135; escape from, 137; framework of, 141; of gender and sexuality, 136; of history courses, 175; and liberal education, 37–55; of mentorship, 106–23; Middle Eastern, 175–76; of teaching, 61, 66; of the Third World Writer, 64; political blasphemy, 93; political spectrum, 156; politics-in-literature, 138; shaping our approaches to texts, 73; Third World students, 116; writing about, 187
Port Moresby, 152
post-Enlightenment subject, 143
Preskill, Stephen, 42–43
protest, 3, 4, 76, 90, 96, 149
public, the, 2, 4, 13, 14, 96, 111,118, 167, 179, 184; education, 111–12; eye, 112; function, 43; good, 25; Greek, 92; intellectuals, 9, 170, 188–89, 190; limelight, 109; peace, 12, 100; prosecutor, 90, 102; public resonance, 3; realm, 5; sphere, 8, 92, 183–84; university, 116–17

racist, 7, 62–63, 151, 159, 90; capitalism, 154, 160; discrimination, 161; hint of, 128; politics of race, 172; racial lingering residues, 175
Rainbow party, 100
realism, 149, 163; realist, 64; realistic fiction, 142
recitation, 45
refugees, 5, 75, 80, 80–88, 151–69
resistance, 46, 49, 156, 157, 177; creative, 154; French, 132; Greek, 97–98; Palestinian, 80–82; student, 16, 125, 132
responsibility, 3, 5, 9, 33, 62, 69, 72, 84, 110, 111, 149, 161, 173, 185
Robespierre, Maximilien de, 129
Robinson Crusoe (Defoe), 141–50

Sabra and Shatila massacre, 174
Sadik, Ahmet, 101
Said, Edward, 9, 14, 16, 63, 73, 110, 128
Salih, Tayeb, 65
Sartre, Jean Paul, 138
schools, 6, 36, 43, 54, 92, 98, 100, 102, 160
Season of Migration to the North (Salih), 65
Second World War, 38, 42, 45, 97, 130
sexuality, 7, 8, 60, 64, 136
Shafik, Doria, 111
Shibli, Adania 72, 74, 79, 83–86
Skopian, 100

Smith, Zadie, 139
social: collectivity, 8, 125; contract, 23–33; fabric, 165; hierarchies, 48; imaginary, 155; life, 29–30; marginalization, 11; media, 13, 167; mobility, 64, 110; momentum, 120–21; movement, 17, 177; sciences, 42–46; transformation, 80
Socratic dialogue, 43, 45, 56
solidarity, 11, 15, 37, 54, 64, 80, 134, 188, 189
Sons and Lovers (Lawrence), 112
sovereignty, 22–31, 75, 152
Soviet invasion, 126–29
Spivak, Gayatri, 58, 62, 69
squash, 108–9
State Department (US), 46
STEM, 44
street art, 157
submission, 24, 27, 36, 157
surreal, 164–65; surrealism, 164; surrealist, 68
Switzerland, 126
syllabus, 112, 115; Arab language courses, 58; Arabic literature, 58–69; humanities, 41–54; Open Syllabus, 73; Palestine, 73–83; reading list, 48
SYRIZA, 94

Tashtego, 28
Ted Lasso, 14
testimony, 61
theatre, 14, 20, 157, 158
therapeutic, 163
Thessaloniki, 89–90
Third Critique, 134
Tower of Babel, 67
translation 7, 17, 58, 59, 67, 69, 70, 75, 156, 183
trauma, 73, 88, 113, 159, 163, 167
Trees for the Absentees (Bsharat), 76, 78, 79, 87
tropes, 156, 160, 169
Tunis, 111, 157, 175
Turgenev, Ivan, 137

unaccompanied minors, 152, 14
The Unbearable Lightness of Being (Kundera), 126–29
unions, 122–23
United Arab Republic, 171
uprisings in Iran, 2022, 153
utopia, 16, 115, 118, 141, 142, 147, 149

Vietnam War, 46
violence, mass, 4, 131; against noncombatants, 130; against refugees, 160
visa, 60, 67
vocation, 2, 6, 8, 9, 12–13, 16–18, 41, 82, 98, 108, 110–23

War on Iraq, 121
Warda (Ibrahim), 68
West Bank, 72, 76, 84, 181
Western Thrace, 99, 101
Wittgenstein, Ludwig, 36, 51

workers, 182; essential, 149; workers' arms, 171; workers' rights, 175; working conditions, 148
workshop, 69, 21, 163, 167, 178
world fiction, 130
world literature, 58, 63, 115, 116, 118

Yugoslavia, 99

Zaydan, Jurji, 110
Zewail, Ahmed, 108
Ziadeh, Mai, 111
Zionism, 75, 181; Zionist, 139, 172

www.ingramcontent.com/pod-product-compliance
Lightning Source LLC
Chambersburg PA
CBHW020410080526
44584CB00014B/1263